/N

LIBRARY

D1422556

Frontiers of
American Culture

Frontiers of American Culture

edited by Ray B. Browne, Richard H. Crowder,
Virgil L. Lokke, William T. Stafford

Purdue University Studies
1968

CHECKED HATHI TRUST
APRIL 2018.
LIMITED (SEARCH ONLY).

© 1968 by Purdue Research Foundation
Library of Congress Catalog No. 68-11976

033393

Contents

WITHDRAWN
from
STIRLING UNIVERSITY LIBRARY

Introduction

Conferences on American culture, or civilization, or studies, are usually free to pursue many organizing approaches—thematic studies, period investigations, examination of methodological problems which beset interdisciplinary studies, and, optimistically, research into areas not yet explored or sufficiently developed. The title of this volume, *Frontiers of American Culture,* will suggest the gentle blurring of focus. The persons responsible for arranging the second Conference on American Culture at Purdue University had as a loosely controlling intention the investigation of unexamined aspects of popular culture. Toward this end outstanding scholars were chosen to discuss aspects of the field which, it was felt, needed closer attention. The result was, and is as expected, a series of papers which are valuable in themselves. They employ a wide spectrum of moods and approaches—speculative, descriptive, provocative, cautious, analytic, and polemical—with intersections of thesis and argument which are perhaps fortunately more a matter of accident than of disciplined intention.

One promising new area, for example, is that of the iconography of the United States. E. McClung Fleming sees six major images— The Indian Princess, the Neo-Classic Plumed Goddess, The American Liberty, Columbia, Brother Jonathan and Uncle Sam—used to identify the American Colonies and the United States between 1775 and 1850. C. Hugh Holman examines two periods in American history in which "cheap books" were widely published. Everybody, Holman notes, who advocates literacy and reading for the masses favors the wide publication of inexpensive books; but he warns against an overlooked danger: "To the extent that 'cheap books' force publishers to measure merit in material terms, they betray the present and emasculate the future. They stifle creativity and originality by asking that it first prove itself in the market place."

Herbert M. Schueller describes the career of William Wetmore Story—art critic, literary critic, novelist, dramatist, poet, author of travel and historical sketches, and a most highly praised nineteenth-century sculptor. The real significance of Story, the man of many talents, Schueller concludes, can be gauged only when "the role of the dilettante in the spread of culture has been estimated."

William Styron's fiction is the subject of Frederick J. Hoffman's essay, "The Cure of 'Nothing!'." Here Hoffman examines the "problem of believing, the desperate necessity for having the 'courage to be' " and discovers that Styron's "most recent novel sets the imagination a-going, in the expectation of an American literature of existentia-Iism." Ray Browne's essay explores the mythology of *Israel Potter* for evidence that Melville, beyond his ambivalent negations, had a final commitment to humanism.

In his essay on Charlie Chaplin, James Sandoe examines three classic Chaplin films and reaffirms that comedy is no "elegant dame," but rather a "Protean bitch with variety more infinite than Cleopatra's." Part of the failure of traditional theories of comedy, Sandoe urges, lies in the inadequate attention paid to inflection ("a line soundly bent for perfect expressiveness or a movement calculated to the same end"). Chaplin, he concludes, "is supremely an artist in his inflection."

Both the American Indian and American geography become mythological in the analysis offered by Leslie Fiedler. Having boxed the compass with Northerns, Southerns, Easterns, and Westerns, the American author is left with but one "frontier"—out of space, out of time, and into or out of mind. Fiedler's essay, the beginning of a study that has since run book-length, presents a torrent of evidence that the "Vanishing American has disconcertingly reappeared" to guide us toward affirmation of our second soul. The importance of another version of soul, that is, the role ascribed to the "mass-female" as educational medium for polemical messages, is analyzed in V. L. Lokke's study of American utopian fiction in the last quarter of the nineteenth century.

Walter Robert's treatment of electronic music does not exactly concentrate on the new soul sounds which characterize the psyche-delic effects attempted in current Beatle releases. The essay does, however, describe the "immense new world [which] has been opened up, something literally unheard of." It suggests also the radical shift of relationships between audience, composer, and performer which will attend any development toward widespread appreciation of the new electronic music. An outline history of jazz as conditioned by jim-crow and crow-jim sentiments is sketched by Leslie B. Rout, Jr., in his essay "Economics and Race in Jazz."

The last two essays in this collection are the only two that were "commissioned" with particular purposes in mind. Studying the lack of folklore courses in the American Studies curricula throughout the country—curricula which supposedly are dedicated to studying all aspects of American culture—Richard Dorson deplores this lack of comprehensiveness and suggests that many aspects of American culture should be explored profitably by folklorists working with the larger discipline.

William H. Gass' polemic against popular culture stirred up the most heated rebuttal of any paper at the conference. Unlike Abraham Kaplan, who looks upon popular as immature but possibly promising, Gass sees nothing but "muck." To him "The objects of popular culture are not art," and the "pleasure they provide among goods, come last." Professor Gass' position, among students of American culture at least, is extreme and therefore offers a properly provocative concluding note for a collection of essays on American culture.

A conference the size of the one from which these papers came is of necessity the result of many people's cooperation. A great debt of gratitude is due to Frederick Eckman (Bowling Green State University, Ohio), to John Jacobus (Indiana University), and to Arthur Mizener (Cornell University) for the presentation of three discussions at the conference which could not be included here. For the assistance they rendered in numerous ways the following Purdue colleagues of the editors deserve thanks: Barnet Kottler, Martin Light, Barriss Mills, Mark Rowan, Henry Salerno, Raney Stanford, Walter Staton, Felix Stefanile, Tom H. Towers. Especial thanks are due to Dean Doner and the office of the Dean of Humanities, Social Science, and Education and to the English Department.

R.B.B.
R.H.C.
V.L.L.
W.T.S.

Lafayette, Indiana
June 1967

Symbols of the United States:
From Indian Queen to Uncle Sam

E. McClung Fleming

A study of the symbolic figures used to identify the American Colonies and the United States between 1755 and 1850 reveals extensive and overlapping use of six major images: The Indian Princess, the Neoclassic Plumed Goddess, the American Liberty, Columbia, Brother Jonathan, and Uncle Sam. A study of these figures yields some useful and interesting suggestions about the culture of the period. A chronological and quantitative analysis of them throws light on successive stages in the rise of American nationality. An iconographic analysis reveals some of the major values and myths associated with the "genius of America" during this period; the cluster of ideals, events, and personalities represented in secondary attributes of these figures that embodied significant aspects of the national presence; and the time and manner in which the popular culture supplemented the genteel culture in personifying the United States. In addition, it is interesting to note the range of the arts—painting, sculpture, the graphic and decorative arts—through which artists sought to meet the growing demand for national symbols. From the 1760's on, these symbolic figures were used in cartoons and political caricatures; as illustrations for magazines, books, and the mastheads of newspapers; for decorative devices on marble statues, ceramic figurines, printed textiles and wallpaper, needlework pictures, ceramic utensils, government medals, and coins.

1. THE INDIAN PRINCESS

The first symbolic figure which arose to represent the American cause was the Indian Princess[1] (Figs. 1, 2). It was the chief figure used to symbolize the American colonies between 1765 and 1776 and

Fig. 1—The Indian Princess. (Paul Revere, detail of The Obelisk. *Boston, 1766. American Antiquarian Society.)*

the United States during and after the Revolution. It persisted, though with diminishing force, as one of the favorite symbols of the United States throughout the nineteenth century. The Indian Princess is usually portrayed as a handsome, vigorous woman in her twenties. She is of noble visage and bearing, has a swarthy complexion and long, dark hair, wears a feathered headdress and skirt or cape and is usually uncovered to the waist. She is customarily armed with a bow and quiver of arrows though sometimes she holds a tomahawk or sword. She is often presented with one or more attributes distinctive of the colonial cause—the rattlesnake, the pine tree, the Liberty Tree, The Sons of Liberty, the Continental Army, after 1777 the American flag, after 1782 the American shield and eagle, and often with both Franklin and Washington in attendance.

During the years 1765 to 1783, the Indian Princess is most often presented in a context involving one or more of three themes—her relationship to Britannia, her association with trade and commerce, and her passionate striving for liberty. In her relationship to Britannia, the Indian Princess is first depicted as a wayward daughter, then a free sister. Through the years just preceding and during the Revolution, the daughter-mother relationship includes every nuance of affection, alienation, parricide, and reconciliation. The theme of economic wealth in trade is symbolized by merchant ships and articles of colonial commerce. The theme of liberty is developed through a variety of symbols. Sometimes the Princess is shown looking longingly at a liberty pole and cap, or reaching out to grasp them, or holding them by her side. She may be shown deserted or accompanied by

The Goddess of Liberty, or standing near the Liberty Tree. Sometimes she is shown with broken shackles at her wrists or a yoke
slipping from her shoulders.

The first personification of the American colonies as distinct from
Great Britain, known to this writer, is in an English print[2] of 1755
celebrating a British naval victory over the French at Louisburg,
which depicts Britain symbolized by Britannia and her "injured
Americans" by a male and female Indian. The first use of the Indian
Princess to represent the American cause appears at the time of the
Stamp Tax controversy. A half dozen prints show how English
cartoonists employed the figure. Perhaps the earliest one is "The
Great Financier" advertised for sale in London in October, 1765. In
it the Indian Princess is a kneeling suppliant with a yoke on her
neck inscribed "Taxed Without Representation." The Boston
Gazette on November 11, 1765, advertised for sale the English print
"The Deplorable State of America" which shows an Amazonian
Indian Princess spiritedly rejecting, with Minerva's advice, the
pandora box of the Stamp Tax held out by Britannia. The earliest
use of the Indian Princess symbol by an American artist, known to
this writer, is in Paul Revere's print "The Obelisk" engraved by
him for use in the great celebration of the repeal of the Stamp Tax
on Boston Commons in the spring of 1766 (Fig. 1). In Revere's typically crude style, it shows the Princess imploring the aid of her
English patrons, headed by Pitt, in freeing her countrymen from
the fetters of the Stamp Tax.

It is significant that a study of the symbolism of images representing Americans rather than Englishmen reinforces the findings of
two recent studies of the symbolism of names referring to the same
subject. Paul A. Varg recently stated[3] that the term "America" was
seldom used before 1759, but in the autumn of that year was frequently used in connection with the festivities celebrating the conquest of Quebec in a way suggestive of a nascent American nationalism. Richard L. Merritt has recently reported[4] that, from his
analysis of self-referent symbols appearing in colonial newspapers
between 1735 and 1775, "it was not until the years after 1764 that
the distinction between 'His Majesty's subjects' or 'British colonists'
and 'Americans' became a real one." At some time in the mid-
eighteenth century there developed on both sides of the Atlantic
a realization of the importance of the American colonies as a force
affecting English domestic politics, British imperial policy, and the
international power struggle; at the same time there developed
among Americans a consciousness of distinctive American national-

ity. The evidence from the symbolism of images suggests that the identification of an American community distinct from the British had taken place by 1755 and was widely accepted by 1766.

Some of the most striking examples of the use of the Indian Princess by English cartoonists during the years 1768-1783 are the prints "The Colonies Reduced" of August, 1768; "Liberty Triumphant or the Downfall of Oppression" of 1775; "The Commissioners" of April, 1778; "The Balance of Power" of January, 1781; "The Reconciliation Between Britannia and Her Daughter America" May, 1782; and "A Political Concert" of February, 1783.

Though the most numerous examples of English use of the Indian Princess are to be found in political prints, equally impressive examples can be found in other media. The Princess appears on a ceramic group known as "William Pitt Receiving the Gratitude of America" shortly after the repeal of the Stamp Tax. During the winter of 1772-1773, the London sculptor Richard Hayward carved a charming Indian Princess in a marble bas-relief on the back of a pedestal supporting his statue of Lord Botetourt which was erected in the piazza of the capitol at Williamsburg, Virginia, in June of 1773. The Princess appears on the frontispiece for the *London Magazine* of February 1, 1775, on two English commemorative medals dated 1776 and 1783, on a commemorative handkerchief of about 1784 designed by Henry Gardiner at Wordsworth, Surrey, bearing at the top the legend "Governors of ye United States of America."

The use of the Indian Princess by Dutch artists and editors to represent the United States is evidenced in two engravings and two medals produced in the Netherlands in 1781 and 1782 in support of American Independence. The earliest is an allegorical engraving by Thomas Koning which appeared on the title page of the first volume of Antoine Marie Cerisier's vigorously pro-American weekly, *Le Politique Hollandais*. The two medals were struck to commemorate the recognition of American independence by the province of Friesland and by the States General of the United Netherlands. The second engraving, by G. Brouwer, commemorates the treaty of friendship and commerce between Holland and the United States negotiated by John Adams in October, 1782. Two engravings which illustrate a similar usage by French artists are the toile de Jouy designed by Jean Baptiste Huet and manufactured at Oberkampf between 1783 and 1790 known as "America Paying Homage to France," and the aquatint dated 1786, designed by Duplessis Berteaux and engraved by Lucien Roger, entitled "L 'Amerique et Les Mers."

Fig. 2—The Indian Princess. (Etching by Jules Jacquemart of Congressional Medal of Honor inscribed to Brigadier General Daniel Morgan cast by Augustin Dupré. Paris, 1789.)

There are many striking instances of the use of the Indian Princess as a symbol of the United States by American artists, editors, and statesmen. Paul Revere has left us at least four examples after the appearance of "The Obelisk" in 1766. These are the cartouche in the lower corner of "A View of Part Of The Town Of Boston in New England and British Ships Of War Landing Their Troops, 1768," engraved, printed, and sold by him in 1770; the vignette which ran on the title page of the twelve monthly issues of the *Royal American Magazine* in 1774 and on its front cover for the first three issues of 1775; his frontispiece "America In Distress" in the final issue of the *Magazine;* and his vignette used on the masthead of Isaiah Thomas' *Massachusetts Spy* from May of 1781 until December of 1784. Another example is in the wallpaper pattern known as "The Lexington Minuteman" probably manufactured in this country during the 1780s. The most important examples are to be found on the three Congressional medals and one Presidential medal commissioned and executed between 1787 and 1791 to commemorate outstanding services to the American cause in the Revolutionary war. Under the supervision of American officials in Paris, the medals were designed by the French Royal Academy of Inscriptions and Belles-Lettres, and executed by outstanding French medallists. The first medal was inscribed to Brigadier General Daniel Morgan for his victory at Cowpens in 1781 (Fig. 2). The Indian Princess is crowning Morgan with a wreath of laurel; in the background the American shield leans against a captured enemy cannon. The second and third medals honored Brigadier General Anthony Wayne and Major John Stewart for their gallant conduct in the capture of Stony Point in 1779. The fourth medal, known as "The Diplomatic Medal" was ordered by President Washington in 1790. The Indian Princess also appears on a pattern coin cast by the Englishman Thomas Wyon of Birmingham in 1785 in accordance with a design that was almost certainly suggested by Thomas Jefferson.

It is evident that, when it became necessary to identify an American interest distinct from the British interest, the Atlantic community turned to the symbolic figure of the Indian Princess. But what explains the choice of this symbol? One factor in the choice is clear— the Indian Princess as a symbol of the American colonies of Great Britain was in part derived from the Indian Queen familiar to Europeans for two hundred years as a symbol of the western hemisphere. It was Martin Waldseemuller's *Cosmographie Introductio* of 1507 which first gave the name "America" to the New World, and which first suggested that this new world was a fourth continent or fourth part of the world supplementing Asia, Africa, and Europe. Since each of the three older continents had for many years been symbolized in the arts by a queenly figure representing the characteristic race of that continent, the European imagination now immediately set to work evolving a symbol of this new world. Quite naturally the new figure was based on the notions that became current with the publication of the first travel accounts of America, of the appearance, habits, and surroundings of the barbarous Indians of the semi-tropical Caribbean region.

Our earliest examples are by Flemish, Dutch, and German artists, but use of the theme by the Italians, French, and English is soon abundantly evident. Though the results were by no means identical, a degree of consensus had been reached as early as 1600. While always having the bearing and address of royalty, the Queen usually was depicted, in visage, as having a swarthy or "tawney" hue; in size, as being Amazonian; in dress, as wearing a feathered headdress and feathered skirt sometimes supplemented by a feathered cape and jewelled anklets. In the early representations, the Queen is armed with a club; in the later ones, with a bow and quiver of arrows. The characteristic animal, usually shown at the feet of the Queen, is an alligator, though in some of the earliest prints it is the armadillo. Other animals grouped around her include a parrot on a branch,

Fig. 3—The Indian Queen. (Lead plaque, German, c. 1580-1590. Rogers Fund, 1960. Metropolitan Museum of Art.)

monkeys, the puma, and the stag. A particularly barbarous touch is the bloody, severed head of a man pierced by an arrow and lying near the feet of the Queen. The idea of the natural wealth of the New World is sometimes symbolized by treasure in the form of ingots, vessels of gold, and chests laden with jewelry heaped around her, by the silver mine of Potosi, or by a cornucopia.

Of the hundreds of examples of The Four Continents theme that have survived, many of them included in the James Hazen Hyde Collection, representative interpretations of the Indian Queen include the engraving by Johannes Sadeler after a drawing by the Flemish artist Dirk Barentz about 1581; a lead plaque cast in Germany between 1580 and 1590 (Fig. 3) which shows a very jaunty Indian Queen armed with bow and arrows, and surrounded with tropical animals (armadillo, monkeys, parrot) and treasure; the woodcut in the first illustrated edition of Cesare Ripa's *Iconologia*

Fig. 4—The Indian Queen. (Woodcut from **Iconologia** by Cesare Ripa. Padua, 1603. Metropolitan Museum of Art.)

published in Rome in 1603 (Fig. 4) in which the Indian Queen, accompanied by a small alligator, places one foot on a severed head pierced by an arrow; the title page of *America: Being the Latest and Most Accurate Description of the New World* published by the noted cartographer John Ogilby in London in 1671, and a seventeenth century tapestry woven in Brussels by G. Paemans after the design of David Teniers the Younger.

Universal acceptance by the Atlantic community of the Indian as a symbol of the Spanish America of the Caribbean did not necessarily guarantee that the Indian would be considered an equally appropriate symbol of the English America that lay between the Alleghenies and the Atlantic seaboard. That this proved to be the case is further evidence of the force which this strange, distinctive, new race exerted on the imagination of the Englishmen who confronted it in the forests of their colonial empire. The values, however, that came to be associated with the Indian were certainly contradictory ones. The negative complex, represented by what Leslie Fiedler has called "the myth of Hannah Dustan and her escape from Indian Captivity," by Horatio Greenough's sculpture "The Rescue Group" which once graced the steps of the East Front of the Capitol, and thoroughly explored in Roy Harvey Pearce's *The Savages of America*[5] was certainly a fact. It is, however, also a fact that, whatever were the negative elements in the first-hand experience of the Englishman with this race, the Indian was almost immediately embraced as a symbol of positive values by Colonial America. He appears on the 1628 seal of Massachusetts and the 1749 seal of the Ohio Company. In 1742, Shem Browne made a famous copper weathervane of The Indian Princess to crown the turret of the Boston Province House which became such a beloved landmark that in an engraving of 1768 Paul Revere could use it as a symbol of Boston itself. It was surely not the image of the ignoble savage that prompted the Sons of Liberty to disguise themselves as American Indians for the Boston Tea Party of 1773, or the shipbuilders of Amsterdam in 1777 to name the warship they were building for the American colonists *The Indian*.

What were the positive values associated with the Indian that made the Indian Princess the official symbol of the United States on the first Congressional Medals of Honor? They were not the values embodied in the myth of Pocahontas,[6] or in the tradition of the Indian as giver of tobacco, or in the millenarian faith of Protestant missionaries zealous to convert the Indian to Christianity.[7] By a simple analogy with the Indian Queen, the Indian Princess stood for the new land of the American continent and the promise of this land, proclaimed by every explorer and settler. Perhaps, also, the new race of men to which she belonged came to suggest the "new man" that—according to observers like Crevecoeur—the European had become in America. Perhaps she served as "a symbol and reminder that there was something in America which could not be hammered into English forms."[8] Above all, through an accident of timing, the American Indian living along the frontiers of the English colonies entered deeply into the European consciousness just when Europe needed a figure to which it could project these ideals of natural nobility and innocence which were both a reaction against and a criticism of the Old Regime.

The Indian Princess, like the Indian Queen, was the Noble Savage[9] of a primitive Eden, but she was something more. She was not the offspring of an alien race but the daughter of Britannia; she was preoccupied not with the hunt and warfare but with the attainment of liberty. If the Indian Princess whom Jefferson helped to place on the early Congressional medals was related to the Indian described in his *Notes on Virginia* of 1785, and in Robert Beverley's *History and Present State of Virginia* of 1705, she may have been the symbol of a way of life more pastoral than primitive. Indeed the Indian of Virginia has been described as a blood brother of the Shepherd of Arcadia. During these years of the founding of the American Republic, could the Indian Princess have embodied elements of what Henry Nash Smith has defined as the prime myth of the American consciousness, the myth of the garden?

2. THE NEOCLASSICAL PLUMED GODDESS

Although the Indian Princess continued to be used as a symbol of the United States, there arose, from the 1780's on, several alternative symbols. One, which represents a transformation of the Indian Princess into a classical deity, might be called the Neoclassical Plumed Goddess. This transformation was an expression of the neoclassical spirit of the late eighteenth century. Popularized in England by the brilliant designer Robert Adam, the new classicism did not take hold in the United States until the late 1780's when it affected poetry, oratory, and dress as well as architecture, painting, sculpture, and the decorative arts. As Howard Mumford Jones has pointed out, the young American nation embraced "a set of classical coordinates to particularize components of its government and its Republican culture," and its elite expressed the fact "in their wallpaper, their doorways, their furniture, their fireplaces, their manners and their social values."[10] Part of this new spirit was a fresh taste for allegory and symbol making. Gentlemen on both sides of the Atlantic set to work borrowing old figures from Greek and Roman mythology or creating new ones to represent the United States. Some favored Hercules and Minerva, for a brief period quite a few took up the Neoclassical Plumed Goddess, almost everyone approved the Goddess of Liberty and a new deity christened Columbia.

The Plumed Goddess is usually depicted near a classical pyramid, altar, pedestal, urn, or triumphal arch, and these are frequently dedicated to the memory of George Washington and other Revolutionary heroes. Sometimes the Goddess is flanked or framed by medallions bearing the profiles of American statesmen and generals, often she is accompanied by an assortment of figures from classical mythology, among whom Minerva, Hercules, Mercury, Liberty, Victory, and Fame figure prominently. Typically she is fully draped in Grecian robes and wears sandals, but her distinguishing mark is an assortment of ostrich plumes in place of eagle feathers worn in a bonnet, helmet, or turban. The ostrich plumes maintain a certain continuity of outward tradition with the Indian Princess while in reality expressing a radical change of spirit. The pyramids and urns, the accompanying deities, and the flowing robes convey the neoclassical spirit, while the basic fact of American sovereignty is indicated by the presence of such symbols as the American flag, escutcheon with thirteen stripes, eagle, and the constellation of thirteen stars. The result is what has been described as "a kind of Indian-Graeco-Roman-American personality."[11]

Good examples of the Plumed Goddess are to be found in the English printed textile of about 1785 known as "The Apotheosis of Washington"; the engraving entitled "America Trampling on Oppression" used as a frontispiece to the Rev. Samuel Cooper's *History of North America* published in England and this country in several editions between 1789 and 1793; the English printed textile of about 1790 known as "America Presenting at the Altar of Liberty, Medallions of her Illustrious Sons"; the engraving by Alexis Chataigner after a painting by Mme. Anthony Plantou called "The Peace of Ghent and Triumph of America" published in Philadelphia in 1815; and a second Philadelphia print of 1815 drawn by John J. Barralet and engraved by Benjamin Tanner entitled "America Guided by Wisdom" (Fig. 5). Here the Plumed Goddess, identified as "The Genius of America," sits regally in her classical robes under the American flag, supporting a shield bearing the arms of the United States with the motto "Union and Independence." At her feet is the horn of plenty; beside her, as protectress and counsellor, stands Minerva, Goddess of Wisdom; to the right is a triumphant arch

AMERICA GUIDED BY WISDOM;

Fig. 5—The Neo-Classical Plumed Goddess. (John J. Barralet, America Guided by Wisdom. *Philadelphia, c. 1815. (Engraving by Benjamin Tanner. Henry Francis du Pont Winterthur Museum.)*

under which, on a pedestal, is a heroic equestrian statue of Washington; in the background stands a benevolent Mercury.

A special use of the Plumed Goddess was as the symbol of "America" in a series of prints of the Four Continents for which there was apparently a popular vogue between 1789 and 1815. In these, the United States clearly represents the entire American continent. The Goddess is usually a youthful, tall brunette dressed in a loose classical gown and cloak and wearing sandals or slippers. The ostrich plumes number from one to ten. In the foreground are such attributes as the liberty pole and cap, the American flag and shield, the eagle, a marble monument to Washington, the rattlesnake, and hogsheads of tobacco. In the background are such American landscape elements as Niagara Falls, cargo vessels, and a mountainous wilderness. Quite often there appears that new American figure—a young African Negro boy dressed in American Indian feathers. A second series of prints in which the Plumed Goddess is the central figure bears the common title "An Emblem of America" and has no reference to the other three Continents.

What values seem to be conveyed by this Neo-Classic representation of the United States? If the Indian Princess embodies the myth that the United States might be the realization of the pastoral ideal, the Plumed Goddess embodies the myth that the United States was, in a special way, the incarnation of Graeco-Roman civic virtues and ideals. This was the culmination of the great dream of antiquity which carried through the entire Georgian epoch to leave a special stamp on the Federal Era. To Jefferson and his contemporaries, writes Alan Gowans,[12] "it seemed as if this new nation, living proof of the classical conviction that men could control their destinies and mould worlds to their will, was the very reincarnation of the grandeur that had been Rome. In the heroes and statesmen of the Revolution, the selfless patriotism of Horatii and Cincinnati lived again; in the new Senate on the Potomac, the old Senate on the Tiber would be reborn; just so, in the new courthouses and capitols and official mansions of America, the monuments of Rome would be rebuilt." The Plumed Goddess expressed a neo-classical moment in the American consciousness when the United States was reviving Roman and Greek architecture on a scale unequaled anywhere else.

3. THE AMERICAN LIBERTY

While some artists, impelled by the neo-classical spirit, were led to transform the Indian Princess into the Plumed Goddess, others selected particular deities whose qualities they wished to associate with the new American Republic. At least three were so utilized— Hercules, Minerva, and Liberty. Use of the first two was limited and cannot here be reviewed. The case, however, was different with the Goddess of Liberty. The story of the steady progress with which Liberty became associated with the American cause goes back at least to the 1760's and is an epic in itself. This association took two visual forms. The figure symbolizing the United States might be shown in the company of the Goddess of Liberty or holding her liberty cap and pole. Or, more important, the Goddess of Liberty might be shown so intimately identified with the American cause as in effect to become "Americanized." This might be by her holding, or being dressed in, the American flag; supporting the American shield; being guarded by the American eagle; or being identified by thirteen stars or the date July 4, 1776. In these cases we have either Liberty representing the United States or the United States interpreted as Liberty. For these reasons this symbolic figure can be called "The American Liberty." (The Statue of Liberty in New York Harbor has no American attributes and therefore cannot be considered an example of the American Liberty.)

A fine early example of this symbolic figure is the obverse of the famous medal *Libertas Americana* designed and ordered by Benjamin Franklin and executed by the great French medalist Augustin Dupré in 1782. The American Liberty is presented in profile as a beautiful young woman with loose hair floating in the wind and carrying the liberty pole and Phrygian cap over her shoulder. Underneath the head is the date of July 4, 1776. Charles Blanc, a member of the French Academie Des Beaux-Arts, perfectly caught the spirit of the composition when he wrote in 1870: "Dupré has represented the new born Liberty, sprung from the prairies without ancestry and without rulers, as a youthful virgin, with dishevelled hair and dauntless aspect...."[13] In accordance with the resolution of Congress of April 6, 1792 establishing the United States Mint at Philadelphia, the American Liberty became the dominant device on the first coins to be minted by the United States government. The cent and half-cent, the only denominations to be struck in 1793, carried a bust of Liberty engraved by Joseph Wright that was copied directly from Dupré's *Libertas Americana*. Later mintings, though different from Dupré's design, can also be considered examples of the American Liberty.

An interesting example of a print of this subject is one entitled "The Goddess of Liberty with the Portrait of Jefferson," engraved in 1807 and published in Salem, Massachusetts. Liberty is seated on the globe, her liberty pole and cap over her shoulder, one foot on the emblem of monarchy, supporting on her knee the portrait of Thomas Jefferson. While pointing to Jefferson, she gazes gratefully at a portrait of Washington on a pyramid in front of her. A glory of sixteen stars surrounds her head and sends its rays across the heavens while a large American eagle sits at her side thrusting his head protectingly over her lap.

The American Liberty was frequently used as a symbol of the United States in decorative sculpture on public buildings. Three good examples were designed for the United States Capitol. For the Hall of the House of Representatives in the South Wing, the young Italian sculptor Giuseppe Franzoni completed an eight-foot statue of Liberty in 1807 under the careful guidance of Benjamin Latrobe. She held the liberty cap in one hand and the Constitution of the United States in the other, with one foot placed on a reversed crown and other emblems of monarchy and bondage, and the American eagle standing at her side. Franzoni's Liberty was destroyed in the fire set to the Capitol by British troops in 1814. In 1817 it was replaced by a plaster statue by Enrico Causici. This regal Liberty, clothed in flowing classical garb, stands gracefully with the extended right arm holding the Constitution of the United States. On her right she is guarded by a splendid American eagle; on her left she is supported by the serpent of wisdom, recalling the American rattlesnake, which encircles a column-like altar. Thomas Crawford's nineteen foot statue of the American Liberty (Fig. 6) which surmounts the Capitol, designed in 1856, grasps a shield bearing the American stars and stripes, and wears at her waist a brooch bearing the letters "U.S." She wears a helmet encircled with stars and surmounted by a crest made up of an eagle's head and an arrangement of feathers derived from the dress of Indian tribes. This is a rare instance of the American Liberty wearing an attribute of the Indian Princess.

Fig. 6—The American Liberty. (Thomas Crawford, Freedom. *Plaster model. Rome, 1856. Architect of the Capitol, Washington, D. C.)*

4. COLUMBIA

The most original, popular, and durable of the symbols inspired by the classical spirit was "Columbia." The figure was conceived as a sort of Graeco-Roman deity personifying the United States, but with a name derived from Christopher Columbus. It was thus a conscious, deliberate creation with traditional as well as novel aspects. Just when and where the name was first used is not clear. Chief Justice Samuel Sewall of the Massachusetts Bay Colony may have been the first to use the name for the New World in 1697. It appears in the *Gentleman's Magazine* in the 1730's, and in a volume of poems published in Boston in 1761. Thereafter it appears frequently in patriotic songs and poems published in colonial newspapers. Two American warships during the War of Independence were named Columbia; King's College became Columbia College in 1784; in 1790 the home of the new national capital was named the District of Columbia. Timothy Dwight's exuberantly patriotic song *Columbia* was written in 1777, Joseph Hopkinson's "Hail Columbia" was composed in 1789, and Joel Barlow's "Columbiad" published in 1807. The name was given to newspapers, magazines, almanacs, towns, counties, rivers, ships, and railroad lines.

The Indian Princess and the Plumed Goddess were created by artists and had clearly recognizable features, but neither had any other name than "America" and neither became a literary figure. On the other hand, Columbia from the beginning was the creature of the poets and was soon embraced by song writers and orators. She kept her own distinctive name though everyone knew she stood for America, but for some time was not given visual expression by artists and only gradually acquired a stable image. The typical Columbia is a regal figure of a woman, beautiful, blonde, fully covered in flowing white garments, and either bareheaded or wearing a laurel wreath, tiara, or liberty cap. She never wears a feathered bonnet or skirt, or an ostrich plume in her hair; she is never portrayed with a bow and quiver of arrows, and the rattlesnake never accompanies her. On the other hand, she is frequently draped in the American flag, or wears a liberty cap decorated with stars and stripes; sometimes she is armed with the spear, shield, and helmet of Minerva. She is frequently shown holding the liberty pole and cap or the American flag on a standard; beside her is often the American shield with its stripes, and the eagle; near her might be the constellation of thirteen stars and an inscription giving the date of the Declaration of Independence.

One of the earliest portrayals of Columbia is the second drawing made in 1782 by William Barton, Philadelphia nephew of David Rittenhouse, at the request of the third Committee of Congress charged with devising a Great Seal for the United States. "On the dexter side," he wrote of this design, "the genius of the American Confederated Republic; represented by a Maiden with flowing auburn tresses; clad in a long, loose white garment, bordered with green; having a sky-blue scarf, charged with stars as in the arms...; and on her head, a radiated crown of gold, encircled with an azure fillet spangled with silver . . ." Barton's proposal was not adopted but several elements in his blazone were to appear again.

The bareheaded Columbia appears in the first three frontispieces of the *Columbia Magazine* or *Monthly Miscellany* which began publication in Philadelphia in 1786. In the second, she is being invited by Concord into a temple which represents the newly ratified Constitution with two of its thirteen columns cracked to represent the non-concurring states. Congressional medals sometimes portrayed Columbia. Though all the earliest ones utilized the Indian Princess to symbolize the United States, Jefferson referred to a suggestion that Columbia be substituted on the Diplomatic Medal of 1790, and Columbia was used on two Congressional medals designed by Moritz Furst awarded to William Henry Harrison and Andrew Jackson for victories in the War of 1812. In 1785, Thomas Wyon of Birmingham, England, designed a pattern coin displaying Columbia with a laurel wreath around her head. Struck in gold, silver, and copper, the obverse bears the inscription *Immune Columbia* and shows the goddess seated on a globe, her right hand holding a large, furled American flag topped by the liberty cap, and her outstretched left hand holding the scales of justice. An early example of the helmeted Columbia is found on the lower half of the printed English toile of about 1785 known as "The Apotheosis of Washington and Franklin." Occupying the center of the scene, magnificently suggestive of power and vitality, Columbia holds in her left hand an oval shield emblazoned with thirteen enormous stars and with her right hand leads Franklin to the Temple of Fame.

When American political cartoons of the early Republic represented the United States, it was usually with the figure of Columbia. One well-executed, anti-Federalist line engraving of 1796 entitled "See Porcupine, in Colours Just Portrayed" shows Columbia sorrowfully bending over a portrait of Franklin which stands on a base inscribed "Independence declared 4 July 1776." Behind Columbia stands a huge American eagle holding the liberty cap and pole under its wings. During a diplomatic brush with Denmark in December, 1809, there appeared a dramatic copperplate engraving made by an

Fig. 7—Columbia (William Charles, Bruin Become Mediator, or Negotiation For Peace. *Philadelphia, 1815. Library Company, Philadelphia.)*

anonymous cartoonist entitled "The Copenhagen Monster Muzzled." It depicts a helmeted Columbia grasping an American flag and accompanied by a fierce American eagle clutching a bundle of spears, defiantly confronting a huge, scaly dragon. In a cartoon of 1815 entitled "Bruin Become Mediator, or Negotiation For Peace," engraved and published in Philadelphia by William Charles, Columbia wears a crown marked "76" (Fig. 7).

Many vernacular treatments of Columbia have great charm and vitality. One, a canvas window shade from a Connecticut tavern painted between 1800 and 1810 by an unknown artist shows a bareheaded Columbia holding the American flag in her left hand, and with her right placing a wreath on the marble bust of Washington while crushing the British crown beneath her foot. Overhead soars the American eagle; the liberty pole and cap grow out of the Tree of Liberty in the background.

A handsome example of the Liberty Cap Columbia can be seen over the east central portico of the United States Capitol in Washington. It is a sandstone sculpture of "The Genius of the United States" executed by the Italian sculptor Luigi Persico between 1825 and 1828 after a design drawn by President John Quincy Adams. Colum-

Fig. 8—Columbia (Wood carving, c. 1850. Marine Historical Association, Inc.)

bia holds a shield inscribed "U.S.A." which radiates a glory. It rests on a pedestal inscribed "July 4, 1776." Columbia points to Justice, who holds the scales and a scroll inscribed "Constitution 17 September, 1787." A large eagle, at Columbia's feet, looks up at her with an alert turn of its head, its wings and talons ready for action.

In addition to its use on Congressional medals, official sculpture, and cartoons, Columbia appears ubiquitously on bank notes, business letter heads, certificates, weathervanes, ship figureheads, and circus wagons. In one example of unidentified outdoor sculpture (Fig. 8), a typical Columbia wears a laurel wreath and liberty cap, and is dressed in a red-white-and-blue blouse and skirt covered with stars. Her right hand probably held the American flag, now missing. Columbia may sometimes show anger, or sorrow, or disapproval, but she is always dignified and a lady, representing the more formal and idealistic aspects of the American character.

Like the Indian Princess, Columbia is a symbol with many meanings for Americans. First of all, she is a more unique and specific symbol for the United States than the Indian Princess, the Plumed Goddess, or Liberty. Secondly, unlike the Indian or the Roman deity, Columbia represents a European force. The core meaning of Columbia has to do with the mission, the achievement, and the symbolism of Columbus' voyage. Part of this achievement is the fact of his discovery of something radically new in the world, indeed, a New World, essentially different from Europe. Part of the mission is the quest for the promise of the East, a promise not just of material wealth and exotic goods but of earth's original paradise. Part of the symbolism of Columbus' voyage is the movement from the Occident to the Orient—the myth of Whitman's *Passage to India*. America, which he discovered, is, in the great westward flow of civilization, the link between Europe and Asia and thus also the final thrust of the impulse which moved man from Asia into Europe, and from Europe into America. The Passage to India, according to Henry Nash Smith, was "the oldest of all ideas associated with America," and a symbol of its freedom and national greatness.[14] Columbia thus symbolized a new world, a new people, a new era, and a mission that was the consummation and fulfillment of history as well as its renewal by a return to man's first Eden. As Alan Trachtenberg has successfully interpreted the half-conscious feelings of Americans for this myth, "In the drama of restoration, America would play a central role. Columbus' discovery was the first act.... America is the appropriate emblem for the new worship, the new brotherhood, the new Eden. On its shores, East and West shall mingle freely, and man shall regain his ancient harmony with nature."[15]

Of the four major personifications of the United States represented in the visual arts during these years—the Indian Princess, the Plumed Goddess, the American Liberty, and Columbia—the Plumed Goddess disappeared with the decline of the neoclassical movement in the 1820's. The Indian Princess, though remaining a popular folk figure throughout the nineteenth century, became less and less identified with the spirit of the United States. On the other hand, as though in response to an impulse to retain and develop the one symbol specifically created to represent the new nation, and one embodying a rich sense of historical mission, Columbia grew in popularity and use. However, as the conviction developed in the young Republic that its single most passionately held ideal was liberty, it was inevitable that increasing use should be made of The American Liberty, and that The American Liberty and Columbia should become fused. There was thus combined in this image of the United States the idea of a great historic mission with a great Moral ideal.

5. BROTHER JONATHAN AND UNCLE SAM

The feminine figures of Liberty and Columbia were created essentially for dignified, formal, and ceremonial occasions, and belonged to the genteel tradition. With the rise of the common man and the growth of the vernacular tradition and the popular arts in the United States between the War of 1812 and the Civil War, there arose several new, masculine figures symbolizing the nation which brought an altogether new vitality, expressiveness and informal robustness to the American image.

Yankee Doodle may have emerged between 1758 and 1775 as a popular, male folk symbol of the New Englanders, but the first male symbol of the United States as a whole was undoubtedly Brother Jonathan. It apparently arose during the early years of the Revolution, and one account identifies the prototype as Jonathan Trumbull the elder, then Governor of Connecticut. As developed between 1778 and 1860 in humorous and satiric literature, in American and English cartoons and on the American stage, Brother Jonathan was a shrewd yankee rustic—trader, pedlar, and sailor by turns; audacious, impudent, witty, and a bit cocky. At first, he was portrayed as short and chunky, later as lean and lanky, and until the eve of the Civil War as clean-shaven.

A fine early portrayal of this figure is the print entitled "Brother Jonathan Administering a Salutary Cordial to John Bull" (Fig. 9).

Fig. 9—Brother Jonathan (Brother Jonathan Administering a Salutary Cordial to John Bull, *attrib. Amos Doolittle, Philadelphia, 1813. Henry Francis du Pont Winterthur Museum.)*

BROTHER JONATHAN Administering a Salutary Cordial to JOHN BULL.

It was issued in 1813 shortly after Perry's victory at Lake Erie, and was probably engraved by Amos Doolittle. In it, Jonathan is a stocky young man dressed in brimmed hat, tail coat, boots, and with hair tied in a long queue. John Bull is blurting out, "oh don't force me to take it, Brother Jonathan. Give me Holland gin, French brandy, anything but this damned Yankee *Perry*." An English cartoon of 1844 again portrays a short, cocky little Jonathan. The time is just after Polk's election, when a showdown over the Oregon boundary was threatened. A bemused John Bull, with his stick under his arm, stands on the English side of the water; across from him threatens a tough, self-confident Brother Jonathan with his dukes up, smoking his "segar," a slave whip in his rear pocket. Gradually, Brother Jonathan grows more tall and lank. The trend can be seen in an English cartoon by Dickie Doyle which appeared in *Punch* in 1847 entitled, "The Land of Liberty—Recommended to the consideration of Brother Jonathan." Jonathan is a rough, long-legged, rakish character in large straw hat and boots. Cigar in mouth, pepperbox revolver in belt, slave whip under his arm, he sprawls on a rocker, his money chest beside him and on it a drink; one leg is stretched carelessly over a fallen bust of Washington. Gradually, in the 1850's, Jonathan acquired a tall beaver hat and striped pants, often with stars on the cuffs. An 1856 cartoon in *Punch* which shows a confrontation between John Bull and Brother Jonathan over the Canadian fisheries shows the latter in this garb, along with his "segar" and slave whip. C. F. Morse published a Civil War cartoon in Washington, D. C. in 1862 which depicts a whole army of clean-shaven, top-hatted, stripe-trousered Jonathans marching on Dixie.

Through a process of unpredictable selection, however, it was another vernacular figure, Uncle Sam, not Brother Jonathan which, by the 1870's was the universally accepted symbol of the United States. This folk figure arose in 1813, during the War of 1812, when army supplies packed and shipped by Samuel Wilson, familiarly known to his friends and acquaintances as Uncle Sam Wilson, came to be labeled "U.S." Soldiers and civilians alike embraced the happy fiction that it was Uncle Sam who was feeding and taking care of the army.[16] Somehow the fiction took root and grew. Well before the death of the actual Samuel Wilson in 1854, cartoons were appearing which portrayed Uncle Sam as head of the national household. The earliest one that we know of is an unsigned lithograph of 1832. Others followed in the thirties. In 1840 appeared a drawing by an anonymous artist, published by Elton, entitled "Uncle Sam's Pet Pups." Uncle Sam is a rather common fellow of middle height, wearing a tall-crowned hat, cut-away coat, and striped pants, but is clean-

Fig. 10—Uncle Sam (L. Wagner, "Uncle Sam Beats All: The Great International Rifle Match," 1877. Henry Ford Museum.)

shaven. In E. W. Clay's cartoon of 1846 called "Uncle Sam's Taylorifics," Uncle Sam becomes familiarly tall and lank. Neatly dressed in beaver hat, long coat tails, handsome cravat and boots, he is clean-shaven, with long hair. By 1860, when *Frank Leslie's Illustrated Newspaper* published the cartoon "The American Eagle in Danger," Uncle Sam was wearing the striped trousers of Brother Jonathan and gaiters. By 1861, as Abraham Lincoln popularized the beard, Uncle Sam came to have whiskers. During the sixties he replaced Brother Jonathan, and by the seventies, in the hands of Thomas Nast of *Harper's Weekly* and then Joseph Keppler of *Puck* the final familiar Uncle Sam emerged to become the country's favorite symbol for the United States (Fig. 10). Columbia was not dropped, and occasionally she was depicted as Uncle Sam's wife, but she remained the rather austere, righteous, humorless matron.

It is not hard to see how the figures of Brother Jonathan and Uncle Sam filled a growing need for vernacular symbols of the country that could express the full range of popular moods and emotions. As for the underlying values conveyed by these figures, it is clear that they embodied a new version of the American pastoral ethos and the ideal of "the middle landscape" that arose in the Jacksonian era and which Americans did not wish to lose. First Brother Jonathan and then Uncle Sam combined astuteness and rural simplicity in such a way as to become a kind of "comic cousin of Jefferson's noble husbandman," thus constituting a version of the pastoral ideal in a distinctively American idiom.[17]

The Indian Princess, the Plumed Goddess, the American Liberty, Columbia, Brother Jonathan, and Uncle Sam give us striking visual clues to a succession of basic values projected to this country by Americans as well as Europeans.

NOTES

1. E. McClung Fleming, "The American Image as Indian Princess," *Winterthur Portfolio,* II (1965), 65-81.

2. "British Resentment, or The French Fairly Coopt at Louisburg."

3. Paul A. Varg, "The Advent of Nationalism, 1758-1776," *American Quarterly,* XVI (1964), 169-170.

4. Richard L. Merritt, "The Emergence of American Nationalism: A Quantitative Approach," *American Quarterly,* XVII (1965), 333.

5. Roy Harvey Pearce, *The Savages of America: A Study of the Indian and the Idea of Civilization* (Baltimore: The Johns Hopkins Press, 1965).

6. See Philip Young, "The Mother of Us All: Pocahontas Reconsidered," *The Kenyon Review,* vol. XXIV, No. 3 (Summer, 1962).

7. See Charles L. Sanford, *The Quest For Paradise: Europe and The Moral Imagination* (Urbana, Illinois: University of Illinois Press, 1961), ch. 5.

8. Oliver W. Larkin, *Art and Life in America* (New York: Rinehart, 1956), p. 45.

9. See Henri Baudet, *Paradise on Earth* (New Haven: Yale University Press, 1965), ch. II.

10. Howard Mumford Jones, *O Strange New World* (New York: Viking, 1964), pp. 233, 244.

11. Jones, p. 242.

12. Alan Gowans, *Images of American Living* (Philadelphia: Lippincott, 1964), p. 247

13. J. F. Loubat, *The Medallic History of the United States of America, 1776-1876* (New York: Published by the author, 1878), I, xxii.

14. Henry Nash Smith, *Virgin Land: The American West as Symbol and Myth* (Cambridge: Harvard University Press, 1950), ch. II.

15. Alan Trachtenberg, *Brooklyn Bridge: Fact and Symbol* (New York: Oxford, 1965), p. 17.

16. Alton Ketchum, *Uncle Sam: The Man and The Legend* (New York: Hill and Wang, 1959), ch. 6.

17. Leo Marx, *The Machine and the Garden* (New York: Oxford, 1964), pp. 132-133.

"Cheap Books" and the Public Interest: Paperbound Book Publishing in Two Centuries

C. Hugh Holman

All art forms are in one sense media to communicate the artist's visions to his audience. For the arts that have mass appeal or commercial aspects these media function both as vehicles for the artist's vision and as entrepreneurial mechanisms. The medium of the painter is oil and canvas; it is also the gallery and the exhibition. The medium of the playwright is made of words, scenery, lighting, and actors; it is also the physical and financial qualities of the theater. Shakespeare's presentation of his view of reality was very much shaped by the characteristics of the Elizabethan theater and audience. Much of the drama on network television is the captive of the mass audience and the advertiser.

In publishing the medium is the book, the magazine, or the newspaper. The magazine and the newspaper have achieved large audiences that have, in turn, effectively shaped their mechanical, substantive, and aesthetic nature. When book publishing began to move toward comparable mass audiences, it needed new means of technical production, different means of distribution, and fresh approaches to its audience. In all these respects publishing for a mass audience differed significantly from publishing as the polite avocation of cultured gentlemen, where personal taste, private whim, and aesthetic courage often determined publishing lists. Christopher Morley once said of the traditional book business, "It is almost the only way, in America, that a man of taste can be sure of losing money with dignity."[1] The mass-media book publisher cannot afford such elegant pastimes.

The development of these new means of printing, distributing, and financing book publication has resulted in the modern book being both a medium and an economic factor which plays a significant role in the nature of the work itself. Yet this role is often ignored by students of literature and of culture. I shall attempt to look at two periods in which American book publishing has consciously aimed at a mass market and at the effects that these efforts produced. I have chosen the "cheap book" development of the 1840's and the paperback book development of the 1940's and 1950's, with the intention of examining the causes which made these developments possible, the paths that book publishing followed during these periods, and some of the implications which these trends appear to have for the public interest, if that interest is identified with both the accumulation of knowledge and wisdom and with the fostering of artistic expression.[2]

1.

The first major movement toward "cheap book" publication in America occurred in the 1840's and was associated in part with paperbound publications. However, the frequent and easy linkage of "cheap books" with paper bindings should not be made. Paper binding was for centuries a common means of assembling printed sheets for those who planned to bind their own books for their libraries, and paper was the standard binding for books in France and in many other parts of Europe. It was widely used in America, both for individual books and for series or "libraries," in the seventeenth and eighteenth centuries. For example, "The Christian Pocket Library," published in mid-eighteenth century America in light blue paper binding, was a series of sermons with forty-eight pages in each number and with six numbers intended to be bound together later to form a pocket volume.[3] Even today the difference between cloth cases and paperbinding for a 300-page book is between fifteen and twenty-five cents, while the difference in retail sales price is often ten times as great in cloth. The production of paperbound "cheap books" in America in the 1840's, frequently called "The Great Revolution in Publishing,"[4] resulted from several factors other than paperbinding.

One important factor was the Panic of 1837, a severe financial collapse that lasted from the spring of 1837 until it reached its lowest point in February, 1843, and then edged upward for four more years before the national economy was back at its original level.[5] This depression caused a virtual cessation of traditional publishing. Henry Charles Lea, in 1885, tracing the history of the house that grew from Mathew Carey's famous firm, said:

The first collection of [Poe's] writings, "Tales of the Grotesque and Arabesque," was published by Lea and Blanchard in 1839 ....it sold so slowly that in 1841 it had not returned the expense of publication....The failure of his early work was not due to any obtuseness on the part of his publishers, but to the financial stringency of the times.[6]

In this shortage of money and this drastic curtailment of normal book sales was a pressure for new markets and lower prices.

The ability to meet these demands came as a result of new, low-cost manufacturing methods. Basic among them were: the production of pulp-paper by the Fourdrinier and the Gilpin paper-making machines, both of which were producing paper in quantity in America by 1830;[7] the development of efficient typesetting machines by William Church in the period after 1822; the perfecting of stereotyping in 1811 and electrotyping in 1841; and the wide-spread use of improved Napier and Hoe cylinder presses in the early 1830's.[8] These mechanical advances made it possible to produce books rapidly and inexpensively. The result was the creation of a new dimension in book publishing and, for a time, an incredible depression of aesthetic quality in bookmaking.

The initial effort to supply books at low prices was by newspapers and magazines. *The Corsair,* a literary miscellany which serialized foreign novels without benefit of payment, began in 1839 under the editorship of Nathaniel P. Willis and Dr. T. O. Parker. It publicly flew the black flag of piracy, declaring its intention to bring "the cream and spirit of everything that ventures to light in England, France, and Germany" in newspaper form at low prices.[9] Before it had gotten fully asail, it was joined in this mission by *Brother Jonathan,* edited by Park Benjamin and Rufus Wilmot Griswold, which published news and sensational fiction, together with other literary materials, poorly illustrated with bad woodcuts. In 1840 another journal entered the field, *The New World,* published by Jonas Winchester and Griswold and Benjamin, who left *Brother Jonathan* to join him. *The New World* was an enormous publication, with "Leviathan" pages sometimes four feet long and eleven columns wide.[10]

The editors found that there was no virtue in serial piracy when extra numbers could present complete novels, and thus they entered book publication. In July, 1841, *The New World* published Lever's *Charles O'Malley* as a "supplement" in regular newspaper format at fifty cents. The first "cheap book" had appeared. *Brother Jonathan* promptly retaliated with the same novel in an "extra" at twenty-five cents, and the "cheap book" war was on. *The New World* began publishing quarto supplements and both journals quickly moved to octavo editions. They were now directly in competition with the regular book trade. They sent forth Dickens' novels in eighty closely printed quarto pages that were certain to injure the eyesight of the readers. They published Bulwer-Lytton, Balzac, Frederika Bremer, Sue, and other pirated Europeans in miserably printed editions with flimsy, bright-colored covers at newsstand prices.[11]

George Roberts began a "mammoth" weekly, *The Notion*, in Boston, and advertised "104 square feet of reading matter." These papers, along with others that joined what the New York *Tribune* called "the Satanic Press,"[12] sold quarto editions of novels on the streets of New York, Boston, and Philadelphia, and sent unbound sheets through the mail at newspaper rates, thus having the best of both worlds. They were clearly exploiting the absence of a copyright law and producing fiction and other literary work at the lowest possible cost and too often in the worst possible taste. Furthermore, they were appealing to the lowest taste in order to sell to an audience that either had no time for books or considered them a dispensable luxury.[13] John Neal declared:

> The present system of cheap literature is playing the very mischief with our country—corrupting the morals—belittling the public mind—spoiling the stomachs—and impoverishing, not only our Native Authors, and the publishers of wholesale books, but even the *Trash-Purveyors* of the day who seem to be fattening upon the offal. . . .[14]

The effect on trade book publishing was severe. Henry Charles Lea said:

> The system of cheap publications, arising from the extreme depression of business between 1839 and 1843, rendered general literature less attractive. It was impossible to sell a work of fiction except in paper, and large stocks of Cooper's novels, bound in cloth and utterly unsalable, had to be stripped of their covers and be done up in paper to find a market.

In 1841, William Gilmore Simms, once a well-remunerated and extremely popular novelist, received from his publishers a letter saying:

> We do not see much hope in the future for the American writer in light literature—as a matter of profit, it might be abandoned.
>   The channel seems to glutted with periodical literature, particularly the mammoth weeklies.[16]

Although some American writers found publishers at greatly reduced prices in these mammoth weeklies—the best known being

Walter Whitman, whose only novel *Franklin Evans* was published by *The New World* on November 23, 1842, at 12½ cents a copy[17] —the bulk of them did not, and those who did wrote novelettes rather than novels. The first massive movement to present the public with literature catering to the lowest taste at very cheap prices and depending on large sales for the moment seemed to dominate the field. Writers like Simms wrote a few novelettes, flirted briefly with the mammoth weeklies, and turned to non-fiction.[18] The mass market seemed to have driven the trade book out of America.

But the matter did not rest there, for the trade publishers began to fight back. Harper and Brothers, at that time the world's largest book manufacturer and publisher, retaliated by joining the fight for the mass market. They had bought the stereotype plates of twelve Bulwer novels. With these plates they launched "Harper's Library of Select Novels," books in two-column, royal-octavo size, bound in brown paper, and priced below cost in the conscious effort to undersell the mammoth weeklies. In addition to Bulwer's novels, the "Library" reprinted other popular British and Continental writers. They sold first at twenty-five cents, then at twelve and a half cents, and sometimes as low as six cents. Harper and Brothers also put its well-established "Family Library," which sold at one dollar and higher in neatly bound paper and sold it for prices as low as twenty-five cents. The firm was using its resources as the world's largest publishing house to drive the upstarts from the field at whatever cost.[19] They won, but they had major—perhaps decisive—assistance from the Post Office, which, in April, 1843, suspended newspaper rates on the mammoth weeklies' "extras" and began charging the higher book rate, effectively increasing the cost of distribution.[20]

Where Harper and Brothers fought fire with fire and outdid the mass market publishers at their own game, Wiley and Putnam, on the other hand, attempted quality publishing at low prices for the regular book trade. They began a paperbound series of reprints of English works, the well-printed "Library of Choice Reading," which contained such works as Hazlitt's *Table Talk,* Hood's *Prose and Verse,* Lamb's *Essays of Elia,* Fouque's *Undine and Sintram*, Peacock's *Headlong Hall* and *Night-Mare Abbey*, and Zschokke's *Tales* at prices ranging from thirty-seven to seventy-five cents. They followed "The Library of Choice Reading" in 1845 with one of the most venturesome of American publishing endeavors, "The Library of American Books," which, under the editorship of Evert A. Duyckinck, published distinguished original work by American authors in attractively printed editions on good book paper, bound in paper but designed to be rebound in cloth. In its eighteen-month history, this "Library" published, among many works, *Tales* by Edgar A. Poe, at fifty cents; *The Raven and Other Poems* by Edgar A. Poe, at thirty-one cents; two volumes of Simms's short stories, *The Wigwam and the Cabin,* and two volumes of his critical essays, all at fifty cents a volume; *Typee* by Herman Melville, at seventy-five cents; *Mosses from an Old Manse* by Nathaniel Hawthorne; and *Etchings of a Whale Cruise* by J. Ross Browne. This must be the most impressive single original publishing endeavor undertaken in the nineteenth century by an American publisher.[21] Not only was the writing quality high, the prices were unbelievably low, and the books beautifully designed and printed on paper of such quality that they remain today, after over 120 years, with practically no foxing or other discoloration. Wiley and Putnam thus attempted to meet the challenge of the "cheap book" with a quality, low-priced trade book.

Hence between 1839 and 1846 came the first attempt to satisfy the mass audience with cheap books, using the magazine and newspaper methods of circulation. It produced successful retaliations by two major book publishers—one with reprints priced to drive the "cheap book" publishers from the market and the other with the publication of original material in paper bindings at low prices. When the fifties came with the richest period in book-publishing that America had ever enjoyed, it came after an upsurge of paperbound book publishing that had so thoroughly left its mark on the American book business that never again was American publishing to be the same. Furthermore, the mass-media book and the quality paperback had each had its successful introduction to the American public.

2.

The years between the late 1840's and the early 1870's were slack times for "cheap book" publishing, but in the period between 1870 and 1890 the movement had a major resurgence. This dramatic rise in the publication of low-priced books resulted from the importing of pirated English books, a major decline in the price of paper which was then being made from ground wood pulp, and a series of sharp economic disasters. Although greater than that of the 1840's in magnitude—in fact, threatening to destroy the normal book trade in the late 1880's—this paperback upsurge had most of the characteristics of the earlier one. It ended abruptly in 1891, partly as a result of the passage of the International Copyright Act and partly as a result of the glutting of the highly competitive market.

In 1939, exactly one hundred years after *The Corsair* set sail, Robert F. de Graff founded Pocket Books and the second major revolution in "cheap book" publishing began. The economic, mechanical, and distributional factors that made Pocket Books possible had remarkable similarities to those that helped create the revolution of the 1840's.[22]

The biggest economic factor was the severe depression which began in 1929. Standard books were again a luxury and attempts to produce very low priced books began again. Charles Boni established a paper book series in 1929, but it failed. Modern Age Books, also in paper covers, was a gallant but futile effort. Late in the 1930's *The American Mercury* began publishing "Mercury Books," frequently abridged versions printed in double columns on pages the size of the *Readers' Digest* and designed for monthly newsstand circulation. Its first title was James M. Cain's *The Postman Always Rings Twice,* and its publication in 1937 was a harbinger of the future, particularly in its mixture of toughness, sex, sadism, and crime. Most Mercury Books were detective or crime stories. The cheap clothbound reprint was flourishing in Grosset and Dunlap's "Popular Fiction" series, and in the mid-1930's Doubleday, Doran began publishing Triangle Books, a 39-cent hard-cover series sold through ten-cent stores and department stores rather than through traditional book stores.[23]

Pocket Books' first list was remarkably varied, aiming at practically every possible audience: James Hilton's *Lost Horizon,* Dorothea Brande's *Wake Up and Live!,* Shakespeare's *Five Great Tragedies,* Thorne Smith's *Topper,* Agatha Christie's *The Murder of Roger Ackroyd,* Dorothy Parker's *Enough Rope,* Emily Brontë's *Wuthering Heights,* Samuel Butler's *The Way of All Flesh,* Thornton Wilder's *The Bridge of San Luis Rey,* and Felix Salten's *Bambi.* Almost every aspect of the present paperbound book spectrum is to be found in these ten titles, except for the subterranean obscene book and the original; and all of these titles were enormous successes, selling hundreds of thousands of copies and, in some cases, millions. By June, 1957, for example, Pocket Books had sold 1,759,000 copies of *Lost Horizon* and 2,101,000 copies of Shakespeare's *Five Great Tragedies.*[24] But its best-selling author was to be Erle Stanley Gardner, thirty-eight of whose titles had sold over a million copies by 1958,[25] and its best-selling book Benjamin Spock's *Baby and Child Care,* first published in 1946, which had sold 19,475,000 copies by the end of 1966.[26]

Mechanically, these phenomenal sales were made possible by new book-making methods: the printing of books on high-speed rotary presses designed for magazines, the production of synthetic adhesive glues that made possible "perfect" binding—that is, binding in which a single sheet is held to other single sheets by a permanent adhesive to which a paper binding can be attached—and the development of a process by which paper covers can be laminated cheaply.[27]

In a distributional sense, Pocket Books' success came through the utilization of magazine distribution methods and companies. Pocket Books uses over 850 independent wholesale magazine distributors to put its products in thousands of retail outlets of every variety all over the nation.[28]

Pocket Books' success called many competitors into the field, notably the British Penguins, Avon Books, Popular Library, Dell, Bantam, Graphic, Pyramid, Lion, and the American house that grew from Penguin, The New American Library. In 1950 Gold Medal Books, a subsidiary of Fawcett, began publishing originals.[29]

The mass market paperback soon was dominated by books dealing with three subject matters—mystery, Western, and sex.[30] Their covers grew increasingly gaudy, emphasizing in unmistakable terms three themes: sex, sadism, and smoking-guns.[31]

In 1948 the paperback book industry invaded the college textbook market when the first of the Rinehart Editions, *The Scarlet Letter*, appeared. This distinguished series of texts, reprinting all kinds of literary works for use in the classroom, has been joined since by many other good lines, notably Houghton Mifflin's Riverside Editions, the Modern Library College Editions, the Scribner's Library, and the Norton Library. The impact upon college teaching may be as great as that of the New Critics and the formalist critics, whose influence the paperback text reinforces.[32]

In 1953 Jason Epstein began publishing a series of paper-bound books for Doubleday called Anchor Books. They were printed on book stock and bound with durable, non-glossy heavy paper covers with modernistic designs. They were designed to sell between seventy-five cents and $1.95 and to be produced profitably in runs of 20,000 copies. Although predominantly a series reprinting quality non-fiction, Anchor Books also publishes some original material and, chiefly in its Dolphin series, works of fiction. In the first twenty-two months of the Anchor Books history, over 1,350,000 copies were sold, with the bookstore being a major distributor. Thus the quality paperback, frequently called the "trade paperback" because it is aimed at the book trade as opposed to the magazine trade, was born. Anchor has been followed by a distinguished group of paperbacks, among them Vintage Books, published by Alfred A. Knopf; Harvest Books, by Harcourt, Brace and World; The Scribner's Library; Compass Books, by Viking, and many, many others.

Paperbound books have thus grown both as mass market books, utilizing the circulation methods of the modern magazine and the paperbook racks in drugstores and novelty stores, and as trade books, designed for sale in bookstores and through other means by which trade books find their purchasers. There has developed, too, as we know to our sorrow, an underground paperback publishing that is most accurately called by the newsdealer's term, "sexies."

The flood of paperbound books has mounted to the extent that the February, 1967, issue of *Paperback Books in Print* lists 42,500 titles in print.[33] In terms of dollar sales, the mass market paperback book is big business; its sales in 1963 were $87,380,000, in 1964 $99,000,000, and in 1965 $106,000,000. In dollar volume the trade paperback is much smaller; its sales in 1963 were $17,000,000, in 1964 $20,000,000, and in 1965 $21,500,000. Thus, measured in dollars, trade paperbacks sell only a fifth as much as mass market paperbacks. If we note that even in today's affluent market the average mass market paperback is priced at sixty-eight cents and the average trade paperback at $2.95,[35] then we must multiply by a factor of 4.3, which means that the mass market paperback is in volume almost twenty-two times as great as the trade or quality paperback. In terms of single title output, in 1963 9,317 titles were issued in paperbinding. In 1966 this number has increased by only twenty-nine to 9,346, and the mass market paperback actually dropped from 2,349 titles issued in 1965 to 2,006 in 1966, while trade book paperbacks rose slightly, from 6,968 to 7,340. As *Publishers' Weekly* said, surveying book production in 1966:

> Paperback titles showed the smallest gain in recent years—only 29 titles over 1965. A sizable drop in mass paperbacks caused the over-all total to drop considerably. While mass market paperbacks decreased by 15 percent in 1966, other paperbacks increased by five percent .... There was a very large increase in original non-fiction paperbacks—some 511 titles over 1965 .... In 1965, paperbacks accounted for 33 percent of all books published; in 1966, they dropped to 31 percent. In 1966, as in 1965, paperback originals accounted for 22 percent of all new books.[36]

Apparently the generation of paperback titles has reached a plateau, and the tremendous energy which the paperbound book has shown may be waning, as it has twice before in American publishing history.

Certainly a number of things point in that direction, in addition to the decreasing number of mass market titles. The large mergers and the "going public" of many publishing houses is making publishing a part of "the communications business," with any single kind of book no longer clearly dominant.[37] The failure of the ambitious—with 700 titles in 1962—"Collier Book" paperbacks and the shift of Crowell-Collier to textbook and trade book publishing under the Macmillan imprint was plainly a straw in the wind.[38] But perhaps the most significant sign of all is the development of clothbound trade book enterprises by the paperback publishers—the NAL Books published by The New American Library, Delacorte Press by Dell, Trident Press by Pocket Books. These paperback publishers are shoring up against a possible storm in the exact reverse of what trade book publishers had done with paperbacks in the 1950's.

3.

But whatever direction the present publication trends may take, the cheap book for the mass market seems to be here to stay, regardless of its kind of binding or the exact method of its distribution. And this incredibly large market for the low priced book has serious implications for the general reader and for the public interest.

The first of these implications results from the fact that the paper binding of books is an outward sign of an economic state rather than a cause of that state. In order to understand the nature of that economic situation, we need to examine some of the financial aspects of book production. The difference in cost between cloth cases and paper binding for the same book is seldom more than fifteen to twenty-five cents; whereas the difference in the cost of the books to the purchaser is from four to twenty times as great for the cloth bound book. In what does this differential reside? If we examine the same book in cloth bound trade and paperbound mass editions, we find that the lower price is the result of the method of distribution and the freedom of the paperback publisher from the payment of sizable royalties, editorial costs, launching the book and advertising it, and similar expenses that the original publisher had to bear. A $5.00 book will pay its author a royalty of fifty to seventy-five cents. Its basic manufacturing cost will be approximately $1.00. Its publisher will spend about fifty cents a copy for launching it and advertising it, and carry the editorial overhead which pays for the selection and editing of books. Distribution costs will absorb the remainder of the $5.00 list price, with about $2.00 going to the retailer. If we consider advertising as a part of the distribution costs—as seems prudent —then the average $5.00 book has substantially more than 50 percent of its retail price invested in its distribution. A substantial portion of the remainder goes into author's royalties, publisher's overhead, and editorial costs—all items of great importance both to the health of publishing and the well-being of authorship.

The paperback reprint publisher pays the author a greatly reduced royalty, depends on the art work on the cover for most of the advertising, distributes through well-established magazine wholesalers, and has a very low cost per unit on very long runs, and is able to produce the same $5.00 book for fifty cents. However, it is obvious that the publisher of the clothbound edition absorbed the major expenses of selecting, editing, and promoting the book, took a financial gamble which had to pay off before the paperback publisher got interested, and made it possible for the reprint publisher to bring out a "cheap book" edition. The publisher and the author have similar roles. They took the risks and established the value of the product. An author usually earns less than one-eighth as much per copy on a paperback edition as he did on the original edition. From his standpoint if a book moves from cloth to paper binding it must sell more than eight times as many copies in the new edition to pay the author the same royalty.[39]

The publication of original works in paper binding, therefore, is possible only when the work seems certain of a fairly substantial market. If it is aimed at the mass market, it needs sales of over 100,000 copies. Gold Medal Books, the most successful of the publishers of mass market original novels, counts on sales of 200,000 copies a title. If the paperback is designed for the book trade, with sales around 20,000, its price must be high enough to cover editorial overhead, higher distribution costs, and increased author's royalties. Furthermore, it must have a reasonable expectation of reaching its 20,000 readers in weeks or a few months, since the sales life of paperbacks is always relatively brief. All of this means that for the average serious author and for most books the safest and easiest path to the market place is that of the high-priced, cloth bound edition. It means, too, that the paperback book is most likely to be successful when it is a reprint of a book that has established itself through the normal media or when it is an original trade book with a reasonably assured audience of substantial size.

At best, new, original, trail-breaking works have usually lost money, but they lose more money today than they did in the past. Small printings of books are costly regardless of binding. In recent years these costs have been mounting. In the 1920's it would cost approximately forty cents a copy to produce a 300-page book in a quantity of 10,000. To produce only 3,000 copies would cost only about fifty cents a copy. Today 10,000 copies of the same book would cost about eighty cents a copy; to produce only 3,000 copies would raise the cost per copy to over $1.10.[40] Hence the publishing of books with small or no audience is becoming much more costly and such books are much less likely to be produced—particularly by large public companies. These economic factors are inevitably strong determinants in what takes place in the publishing world. They are not new; many of them in simpler form were stated in the arguments over "cheap books" and the international copyright law in the 1840's;[41] but when publishing moves from a question of the taste and judgment of the gentlemanly publisher to a matter of concern to the stock market and the banking combines, they carry added weight.

4.

All mass media for the arts, including paperbound books along with television, radio, motion pictures, large circulation magazines, and other such devices, inevitably impose their own criteria upon the material which they disseminate. These criteria are not necessarily bad, but they are frequently unrelated in basic principle to the intention of the creator or the needs of the audience. Thus paperback books, like television and motion pictures, are media for transmitting a form of culture to the millions, but, in the very act of being such a transmitting mechanism, they lose their neutral quality and become more than a transmitter. They become, for better or worse, molders of artistic form, censors of content, and all too often quasi-creators. Thus the nature of the medium determines the cultural fare which it makes available to the mass audience.

We hear a great deal about the cultural impact of the paperback book on the mass audience, about the availability to millions of fine works of art at incredibly low prices. What we hear is true. William Faulkner and Ernest Hemingway, Thomas Wolfe and F. Scott Fitzgerald have reached audiences of incredible size. And this is good. But, had the demands of satisfying this mass audience been necessary to the initial publication of Hemingway and Faulkner, of Wolfe and Fitzgerald, none of these writers would have been economically feasible risks. That is merely another way of saying that the greatest threat of the publication of books for the mass market is in the tendency of such publication to stifle the publication of books needed by particular but limited audiences, of books that are the first work of promising but highly original writers, of books that do not seem to promise any profit to their publishers.

The ultimate interest of the public is in both artistic quality and the wide-spread dissemination of works of established merit. To the extent that paperbound books aid in these efforts they serve the public interest well. But I am reminded of the wise words of that eminently sane lady, Gertrude Stein:

For a very long time everybody refuses and then almost without a pause everybody accepts. In the history of the refused in the arts and literature the rapidity of the change is always startling. Now the only difficulty with the *volete-face* concerning the arts is this. When the acceptance comes, by that acceptance the thing created becomes a classic....The characteristic quality of a classic is that it is beautiful....when that first rate work of art becomes a classic because it is accepted the only thing that is important from then on to the majority of the acceptors...is that it is so wonderfully beautiful. Of course it is wonderfully beautiful, only when it is still a thing irritating annoying stimulating then all quality of beauty is denied to it.

Of course it is beautiful but first all beauty in it is denied and then all the beauty of it is accepted.[42]

It is also in the public interest that we not only be enriched by the past, sharing widely the great works which have with difficulty won their way to recognition, but that we also keep alive a viable environment for the creation of original works, whose beauty is hidden from the public eye and counter to the current taste. To the extent that "cheap books" force publishers to measure merit in material terms, they betray the present and emasculate the future, they stifle creativity and originality by asking that it first prove itself in the market place.

NOTES

1. In *Saturday Review of Literature,* July 18, 1925, as quoted by Herbert R. Mayes, "Trade Winds," *Saturday Review,* L (February 4, 1967), 14.

2. The historical data upon which this paper rests are drawn from the following studies: Marshall W. Best, "In books, They Call It Revolution," *Daedalus,* Winter, 1963, pp. 30-41; Eleanor Blum, *Paperbound Books in the United States in 1955: A Survey of Content* (Unpublished Ph.D. dissertation, University of Illinois, 1958); O. H. Cheney, *Economic Survey of the Book Industry 1930-1931,* with 1960 Introduction by Robert W. Frase (New York, 1960); Robert W. Frase, "Economic Trends in Trade Book Publishing," in *Books and the Mass Market* (Urbana, Ill., 1953), pp. 21-42; Freeman Lewis, "Paper-Bound Books in America," *Bowker Lectures on Book Publishing* (New York, 1957), pp. 306-335; Charles A. Madison, *Book Publishing in America* (New York, 1966); Dan Lacy, "The Economics of Publishing, or Adam Smith and Literature," *Daedalus,* Winter, 1963, pp. 42-62; Hellmut Lehmann-Haupt, Lawrence C. Wroth, and Rollo G. Silver, *The Book in America,* 2nd ed. (New York, 1951); Frank Luther Mott, *Golden Multitudes: The Story of Best Sellers in the United States* (New York, 1947); Frank Luther Mott, *A History of American Magazines 1741-1850* (Cambridge, Mass., 1930); Frank L. Schick, *The Paperbound Book in America* (New York, 1958); Raymond H. Shove, *Cheap Book Production in the U.S., 1870-1891* (Urbana, Ill., 1937); Theodore Waller, "Expanding the Book Audience," *Books and the Mass Market* (Urbana, Ill., 1953); Thomas J. Wilson, "American Book Publishing: Hazards and Opportunities," *Daedalus,* Winter, 1963, pp. 78-91; and *Publishers' Weekly.*

3. Schick, pp. 38-39; Lewis, p. 307.

4. By Frank Luther Mott, among many others; see *Golden Multitudes,* pp. 76-69.

5. Commodity prices, based on the Warren-Pearson whole-price index for all commodities (New York, 1910-1914 equated to 100) fell from 110 in 1838 to 75 in 1843 and rose to 82 in 1848. See Richard B. Morris, *Encyclopedia of American History* (New York, 1953), pp. 508-509.

6. *One Hundred Years of Publishing* (Philadelphia, 1885), as reprinted in revised form in *One Hundred and Fifty Years of Publishing 1785-1935* (Philadelphia, 1935), p. 25.

7. The first American book printed on American machine-made paper was Lavoisne's *Atlas,* published by Mathew Carey in 1820 (Lehmann-Haupt, p. 87).

8. Lehmann-Haupt, pp. 72-84.

9. Mott, *History of American Magazines,* pp. 356-357.

10. *Ibid.,* pp. 359-360.

11. *Ibid.,* pp. 359-361.

12. *Ibid.,* p. 361

13. *Ibid.,* p. 362.

14. *Brother Jonathan,* VI (Nov. 18, 1843), 322

15. Lea, p. 25.

16. Letter from Lea and Blanchard, Dec. 16, 1841, quoted in Earl L. Bradsher, *Mathew Carey* (New York, 1912), p. 13.

17. Gay Wilson Allen, *The Solitary Singer* (New York, 1955), p. 57. *Franklin Evans* was said to have sold 20,000 copies.

18. See *The Letters of William Gilmore Simms,* Mary C. S. Oliphant, A. T. Odell, and T. C. D. Eaves (Columbia, S. C., 1952), I, 246 ff. During this period Simms stopped writing full length novels and turned to history and biography.

19. Eugene Exman, *The Brothers Harper* (New York, 1965), pp. 158-182, gives a detailed history of Harpers' struggle with the mammoth weeklies.

20. Mott, *Golden Multitudes,* p. 78.

21. John Stafford, *The Literary Criticism of "Young America": A Study in the Relationship of Politics and Literature, 1837-1850* (Berkeley and Los Angeles, 1952), pp. 23-24; Perry Miller, *The Raven and the Whale* (New York, 1956), pp. 135-167; *The First One Hundred and Fifty Years: A History of John Wiley and Sons* (New York, 1957), pp. 16-19. A surprising amount of information about this series is to be found in T. O. Mabbott's Introduction to the Facsimile Text Society edition of *The Raven and Other Poems,* by Edgar A. Poe (New York, 1942), pp. vi-xviii, which is my basic source.

22. Lewis, pp. 308-311; Madison, pp. 547-549, Schick, pp. 125-137. Shove is a history of the 1870-1891 period.

23. Madison, pp. 290-291; Lehmann-Haupt, p. 337; Schick, p. 130.

24. Schick, pp. 128-129.

25. Schick, p. 132.

26. *New York Times Book Review,* Part II, Feb. 26, 1967, p. 35.

27. Lewis, p. 307; Schick, pp. 96-108.

28. Schick, p. 129.

29. Schick, pp. 171-172.

30. Blum, pp. 84-100.

31. Schick, p. 85.

32. Schick, pp. 201-225.

33. New York, 1967.

34. "1966 in Review," *Publishers' Weekly,* CXCI (Jan. 30, 1967), 47.

35. *New York Times Book Review,* Part II, (Feb. 26, 1967), p. 2.

36. "1966: Subject Analysis of American Book Title Output," *Publishers' Weekly,* CXCI (Jan. 30, 1967), 35-36.

37. Wilson, pp. 79-80.

38. Madison, pp. 458-459.

39. For the basic data upon which these statements are based, see the *Daedalus* articles by Best and Lacy, particularly pp. 33-35 and 48-56.

40. Best, pp. 31-32.

41. See Miller, Schick, and Benjamin T. Spencer, *The Quest for Nationality* (Syracuse, N.Y., 1957), for detailed treatments of the copyright controversies.

42. "Composition as Explanation," *Selected Writings of Gertrude Stein* (New York, 1946), p. 435.

An American in Rome:
The Experiments of W. W. Story

Herbert M. Schueller

On January 23, 1864, John Addington Symonds, then a young man of twenty-three on a visit to Rome, wrote thus to his friend Henry Graham Dakyns: "I have had some conversations with the sculptor Story, and have received from him strong confirmation of my theories respecting the parallel between sculpture and music. He believes in it fully and improvises at the piano before he models the clay." William Wetmore Story (1819-1895) was then forty-five years old and a celebrity in England, if only partially one in his home town of Boston. The son of Joseph Story (1779-1845), one time Associate Justice of the Supreme Court of the United States, he was himself an able lawyer who had written legal treatises.[1] Early in life he was discovered to have a talent for sculpture, and after his father's death, he was commissioned to do a bust of him. In 1847 he had gone to Rome to study his art and craft, a move which was destined to become permanent in 1856. At first he had little success. Then in the London Exhibition of 1862 he made his name with his *Cleopatra* and his *Libyan Sibyl,* the latter a work Henry James thought he never surpassed. Thereafter he was one of the popular sculptors of his day, and before he died in 1895 was made D.C.L. by the University of Oxford, a Commander of the Crown of Italy, a Member of the Academia della Sta. Cecilia, a Member of the Society of the Arcadians, a Member of both the American Academy of Arts and Sciences and the Massachusetts Historical Society, a Member of the Athenaeum Club of London, and an Officer of the French Legion of Honor. One of the now almost forgotten men of the nineteenth century, he functioned not only as a sculptor,[2] but also as a poet,[3] as a writer of fiction,[4] of travel and historical sketches,[5] and of historical closet drama,[6] and also as a critic, of sorts, of art and literature.[7] Like

Symonds himself he was in large part a talented dilettante,[8] a man of wealth who composed in many forms and in several media and in an incidental way served his reading public as popularizer of the great artists of the past. Reported to have been a man of few pretences, Story was not himself as convinced of the importance of his work as were his contemporaries who rewarded him well for it.

His rather impressive accomplishments received the ultimate compliment in the publication of two books about him: Mary E. Phillips' *Reminiscences of William Wetmore Story* (1897) and Henry James' two-volume *William Wetmore Story and his Friends* (Boston, 1903). The former is unblushingly adulatory, but it is clear that the latter was written with a certain distaste. In a letter sent to Charles Eliot Norton in 1873, James in speaking not of the man, but of the artist, remarks: "So you're acquainted with Story's muse—that brazen hussy—to put it plainly. I have rarely seen such a case of *preposterous* pretension as Story. His cleverness is great, the world's good nature to him is greater."[9] Could James have been envious of Story's supposedly undeserved success? It may be so. Mark Twain, whom Story listed as one of the finer American writers and who would rather have been condemned to John Bunyan's heaven than to the reading of a James novel, might have thought so. Though Mark Twain would have deplored Story's tourist-type of culture-seeking, he would have admired his independence of thought and his calm and modest way of pursuing his own interests without any anticipation of a universal recognition of his genius or greatness. One may see Story as the typical nineteenth century American of both wealth and artistic leanings who emancipated himself from the limitations of his country. What were his accomplishments in fact, one may ask, and why did he find it necessary to leave America to achieve them?

1.

His purported accomplishments were of course in sculpture, and here he was what is nowadays called an experimenter. He was clearly dissatisfied with the sculptural art of his own day. "While painting has advanced," he wrote in 1844 in a note to his poem "Nature and Art," "sculpture has stood still" because "Modern sculpture is so subservient to Grecian, that the human face is generally treated as if it were of no moment in the expression of passion and character. ...We have thousands of Venuses, but no women....Sculpture is almost nothing but imitation." The exception he thought to be Hiram Powers.[10]

He was careful to say what he thought sculpture was. True, he was never primarily a theorist, and his aesthetic principles and stances as he discusses art are implicit rather than explicit. But he did make it plain that in the idealism-realism controversy of his day, he took a middle position. "Sculpture in the highest sense is a serious art," he wrote in his 1878 report for the American Fine Arts Commission of the Paris Universal Exposition, "and demands simplicity, concentration, and style. It is also a limited art. . . . It disdains the merely picturesque; it is degraded by the contact of *genre*. . . . Its province is restricted to form, and its dealings should be in the ideal. . . . With its feet planted on the real it must lift its head above the common into the ideal. . . . Its aspect is calm and serious; it is forbidden it to laugh, and almost even to smile. Its spirit is tragical and not comical. It has to do with character, not anecdote. . . ."[11] Story's attitude towards realistic art was uncompromisingly negative. Here, he thought, technical mastery prevailed and not the poetic which one should expect of art. Brutality, innuendo, pruriency, lack of discipline, a striving for individuality and novelty, and even a debauched taste were among his discoveries in the art of 1878. Though these opinions are part of the history of taste and not directly relevant here, yet they do point to his insistence that art have a realistic base but an idealistic aim. "Poetic" was his magic word.

In 1882, twenty years after his initial success as a sculptor, Story wrote an apology to Oscar Wilde about an "offending passage," presumably in a lecture or letter he had written. Wilde wrote back with a certain unctuousness that "sneering satire of art was a thing impossible for one who has made marble musical in harmony, and poetry in its perfection Parian." The obvious and possibly undeserved compliment had in it a certain truth. Despite the nature of his conversations with Symonds, Story disliked the English and Whistlerian use of terms like "symphonies," "nocturnes," "harmonies," and so forth, and had a contempt for a mixture of the arts. Yet he did seem to attempt to translate the arts into one another. He is termed one of the literary sculptors by Margaret Farrand Thorp,[13] and so he proves to be from first to last. He did make his sculpture "poetic."

The Arcadian Shepherd Boy (1852) (Fig. 1), one of his earliest pieces, has all the smoothness of late classical and Roman art. The figure is simple and graceful and suggests an unconsciouness of self. But it has little character or individuality; its decorative aspects are more marked than its intended expressiveness. It displays the native talent and skill of a sculptor who yet produces a rather conventional work arousing a rather complacent, unruffled effect. One need not know the models to realize that it is an imitation, and a "literary"

Fig. 1—Arcadian Shepherd Boy. *(Boston Public Library.)*

one at that. Fortunately, it is not typical of Story's work.

His first two successes (apart from the bust of his father) were made in 1860 and exhibited, as has been said, in 1862. (The transportation of these figures was paid for not by America or Americans, but by the Italian government.) Both reveal an attempt at expressing a brooding internality, a certain dramatic unintimacy which the observer encroaches upon. *The Libyan Sibyl* (Fig. 2) is reputed to have been inspired by a discussion between Harriet Beecher Stowe and Story about Sojourner Truth, the freed slave who preached widely about emancipation and women's rights. Story never met her, but he represents her face as coptic, she wears the tetragrammaton on her neck, and she is nude to her hips. Having a large face, large arms, full lips, and placing her elbow on knee and hand on chin, she gives the effect of immobile, spartanic brooding. The entire figure is large, heroic, large-bosomed and large-shouldered. She represents African slavery, specifically that of Libya. The drapery covers her crossed knees, their crossing probably symbolizing reticence and secrecy. Story himself, Winckelmann-like, thought of her as "looking out of her black eyes into futurity and [seeing] the terrible fate of her race."[14] She is no girl, but a middle-aged woman of untold experiences.

The *Cleopatra* (Figs. 3, 4, and 5) seems to have the same face as that of the *Libyan Sibyl*. She too is no classical Venus, but a middle-

Fig. 2—The Libyan Sibyl. *(National Collection of Fine Arts, Smithsonian Institution.)*

Fig. 3—Cleopatra. *(Metropolitan Museum of Art.)*

Fig. 4—Cleopatra.

Fig. 5—Cleopatra.

aged woman whose concerns are her inner thoughts at the moment at which she has been "caught." It is she who is described by Hawthorne,[15] Story's great admirer, in Chapter XIV of the *Marble Faun* (1860):

> A marvelous repose—that rare merit in statuary, except it be the lumpish repose native to the block of stone—was diffused throughout the figure. The spectator felt that Cleopatra had sunk down out of the fever and turmoil of her life, and for one instant—as it were, between two pulse throbs—has relinquished all activity, and was resting throughout every vein and muscle. It was the repose of despair, indeed; for Octavius had seen her, and remained insensible to her enchantments. But still there was a great smoldering furnace deep down in the woman's heart. The repose, no doubt, was as complete as if she were never to stir hand or foot again; and yet, such was the creature's latent energy and fierceness, she might spring upon you like a tigress, and stop the very breath that you were now drawing midway in your throat.
>
> The face was a miraculous success. The sculptor had not shunned to give the full Nubian lips, and other characteristics of the Egyptian physiognomy. His courage and integrity had been abundantly rewarded; for Cleopatra's beauty shone out richer, warmer, more triumphantly beyond comparison, than if, shrinking timidly from the truth, he had chosen the tame Grecian type. The expression was of profound, gloomy, heavily revolving thought; a glance into her past life and present emergencies, while her spirit gathered itself up for some new struggle, or was getting sternly reconciled to impending doom. In one view, there was a certain softness and tenderness—how breathed into the statue, among so many strong and passionate elements, it is impossible to say. Catching another glimpse, you beheld her as implacable as a stone and cruel as fire.
>
> In a word, all Cleopatra—fierce, voluptous, passionate, tender, wicked, terrible, and full of poisonous and rapturous enchantment—was kneaded into what, only a week or two before, had been a lump of wet clay from the Tiber. Soon, apotheosized in an indestructible material, she would be one of the images that men keep forever, finding a heat in them which does not cool down, throughout the centuries.

Story seems to have been haunted by the personalities of the people he represented in sculpture. Like the Pre-Raphaelites, he occasionally wrote poems on the same subjects as his sculptural works. Thus he wrote a "Cleopatra" poem,[16] and when he was told that the poem and the statue did not correspond, he produced, in 1884-85, a new Cleopatra reclining on a couch, as she does in the poem.

We must deal briefly with *Medea Meditating the Death of Her Children* (1864) (Fig. 6), *Salome*, (1869-70) (Fig. 7), and *Jerusalem in Her Desolation* (1870-71) (Fig. 8). The first, a fully clothed figure looking more masculine than feminine, represents pent-up passion

Fig. 6—Medea. *(Metropolitan Museum of Art.)*

added to quiet desperation, the inner storm all suppressed. The second figure has a certain languor as if the moment represented followed not long after Salome's dance before Herod. This figure seems practically the same as those of Cleopatra and the Libyan Sibyl, the face being markedly non-"Grecian" and the bosom being well developed. The third wears the tallith, and her face, and especially the nostrils, express bitter grief, despair, and hopelessness. She too appears in poems by Story: "Jerusalem's Desolation,"[17] "The Desolation of Jerusalem,"[18] and "A Jewish Rabbi in Rome."[19] All of these works combine expressive interest with historical detail. Story's *Cumaean Sibyl* (1872-73) wears the winged dragon of Eternity, and, indeed, if there is one dominant quality in Story's sculpture, it is the oracular.

2.

The same cannot be said of Story's poetry, which appeared in the *Atlantic Monthly,* the *North American Review,* and *Blackwood's* before it appeared in book form. Indeed, his poetic career antedated his sculptural one, and, after his first poetic venture for Phi Beta Kappa at Harvard, Browning, his friend for forty years, and Landor, whom he befriended, and occasionally Keats, were clearly his influences. The Browningesque dramatic monologue is a persistent form, and the Landorian lyric is sober, dignified, decorous, sensi-

Fig. 7—Salome. (Metropolitan Museum of Art.)

Fig. 8 — Jerusalem in Her Desolation. (Philadelphia Memorial Park, Frazer, Pennsylvania.)

tive, elegiac, but not so cold as Landor's. The over-all effect is a persistent geniality and a passionate feeling modified by reason. The emotions are not single-faceted or overwhelming; they embody not only themselves but also a sense of tolerance. A certain gentility pervades everything. Revolutionary the poems are not. A certain monotony accompanies the reading of them, as it probably does in one's close absorption in any one poet's work at any single sitting.

This monotony is partly the result of the pervading and sometimes "clattering" iambic pentameter, sometimes rhymed, sometimes un-rhymed, and the unsubtlety of the content and the imagery. They may be called the amusements of a legal mind interested in human relationships.

The Browningesque dramatic monologue is both personal and impersonal, both subjective and objective, and requires one's think-ing "into" people and the situations in which they find themselves. Imaginary conversations or imaginary monologues of historical personages are especially fitted for such poetic treatment. Story thus seems to be a less skillful and subtle, but more legal, Browning. Yet other elements are present too, especially a kind of gossipy realism. "By Way of Introduction"[21] is addressed to "Frank" [Heath?]; it emanates from an old convent, and like most of Story's poetry, combines the direct statement ("We all dine in the old refectory") and a certain colloquial language ("he [Christ] grew half-cracked at last") with Browningesque description and a Keatsian relish for sensuous impressions, especially those of flowers and smells. In many of his poems garden-descriptions, loved by the English, abound; there are also touches of the exotic-precious and, of course, of the fallacy which attributes human emotions to nature. The scholarly is also ever-present, however, as is the "dropping" of classical names— those of Tacitus, Sappho, Euripides, Flora and Bacchus, Aeschylus (to create an unpalatable mixture), in the manner of minor Victorian writers, and even some of the major ones. Thus all of the realism, which is blended with a certain Pre-Raphaelite literalism, is covered with a vaguely romantic film.

The historical imagination through conversations gives color to the realistic and literal details. The subject-matter is always—or in the dramatic monologues usually—Biblical and antique. In "A Roman Lawyer in Jerusalem: First Century" the case of Judas is reconsidered, Judas now being thought to be the only disciple of Jesus convinced of His divinity and the one passionately determined once and for all to prove that divintiy.[22] In "A Jewish Rabbi in Rome: With a Commentary by Ben Israel" Jerusalem in her desola-tion is discussed as caused by the Christians. A primitive Christian in "A Primitive Christian in Rome" is torn between Christ and Paul on the one hand and the great pagan thinkers like Plato, Aristotle, and Cicero on the other. Other monologues represent "Phidias to Pericles," "Marcus Aurelius to Lucius Verus," or are spoken by an imagined Pan (in love), Cleopatra, Marcus Antonius, Cassandra, Orestes, Praxiteles, Chersiphron (the Cretan architect), Tantalus, Padre Bancelli (the Florentine sculptor and painter),

Duke Ludovico Sforza "prosing" about Leonardo da Vinci (who tries too many things instead of sticking to one single art), Leonardo "poetizing" to the Duke in his own defence, the Duke of Urbino ("A Contemporary Criticism") judging Raphael; and there are poetical speeches by numerous monsignors, priests, novices, abbots, curates, Catholic converts, and other Roman persons. Along with these medieval and antique persons and situations there are modern ones which it would be tedious to enumerate, though only the title of "An English Husband to His Italian Wife" will suffice to make my point about one of Story's sources.

In the midst of confessions, nature-descriptions, and constant references to mythological, and Italian subjects, and especially Italian art, are the usual poetical moralizings, in the nineteenth century quite explicit and in the present one more carefully hidden, about man and his destiny, those comments about the constancies (the "universals") of human life of which literature is full. There is the ubiquitous love:

> At times he'd rise and come
> And sit beside me, take my hands in his,
> And call me best and dearest — heaping names
> Of love upon me — till beneath their weight
> I bent, and clung unto his neck, and wept;
> Oh! what glad tears he kissed them all away.
> ("The Confessional," II, 134)

There are Wordsworthian echoes about the dullness of the senses:

> We are divorced from nature; our dull ears
> Catch not the music of the finer spheres,
> See not the spirits that in Nature dwell
> In leafy groves through which they glancing look . . .
> ("In the Glen", II, 165)

and about the "knowledge" of children:

> Ah Heaven! we know so much who nothing know!
> Only to children and to poets' ears,
> At whom the wise world wondering smiles and sneers,
> Secrets of God are whispered below.
> (*Ibid.*, II, 169)

Mutability is there (with echoes of Fitzgerald's translation of the *Rubaiyat*):

> Where once great lords and ladies lived and laughed,
> And fought, loved, danced, long centuries ago,
> That are but dust now — and their crumbling courts

> Where once glad voices rang and pageants passed,
> Are dreary lairs of vermin and filth
> Haunted by hooting owls and silent ghosts.
>> ("By Way of Introduction," I, 5)

and in describing it for mankind Story is both Biblical and Whitmanian:

> Such thoughts come over me, oppressed and sad,
> As 'mid Rome's ruined tombs I meditate,
> Feeling how transient a thing is man,
> Whose life is but a shadow on the grass
> That comes and goes, or like a passing wind,
> Or like a voice that speaks and vanishes.
>> ("A Jewish Rabbi in Rome," I, 77)

Life is a riddle ("By Way of Introduction"), nature is indifferent ("A Jewish Rabbi in Rome"), and faith is unstable ("A Primitive Christian in Rome").

But all of these observations are in keeping with the characters who make them and are not self-consciously "philosophical" excrescences on the text. This is because the concrete and the artistic material, and not theories and ideas, were Story's first concern. His text has surprisingly little of that poetic stuffing termed the personification. Beauty, Virtue, Fame, War and Peace are conspicuously absent in the upper-case splendor with which the eighteenth and nineteenth centuries invested them. In "By Way of Introduction" (I, 15-16) he says he wishes he had the luck to find Agrippina's diary with its

> portraits sharp
> Of men and women as they lived, talked, loved,—
> Not as in History's limbo they appear. . . .

and he means by this the concrete and the specific.

Story's poems are based on personalities and reveal their opinions and their problems. The dialogue, either explicit or implicit through monologue, is the basis of his literary work—not only of his poems, but also of his critical writing and his fiction. His poems are meant to be heard, not merely over-heard. In *He and She* and in *A Poet's Portfolio: Three Years After* (the latter a "sequel" to the former) the basic form is an extended series of talks between a man-poet and a woman-listener; interlarded with the prose are poems by the man read aloud by him at the woman's insistence. The result is a pleasant, desultory kind of reading of the "summer" type; every subject is possible, and each one is disposed of with dispatch. The atmosphere is a kind of sophisticated bucolic, that of a kind of *Shepherd's*

Calendar, in a sort of "georgic" language. Language which jingles is not wanting; some of the images today seem unattractive ("the jewels dance on your bosom," "In your eyes is a dewy trance," "the blushing poppy"); one poem ("Io Victus," *He and She*, pp. 91-93) has been anthologized. For the most part the method of organization is that of free association. The subjects, as a result, come in a pell-mell fashion: loveless sex; the kind of poetry which endures; the unreality in poetry of specifically named persons ("Nina" in Story's poems) who do not exist but might have done so; the desirability or undesirability of a poet's reading his works aloud; the harshness and fickleness of nature; and the characteristics of Donne's poetry. He agrees with Goethe about the "occasional" character of some poetry. But his interests go beyond art to the difficulty of one's truly loving and hating, to the nature of the self-centered Byronic person, and to the fallacy of the Faustian desire for youth recaptured. Rather unusual is his notion of the close association between memories and odors, but more in keeping with his "strenuous" nature is his conviction that hard work and ideas are required in art. He finds inadequate the idea of artistic inspiration, and he believes the nature of spirit to be a mystery. With Montaigne he says, "Que sçais-je?" and makes observations, with a certain approval, about the weakness of religious faith in his own time and about the probability that man is only an instrument of nature, and not a creator at all. Thus he finds that superstition is occasionally efficacious and that in different periods of time God is "created" in different ways after man's own fashion. But he shifts back and forth from serious matters to those of less moment, like the extravagant claims made for current writers (especially in America) in advertisements, for instance, and for dead men as described in their obituaries; like the inadequacy of all translations; and like the notorious claims in travelers' stories about their exploits. But again and again he returns to the poet, who, he says, need not and cannot tell the truth and is especially false when he speaks of dying for love; who is free from the demands of accuracy and need not base his work on personal experience because "one may fall in love with imagery as well as with persons" (*A Poet's Portfolio*, p. 256): in fact, the poet's pursuit *is* like falling in love—both imagery and poetry being in the imagination. Story finds mankind itself in one sense to be unique in that laughter is a human characteristic and alien to nature, which, in any case, Story finds to be a vague term. Equally as native to man as laughter, which Story observes to be ugly in sound, is man's discontent with the present. Like Henry James, however, Story finds the variations of life, nature, and beauty to be infinite— as infinite as the differences among men's minds themselves. Thus the subjects treated in *He and She* and *A Poet's Portfolio* almost defy organization, but reveal a mind curious, alert, open, and catholic.

Were this paper a study in the history of ideas, one would have to identify "sources" and echoes. One would also have to identify antici- pations. At one point, for instance, Story says what Proust attempted to illustrate: I refer to the association of memory and odor. And thus one would have to observe that writers distinctly minor do indeed anticipate those who are as distinctly major.

In his dramas, however, in which past events and historical per- sonages are viewed in action, there are no anticipations, and he is obviously following other writers. There are only two of these plays, both published in 1875.

His *Nero: An Historical Play* was dedicated to "Fannie" Kemble, who had, before its publication, invited people to a private reading of it in her home. During the course of the proceedings, an earth- quake took place. This, Story himself admitted, was "in strange ac- cord with the story," which follows the traditional accounts of Nero well, though it reads like a watered-down imitation of Webster, Shakespeare, and Shelley in *The Cenci*. The elements include mur- der, incest, suicides (including Nero's own with his reputed cry, "Think what an artist perishes in me!"), treachery of every sort, adultery, homosexuality, greediness for money and power, conspiracy, persecution (of the Christians), dream-premonitions, the disloyalty of friends, and scenes of torture. The verse—iambic pentameter un- rhymed, of course—is facile. The lines are clear in meaning, and one has no doubt that the uninitiated audience might easily take the play for Shakespeare's. The line is not unpleasant, and the handling of the caesura is attractive. But the richness of imagery is lacking, subtlety is wanting, and for the sophisticated audience everything is too direct. Yet, as one reads the work, the versification seems not to be monotonous. Of moralizing there is plenty, though no more than in the great models; but it is the usual moralizing about the more common themes of the transitory character of life and of the inevitability of death, no matter how arrived at.

The characterization is fairly sharp. Seneca is a kind of longer- speaking Polonius, and Agrippina is not unlike Volumnia. As one might expect, Nero himself comes forth as the person best defined. He is childish, vain and fickle, impatient, violent in his lusts for sex and power, ruthless in every respect, desirous of every kind of flattery, childlike in his self-indulgence, and corrupt in his debauchery. He sees to the murder of his mother, destroys both friends and enemies, takes the wife of his friend, and intends to marry a male favorite. His "great" speeches of fear in general and of the fear of death in particular are in imitation of Shakespeare at his most operatic.

Story's drama of Nero was based on Suetonius and Tactitus, but over and over again the Shakespearian echoes predominate. Like many Shakespearean heroes, Nero expresses the weariness of the wearer of a crown, and Anicetus, in speaking of the transporting of Agrippina to her death, sounds like a comparatively unimaginative Enobarbus:

> Send then a galley for her use.
> If she accept, it shall be trimmed and decked
> Fit for an empress. From its prow and poop
> Let silken streamers flutter. Let her couch
> 'Neath a pavilion cloth of gold be spread
> With soft embroidered cushions—while the oars,
> All tipped with gold, keep even rise and fall,
> To music's low recurrent pulse, and bear
> The empress on to Caesar. . . (III, 5).

Caesar at his most effeminate sounds sometimes like Cleopatra herself:

> Ay, 'tis time to think
> How I shall dress. Your counsel; shall I wear
> Apollo Citharaedus' glowing robes,
> Broidered with gold, and sweeping to the ground,
> Pure perfect white? Will that become me best?
> Or shall I wear the Asian dress, all loosed,
> Without a girdle, and with drooping sleeves? (IV, 1).

Cleopatra-like, he even asks that his attendant bring him his robes (IV, 3). But he is also a Hamlet, though others among the characters of the play, and especially Agrippina, share his sense, as Poppea says, that

> All I have gained I played for - all is mine;
> And yet how stale, and dull, and flat it is!

He sounds like Shakespeare's tyrants when they defy their enemies, have illusory visions of their future acclamations by the crowd, and contemplate themselves in imagined death. In a hallucinatory declamation at the end of the play when he sees his past parade before him, he sounds like Macbeth:

> How cold! how cold it is, I shiver here!
> Great God, who's there? Britannicus? No, no!
> Away! I did not kill you—'twas a fit.
> Shake not your head—lift not your threatening hand.
> You, too,—my mother,—do not smile on me,—
> It is too ghastly. . . . (V,9).

But there are more apparitions, and there is also a brief Shakespearean requiem for Nero himself. What stands out, however, is his fiend-
ish delight at the persecution of the Christians and his regret that
with his death an artist will be gone: He will never act again, or play,
or sing, or model, or paint (V, 11). Perhaps Story's interest in writing
on this subject may have been motivated by his sympathy for someone of whom it could be said,

> He is an artist,—that we must admit.
> Pity he tries so many forms of art.
> Were he content with one he might excel. . . .
> . . . .
> Life is not long enough for every art (IV, 1).

About *Stephania*, which was privately printed, I shall not go into
detail. It too has a historical subject: Stephania, wife of Crescentius,
head of the Roman government under Otho III (980-1002), after the
murder of Crescentius by Otho at the Castle of St. Angelo, by design
becomes the latter's mistress and eventually his murderess. The play
is "psychological" in the manner of Story's sculpture. James thinks of
"Owen Meredith" as someone who might have relished the situation
and the emotions. But even more apropos is James' remark about
"that operatic side of the picture in which the idea of 'crime' recurs
very much as one of the indispensable rhymes of the libretto...
[He strikes] with predilection the note of passion let loose. It was
in their dangerous phases that the passions most appealed to him."23

Story's fiction need not detain us. Just as his plays seem to be in the
line of *The Cenci* (1819) and *A Blot in the 'Scutcheon* (1843), so "A
Modern Magician" reminds one of innumerable stories of the occult,
and also of Elizabeth Barrett Browning's interest in mediums and
her husband's "Mr. Sludge the Medium." In it an American boy goes
to Rome with a letter of introduction to a magician, Signore Curio.
Introduced by descriptions of fever-induced hallucinations and by
impressionistic descriptions of Rome, the plot reaches its climax in a
transformation of all the nineteenth century people present at a
seance into figures of Greek mythology; the remaining question is
whether the event was psychological and wine-induced or the creation
of Signor Curio. The novel *Fiammetta: A Summer Idyl* is a story about
a mountain girl who dies of unrequited love for the painter for whom
she acted as model but who valiantly restrains himself from seducing
her. It sounds in part like *The Marble Faun* (except that Story's own
Cleopatra, mentioned in *The Marble Faun*, is replaced by, presumably, his own *Judith* [1860] transformed into a painting) and in
part like the lesser efforts of Henry James.

3.

In his artistic endeavors, Story may thus be considered a "generalist," a skillful also-ran. His critical writing is no less capable in a general way. Van Wyck Brooks called him a chameleon in verse. He is not so in prose. *He and She* and *A Poet's Portfolio* are replete with critical comments which I have here recorded. In his *Conversations in a Studio* (1890) and *Excursions in Art and Letters* (1891) Story reveals himself as a possible respectable English don devoted to the arts, or even as a possible academic "humanist" of today. His tone is Saintsbury-like: that is, conversational; and his models are possibly Landor's *Imaginary Conversations* or Wilde's *Intentions* (1891). James reports that Story himself was a great talker and that his books are all talk. Yet he uses the conversational method, not to avoid taking a position, but rather, by means (as in the Platonic dialogues) of a "fall guy," to sharpen it.[24]

At times it almost seems as if Story's "conversations" were written about the twentieth century. Prices of art-works, he thinks, are too extravagant, as they were (here Story documents the facts) in ancient days. Artists are not underpaid; nor were the great ones of the past underpaid either. Millionaires are in part responsible for the current state of affairs. Like most Americans, they are ignorant of art, but patronize it because art is the fashion. Yet it must be remembered that changes in taste occur rapidly and that "Fashion has a great deal to do with success, and humbug, perhaps, even more" (I.2). What is true for art is also true for poetry: fashion governs the decisions, and popularity is no guarantee of fame. Look at Robert Treat Paine (1773-1811), the most popular American poet of his day, now forgotten. Still, taste and knowledge are growing in America. And, in any event, bad taste is better than indifference (or no taste at all).

Story was of course aware that there is no such thing as communal taste, but that there are only individual tastes which in the abstract seem to blend into groups or even into a single one. He knew that one's own taste undergoes great changes as one travels from childhood to advanced adulthood; that even our houses are parts of ourselves and reflect our taste through the choices we make; that what we need, he thinks, as a basis for taste, if we are properly to criticize art works, is knowledge. Criticism is largely a matter of personal feelings and fashion, he indicates, but knowledge, and always more knowledge, is needed if one is to praise rather than merely to find fault. Artists have a right to be judged by their best work, not by their worst, and whether we call ourselves amateurs or connoisseurs—terms which

Story thoroughly dislikes——, we need to combine taste with knowledge to discover the best in any artist's work.

But it is of the artist's work itself that we must have a knowledge. Artists themselves seldom conform to the idea we have of them from their productions, though no life is happier than theirs. Every other life is flat and tasteless, but the life of art is the life of a constant learning. The beginnings of art-production are easy, though great facility is not always a boon, and technical drilling is a necessity. Nevertheless, germs of thought and feeling are what really are of ultimate importance. Poetry, for instance, develops early in a person, but the greatest of the world's poems were written in their authors' advanced years: major works by Chaucer, Milton, Dante, Homer (perhaps), and others are Story's examples. Creativity is much in evidence in old people because culture and much education are as necessary to the great artist as they are to the critic; equally necessary are devotion to work and a love for it. True, every art has its mechanical part, and it is still a mystery how ideas enter an art. But, then, creativity itself is a mystery.

Story has no ready-made explanations of the nature of creativity, which he calls a riddle. Nor does he care enough about theory as such to construct his own psychology of it. He suggests what he thinks to be the nature of the artist's function without explicitly describing it, and he does so by defining art itself. The result is conventional enough: Art is neither real nor illusory; it is an expression and embodying forth of the artist. It is not factual because facts in art may be untrue, nothing being true there unless "it be assimilated by the imagination to the idea which is the soul of the work" (II.330). It requires both consecration and the poet's dream, is the master of nature—not its slave, and offers us the suggestion—which is often better than the statement. For Story realism is anathema and Zola is its disciple. Beauty and dignity, he says (apparently pursuing a platonic absolute), cannot be produced by the ugly and the uncouth; and he opposes Ruskin's idea that forms and lines are beautiful because they are taken from natural products like leaves and flowers. They are beautiful simply because they are beautiful (II.348).

Thus, distrustful of general theory and of the vague inclusive terms it employs, Story seems to take an art-for-art's-sake position without ever using the term. His idea, as discussed with Symonds, of the parallel between sculpture and music might suggest a possible Hegelian notion that the arts are One. But no: It is the principle of harmony which unites them. ". . . [H]armonies of forms and lines are felt to be allied to music, though we cannot explain the relation. Proportion is harmony; symmetry is nothing but the harmonious relation of meas-

ures; and I have no doubt they have an absolute mathematical relation, as much as the pulsating of strings" (II.343).[25] He almost becomes Hegelian in maintaining that ". . . the harmonies of color, and
forms, and tones, and words, are closely related to each other, and but
expressions of merely the same thing. A sculptor's work will be cold
if he is not sensitive to color and music" (I.143). But to see parallels
between several arts and to think that their aim is similar are two
different things; one art cannot be substituted for another. He thinks
that sculpture is perhaps a higher art than painting because its limitations are greater and its "requisitions" higher. Yet each art has its
own materials, laws, and difficulties; each art is an individual matter.
Thus he deplores the aesthetic tendencies in nineteenth-century art,
especially in England, where the boundaries of the arts seem to be
confused—"or so at least the current jargon of art would seem to indicate. We have symphonies in color, recitations in music, tone-
poems, harmonies of verse, etc. Picturesque sculpture is a mistake. So
is sculptural painting . . ." (II.467). One might ask if Story is speaking
of his own sculptural experiments.

While, then, he deplores certain tendencies in English art, he is
even more pessimistic about those of America. In his report of the
Paris Exposition of 1878 he does mention Emerson, Longfellow,
Lowell, Hawthorne, James, Howells, and Mark Twain as making up
a real American literature; but he can only mention the unrecognized
Washington Allston among painters and Hiram Powers among
sculptors as possibly being on their plane in the non-literary arts. In
his critical writings American names are comparatively absent, and
those which do appear are not primarily those of artists: his father,
John Quincy Adams, George Peabody, Agassiz, William Pinckney,
and Prescott the historian.

His idols are the universally accepted great: Donne, Dante, and so
forth. In one respect he takes a place even among Shakespeare critics.
He quotes Shakespeare profusely, and thinks of him as a man of no
vanity who had a mind in which "all things turned to poetry. . ."
(I.76); as an unconscious genius of the first order; as a writer who
was superior in the use of rhythm and whose plays seem to grow,
while other playwright's works seem merely constructed. Story thinks
of him as the most impersonal of writers, who, however, has been mis-
interpreted on the English stage. What we think of Shakespeare's
characters, Story asserts, is only what English actors have conditioned
us to think. To demonstrate this point, he wrote a long essay of the
textual-critical type, "Distortions of the English Stage as Instanced in
'Macbeth,' "[26] in which he shows that Macbeth and his lady are one
thing in Shakespeare but another as played by Mrs. Siddons and the

Kembles. Macbeth is the villain, insatiable in crime, remorseless, not disturbed by regrets and doubts. Filled with ambition, he is cruel, pitiless, and bloody—and hypocritical. Lady Macbeth, however, is essentially a woman, misled by her husband and ambitious only for him, practical, impulsive, and remorseful, despite her weak moral sense, for her crime.

And almost as mistaken, Story thinks, as the English way of playing Shakespeare are the Baconian theory of the authorship of Shakespeare's plays and Goethe's theory of Hamlet's indecisiveness. But, then, he disliked most of the Germans, except for Jean Paul Richter, Heine, and occasionally Schiller. Goethe is almost his *bête noire*. "Pegasus," Story writes, "never ran or flew away with him" (I.96); furthermore, the Faust of the introduction of Goethe's primary work would never have sold his soul for mere youth. None of the Germans, including Goethe and the Schlegels, understood Shakespear better than the English did: their criticism is as bad as Voltaire's, and Goethe's is especially poor. Reversing an opinion broadcast in the last thirty or forty years of our century, Story said that Schlegel got all of his notions from Coleridge. But a German is apparently *sui generis*, and his capacity "for boring and of being bores is inexhaustible" (I.281).[27]

One can only admire Story's versatility. Not content to experiment with two of the major arts himself, he even tackled the subject of language. Though he conjectured about the idea that art is a language, he conjectured too about language itself. He wrote a philological essay on the origin of the Italian language,[28] made the observation (hardly new in his day but treated in the last several decades of the present century as though it were only now being discovered) that language changes, made extensive comments on the meanings of certain nouns, and discussed newspaper language, "lawlessness" in the handling of language, and so forth. He contrasted English, German, Italian, and other types of English pronunciation, and was especially thorough as he spoke of the extent to which verbal formulas, repetition, and jargon act to crystallize thought so that the trouble of thinking is minimized.

Thus Story was a man intelligent, congenial, facile, and not ashamed to test his talent in public display of his sculpture, poetry, drama, and criticism. But he was not the experimenter he thought.

4.

If Story were alive today, he would not be taken seriously. He was too much of his time, not enough outside it. Yet he was more than a

"Sunday painter" and took his own work very seriously. When one compares his work with that of his contemporaries, however, it is easy to see how uninventive he was despite his "experimental" use in sculpture of non-hellenic types and in poetry of fairly "realistic" modes of speech. His art is too full of reminders of the work of others; his style is not distinctive enough to convince one that he achieved the individual expression for which he strove.

It is of course easy to be unfair to a man like this. His own complete correspondence, if it is ever published, may possibly reveal a greater consciousness of art contemporary with his own than do his published writings. It is almost inconceivable that a sculptor of his popularity should have been unaware of the work of Rodin. Said to be musical and the possessor of a good baritone voice, he never mentions Verdi or Wagner, to give one example of musical composers of his day, though Beethoven, long dead when Story was an adult, was the object of one of his poems. He may have been unaware of the existence of Ibsen. His interest in Italy and its past did not cause him to mention the writings of Pater or Symonds. He does not mention Flaubert, Tolstoi, Hardy, or Meredith—to name only a few, though he knew Henry James personally. Only Zola receives his displeasure in print.[29] It is not a matter of his agreeing with posterity's estimate of these men, but of his not mentioning their names at all.

Even his silence is a judgment, and if the art-work of his own present was not to his taste, he had to settle into the more comfortable and distant past. As an American who never forgot Boston while he consciously rejected her, he lived in the realms of art which Europe, but not America, had had the time to create. A devotee of the notion that art is expression, Story lived in a dream-world of expression as realized, and not in the world of expression struggling for life. He had no illusions about the technical difficulties of art, of their day-by-day demands on the artist. Like Goethe and Carlyle, he implicitly and explicitly followed the doctrine of work. But he had a "fatal facility," as Symonds said in connection with his own writing of poetry; everything came too easily. But what he had to transcend, if he could, was what had already been achieved. This was European art which was already there, which had actually been accomplished through the preceding centuries.

I daresay that Story's American contemporaries in his circle in Rome were in much the same boat: they resented the fact that America, a country only two hundred years old, did not possess an art such as Europe had created in the course of nineteen or twenty centuries. Therefore many of them did not stay home to "create," but went off to Europe to "appreciate" what had been there for hundreds of years. On pages 179-180 of his report of the 1878 Universal Exposition in Paris, Story wrote:

> We as a nation have built our house. It is useful. It is commodious. To its practical departments we have given much thought. But art as yet has no place in it. We claim to be a practical people. We insist that use is better than beauty; that if our national house is not decorated and beautified, it is because beauty is of no practical benefit to men. We talk perpetually of our being a new country, whose business it is to fell forests, open new paths, plant sawmills, build towns and railways, and attend to business. Undoubtedly this is our duty, but not all our duty, nor the highest and best part of it. A new country, forsooth! As if any people of Anglo-Saxon origin—with all its world of inherited literature behind it and Shakespeare for an ancestor; with all its history stretching back in direct line two thousand years; with all its religion and law derived from the past—could possibly be called young! As if the mere facts of place made a people young! As if we should all be old if we were on European soil, and are only young because we are on American soil! Do we plead ignorance of finance, or war, of trade, of commerce, of mechanics, on that score? Is there any nation that stands more forward than we in these departments? Why, then, should we excuse ourselves for deficiencies in higher culture by such a plea? We know that it is false. We know that it is only an excuse. So far from this being the case, we are one of the most luxurious nations in the world; one of the most developed in all that related to convenience and the practical requirements of life, one of the most accomplished in all the so-called useful and mechanical arts; but in the ideal spheres of art we have accomplished little, because we have desired little; our needs and necessities have been amply supplied, but the heart and soul have been fed upon husks. Use has its buildings and habitations, but beauty has not yet its temple.

Behind this nineteenth century rhetoric there seems to be too great a protest. True, it is easy to forget that, today, American museums contain a good share of the world's art, that books are available everywhere, and that radio and phonograph have introduced to American ears music which was not available in such plenty even in the Europe of Story's day and even for people wealthy enough to live abroad. Therefore the protest was relevant and true. Story went to Rome not merely to get away from Boston (there are no self-conscious posings of alienation in any of his remarks). He went to Rome to become part of Europe, but not of contemporary Europe.

The fact is that Story was historical, anthropological, humanistic, and anthropomorphic, and that his popularity was due in large part to the fact that his efforts in stone were expressive, "exotic," and unusual—because he pursued not the classical Greek, but the Coptic, the Egyptian, and the Semitic, because his Cleopatras, Medeas, Judiths, and so forth, awkwardly machine-made as parts of them (and especially the drapery) seem, were yet expressive of psychological states and at the same time had the character of the out-of-doors public monument. They combined a vague romantic symbolism with an "operatic" and a picturesque historicism of costume.

They are therefore historical-scholarly in character, and less representative in a way of the "totality" which is Story than are some of his writings. His *Roba di Roma*—there is a poem by the same title (*Poems*, 1886, I, 228)—is in a sense his most typical work. Originally in two volumes, then reduced to one, and then enlarged in size in the one-volume printing as it went through various editions, it includes personal reminiscences and impressions of Rome, detailed descriptions of the city's street-music, beggars, holidays, religious seasons, games (including betting), the appearance of the city at various times, its cafes and theaters, its markets, the ghetto, athletic occasions, customs surrounding births, marriages, and funerals, and of course the places which are the tourist's delight—the Colosseum, the Campagna, and so forth. Everything is subjected to historical scrutiny, and no detail is too minute for mention. The result, somewhat in the nature of a hodge-podge, is that anthropological and folk-loristic materials are markedly present. Literary quotations abound, but so do facts and figures, the most notable of the latter being in a large chapter on the population of ancient Rome. Story appends musical notation for a song and also statistics about the finances and population of modern Rome. Another book, *The Castle of St. Angelo and The Evil Eye* (1877) is made up of additional chapters to the *Roba*, the second essay having appeared in slighter form in first editions of the work. The first, about the Mausoleum of Hadrian, is a thorough historical study with references to classical historians and descriptions of the mausoleum in Story's day. Like Symonds in the first volume of his *Renaissance in Italy* (*The Age of the Despots*, 1875) Story has a peculiarly detached, but fascinated, sense of (non-religious) evil, which he seems to relish. *The Evil Eye* is a study in folklore and superstition, and like the *Roba di Roma* as a whole and Story's sculpture and poetry in particular, reveals an insatiable interest in detail no matter how "realistic." Here is the curiosity of the scholar; and here the writing, no matter how much inspired by the romantic past, is less like that of Carlyle than like that of Gibbon.

The man's industry is incalculable. In *Excursions in Art and Letters*, he wrote a long essay on Michelangelo, semi-factual, semi-impressionistic, appreciative. In the same work, in showing that

Phidias did not create the Elgin Marbles, he could not overlook any fact; and his technique is that of the scrupulous scholar as he denies that the ancient Greeks and Romans possessed the art of casting in plaster. And then, for variety's sake, he imagines that he has a conversation with Marcus Aurelius; in this there is a critique of Christianity which creates the opportunity for the agnostic to confront the historian. Story's predominant passion was a Schlegel-like historical sympathy, and his every aim was to reconstruct the past. His historical writings must be judged by the historian, his comments on art and life are part of the extensive background of the history of ideas, and his sculpture and poetry are part of the significant backdrops of the history of art. How significant will be realized only when the role of the dilettante in the spread of culture has been estimated. But the reference works still call him a sulptor. *Sic transit gloria*: One popular encyclopedia of today records: "They were the most admired sculptures of his time."

NOTES

1. *Reports of cases argued and determined in the Circuit Court of the United States,* for the first circuit. Vols. 1, 2 (Boston, 1842, 1845).

   A Treatise on the Law of Contracts not under Seal (Boston, 1844; 5th ed., 1874).

   A Treatise on the Law of Sales of Personal Property (Boston, 1847; 4th ed., 1871).

2. Phillips, mentioned in my text, has a presumably complete list. Among the best known are those mentioned and to be mentioned in my text. Among commissions are those of his father (formerly in Mt. Auburn Chapel, Cambridge, Mass., now in Harvard University Law Library), George Peabody (London), Edward Everett (Boston), Chief Justice Marshall and Joseph Henry (both Washington, D. C.), and, as a climax, the Memorial to Francis Scott Key (San Francisco).

3. *'Nature and Art': A Poem Delivered before the Phi Beta Kappa Society of Harvard University; August 29, 1844* (Boston, 1844). Story was dissatisfied with this work and at first resisted pressures to publish it.

   Poems (Boston, 1847).

   Poems (Boston, 1856).

   Graffiti d'Italia (Edinburgh and London, 1868).

   Ode on the Fifth Half Century of the Landing of Gov. John Endicott, delivered before the Essex Institute of Salem, Sept. 18, 1878 (Salem, 1878).

   He and She; or, A Poet's Portfolio (Boston and Cambridge, Mass.; Edinburgh, 1884).

   Poems, 2 vol. (Boston and Cambridge, Mass.; Edinburgh and London, 1886).

   A Poet's Portfolio: Later Readings (Boston and New York; Edinburgh and Cambridge, Mass., 1894).

4. "A Modern Magician," *Blackwood's,* CVI (May, 1867), 552-576. (Unsigned).

   Fiammetta: A Summer Idyl (a novel) (Edinburgh and London, 1886).

5. *Roba di Roma* (London, 1862, and 7 later editions, the last in 1887).

"Mystery or Passion Plays," *Blackwood's*, CVI (Dec., 1869), 671-693. (Unsigned).

The Castle of St. Angelo and The Evil Eye: Being Additional Chapters to *Roba di Roma* (the latter formerly a chapter of that book) (London, 1877).

"Vallombrosa," *Blackwood's*, CXXIX (April, 1881), 483-508.

"The Corso of Rome," *The Great Streets of the World* (New York, 1892).

6. *Nero* (Edinburgh, 1875).

Stephania (Edinburgh, 1875).

7. *Conversations in a Studio*, 2 vol. (Boston and Cambridge, Mass.; Edinburgh and London, 1890).

Excursions in Art and Letters (Boston and New York; Edinburgh and London, 1891).

8. Several additional works should be mentioned: In 1842, before he turned to art from law, he contributed to the *Boston Miscellany*, which was edited by Nathan Hale, one of his friends; and in 1843 he wrote and designed illustrations for the *Pioneer*, edited by James R. Lowell and R. Coster; in the latter he used his own name and also the pseudonym of I. B. Wright. One-third of the third issue of the *Pioneer* is largely Story's.

He also edited *The Miscellaneous Writings of Joseph Story* (Boston, 1852); and The *Life and Letters of Joseph Story*, 2 vol. (London and Boston, 1851).

He expressed himself also on political matters, chiefly in the London *Daily News:* "The American Question," Dec. 25, 26, and 27, 1861; reprinted in *Political Pamphlets* (Manwaring), XCII, no. 9 (London, 1862).

9. Leon Edel, ed., *The Selected Letters of Henry James* (New York, 1955), p. 45. James agreed to write his book on Story in 1897. Waldo Story, also a sculptor and one of the two sons of William Wetmore, and his wife pressed James to do it; still, he did not go at it immediately, his last three novels having in fact been completed before it appeared in 1903. James' reluctance is clear: from the result Story seems more shadowy than his friends and is almost only an abstract focal point around which circle his age, its climate of opinion, and its mores. When the Duchess of Suther-

land congratulated James on the publication of this work, he called it his "effort to perform in that record, in a manner, the operation of making bricks without straw and chronicking (sometimes) rather small beer with the effect of opening champagne. Story was the dearest of men, but he wasn't massive, his artistic and literary baggage were of the slightest and the materials for a biography *nil*. —However (once I had succumbed to the amiable pressure of his children), I had really to *invent* a book patching the thing together and eking it out with barefaced irrelevancies—starting above all *any* hare, however small, that might lurk by the way" (*ibid.*, p. 194). James, indeed, fills page after page in avoidance of his subject. There are commentaries on family diaries, the history of Rome, Story's forebears, the Palazzo Barberini (where Story lived), and an immense cast of characters: James Russell Lowell, Charles Eliot Norton, Margaret Fuller, Longfellow, Thackeray, George Curtis, Powers the sculptor, the three Brownings, F. Marion Crawford, Hawthorne, Dickens, Carlyle, Mazzini, A. W. Kinglake, Charles Perkins, Garibaldi, Landor, Von Humboldt, Ranke, Bettina von Arnim —almost everyone in Story's circle and outside it except Story himself.

10. "Nature and Art," p. 48. It should be noted, however, that Story's estimate of Powers' work was not high. In a letter written on March 21, 1849, to J. R. Lowell, Story writes: "[Powers] is a man of great mechanical talent and natural strength of perception— but no poetry is in his composition and I think no creative power" (Gertrude Reese Hudson, ed., *Browning to His American Friends* [New York, 1965], p. 242).

11. "Report on the Fine Arts," *Reports of the United States Commissioners to the Paris Universal Exposition, 1878,* Vol II (Washington, 1880), p. 117.

12. November, 1882; *The Letters of Oscar Wilde,* ed. Rupert Hart-Davis (New York, 1962), p. 131. Incidentally, Story, Symonds, and Wilde, if they were alive today, would find much of interest in Donald Hatch Andrews, "The Music of Sculpture," *Main Currents in Modern Thought,* XXIII, No. 2 (November-December, 1966), 31-37.

13. *The Literary Sculptors* (Durham, N.C., 1965).

14. Henry James, *William Wetmore Story and His Friends,* 2 Vol. (Boston, 1903), II, 71.

15. In *The Marble Faun* Story is presumably represented by Kenyon,

and his Roman studio is supposedly described in Chapter XIII: "A Sculptor's Studio."

16. *Grafitti d'Italia*, pp. 147-154; and *Poems,* 2 Vol. (1886), I, 129-134.

17. *Poems*, I, 77-82.

18. *Ibid.*, I, 254-257.

19. *Ibid.*, I, 56-82.

20. "Nature and Art." Here the influences are neoclassical. The basic verse-form is the heroic couplet from which the ear is relieved by several stanzas in imitation of the ode and by one 10-stanza set of quatrains. The poem is a kind of Popeian essay, much of it in "poetic diction," on man in nature and in art; it contains an apostrophe to poetry, quite conventional notions about its subject-matter, a great number of personifications (Hope, Memory, Fancy, Passion, Love, Custom, Death, Time, Freedom, Beauty, Earth, Art, Faith, *et al.*), a judicious but rhapsodical tone, concern for the use and abuse of art, and conviction of art's lofty aims. There is the usual catalog, not of ships or literary critics or even merely of writers, but of artists of several varieties: writers from Pindar to Euripides, from Virgil to Ariosto, from Chaucer to Shakespeare, including Goethe and Schiller; musical composers from J. S. Bach to Rossini; painters from Raphael to Rembrandt (with a nod in the direction of Washington Allston); sculptors from Phidias to Michelangelo. The conventional eighteenth-century characteristics of the poem make it in almost every respect atypical of Story. It was of course written by a young man of twenty-five for an occasion which must have been stuffy, to say the least.

21. *Poems*, 2 vol., I, 1-17. Further references to these volumes are in the text.

22. This poem, first printed in *Blackwood's* in 1886, was twice separately reprinted, in 1870 and in 1902, the latter edition being called "In Defense of Judas."

23. James, *op. cit.,* I, 194.

24. I shall discuss chiefly the ideas in *Conversations in a Studio,* but I shall not identify the page-source for each opinion because I have tried to organize Story's opinions and not present them in the casual way he himself assumes. Direct quotations are identified by volume and page numbers in the text.

25. Story indeed tried to show "the true relations of proportion in general as well as in the human body...." There were "the relations of the diameter, square, and equilateral triangle to the circle in which they are inscribed. ... This ... [is] the occult meaning of the symbol called the Seal of Solomon, which is the triangle inscribed in the circle." The reasons are "the mathematical as well as the symbolical, the mystical, and the geometric. The laws of numbers, of forms, and of magic . . . [coincide]" (II, 481).

    Here Story is discussing his work, *The Proportions of the Human Figure, according to a new canon of Polycletus, and of the Principal Ancient and Modern Systems* (London, 1866). He was not alone in his endeavor. George Field (1777?-1854), a chemist, David Ramsay Hay (1798-1866), a decorative artist, and Dr. John Addington Symonds (1807-1871), a physician, all were entranced with the ancient notion of an absolute principle, in the arts, of proportion mathematically expressed.

26. *Excursions in Art and Letters,* pp. 232-286. The essay first appeared in the *National Review*, XVII (Oct., 1863), 292-322.

27. Even earlier in his Phi Beta Kappa poem, "Nature and Art" (1844), Story took his clear and independent stand on Goethe, whom he thought of as a genius all right, but primarily as a poet of *what is* devoted to the gospel of work; as a man of many capacities, yet essentially "an iceberg, cold, transparent, gigantic, but serene, and glittering with the prismatic hues of poetry" (p. 46). And writing to J. R. Lowell in 1856, he said, "The wise Goethe has talked as much twaddle as any man I know. When people jabber so much about Art as they do here and have all their terms so cut and dried they are only playing cards on Art's coffin—just as Aristotle's Poetics was the funeral oration of Greek poetry" (James, I, 315). Apparently Story thought that when art lends itself to formula, it is on its death-bed, and that Goethe's formulizings—like Aristotle's—prove the point.

28. *North American Review,* CXXVI (Jan.-June, 1878), 97-110.

29. It might be interesting to conjecture about his possible reaction to Max Nordau's *Entartung* (1892), translated as *Degeneration* (1895). He disliked Byron, for instance, and deplored the effect in music of Offenbach!

The Cure of "Nothing!":
The Fiction of William Styron

Frederick J. Hoffman

1.

While William Styron has quite correctly refused to be called a "Southern writer," in an interview for the *Paris Review* he did admit that the South supplies "wonderful material."

> Take, for instance, the conflict between the ordered Protestant tradition, the fundamentalism based on the Old Testament, and the twentieth century—movies, cars, television. The poetic juxtapositions you find in this conflict—a crazy colored preacher howling those tremendously moving verses from Isaiah 40, while riding around in a maroon Packard. It's wonderful stuff and comparatively new, too, which is perhaps why the renaissance of Southern writing coincided with these last few decades of the machine age.[1]

It is futile to stir up the old cliches about "decadance," "Southern tradition," the "Southern model," etc.[2] Styron has better and larger fish to fry. He is, above all, concerned with a basic and timeless issue, though it surely has its place in twentieth century literature.

It is, in brief, the problem of believing, the desperate necessity for having the "courage to be." Almost all of his fiction poses violence against the human power to endure it and to "take hold of himself" in spite of it. The pathos of his creatures, when it is not directly the result of organizational absurdity,[3] comes from a psychological failure, a "confusion," a situation in which the character, trying to meet an awkward human situation, makes it worse and (almost invariably) retreats clumsily or despairingly from it.

Writing to the *Paris Review* (of which he was an Advisory Editor) for its first issue, on the ever-present questions of "the times" (*are* they worth, or *do* they promise good literature, etc.), Styron said:

> I still maintain that the times get precisely the literature that they deserve, and that if the writing is gloomy the gloom is not so much inherent in the literature as in the times. . . . The writer will be dead before anyone can judge him—but he *must* go on writing, reflecting disorder, defeat, despair, should that be all he sees at the moment, but ever searching for the elusive love, joy and hope—qualities which, as in the act of life itself, are best when they have to be struggled for, and are not commonly come by with much ease, either by a critic's formula or by a critic's yearning.[4]

There is nothing very complicated about this. It is a fairly simple set of human explorations. In a way, it is a twentieth-century restatement of Baudelaire's "Le Gouffre." Only here, in Styron's fiction, it takes on a far less subjective, isolative character. Lack of belief causes great cracks in the human landscape; and men look, desperate and afraid, across them at each other. Most of what they do has the character of trying to heal the wound, close the gap, but by means of ordinary secular devices. Alcohol has an important role in the lives of Styron's characters, but it is not a way of closing the fissure; it temporarily makes things *appear* improved, but it may ultimately lead to disaster. It is simply not a surrogate of God, though God's absence is surely responsible for the increase of its use.

I do not mean to suggest that Styron inhabits or has created a simple-minded world. It is perhaps the most difficult feat of all, this one of asserting not only the pre-eminence of values (love, joy, and hope[5]) but of creating meaningful situations in which men and women struggle to gain them, or even to understand them. The "modernness" of Styron's world, then, is not related to nihilism, but to humiliation, and to struggle: the ghastly struggle just to *assert* one's humanness, to get over the barriers to understanding, to clear one's personality of obsessions. Another way of putting it is that the Styron hero is trying for a clear view and a steady hand, like the hand of Cass Kinsolving *after* he has freed himself of the imprisonment within despair and within the obsessive indulgences used temporarily to combat it.[6]

2.

Styron's minor prose is largely confined to asserting those essentials, as though the essays and sketches were a clearing-house, to provide the novels a freer range of observation and action. The brief sketch of the funeral of William Faulkner, in *Life* magazine of July 20, 1962, puts a cap upon the lot; he speaks reverently, not only of his dead hero, but of the very substance and center of Yoknapatawpha County: the famous square in downtown Oxford, the court house and jail, the statue of the Confederate soldier.[7] Even a very early short story, "The Long Dark Road," selected by his teacher, William Blackburn, for inclusion in a Duke University anthology, concerns one of those calamitous explosions of human irrationality (in this case, a lynching) which Styron repeatedly described afterward in his two major novels.[8] His essays include one against capital punishment, in which he puzzles over why it is that the poor are condemned so much more often than the rich, and meditates upon "the soul" of the victim, which "will have been already so diminished by our own humanity" by the time it is "taken."[9]

The Long March gives an insight into the simplest variant of Styron's moral speculation.[10] If we assume that the human creature deserves (or can rise to) dignity and even nobility, but is often the victim of accident and absurdity, *The Long March* illustrates our assumption with the simplicity of a blackboard demonstration. As the novel opens, we see, "in the blaze of a cloudless Carolina summer," in a Marine training camp,

> What was left of eight dead boys [which] lay strewn about the landscape, among the poison ivy and the pine needles and loblolly saplings. . . . (p. 30)

Apropos only of the general absurdity of this military world, the "bone, gut, and dangling tissue" point to a haphazard regime, and even to a mad one; at least, its absurdity is a compound of accidental and humanly willed disasters.

In subsequent events, the Colonel (Templeton) of the Marine troop orders his men on a 36-mile hike, to prove nothing at all except that his men can and should walk the distance. Lieutenant Culver, the novel's hero, is also its center, because he is the only one whose personality is seen in more than one dimension. There is a phrase from Haydn, recalled from a brief peacetime stretch in Washington Square, with a wife, a cat, and a record-player, which haunts his mind throughout and is apparently to remind one of a saner world beyond this spectral and weird military enclosure. The Haydn plays a role roughly similar to a recording of Mozart's *Don Giovanni* in *Set This House on Fire,* which Kinsolving uses to "blast" the "ghosts" of his neighbors in Sambuco. In any case, it is one of Styron's frequent insertions from the "cultivated world" which always make one wonder if they are necessary.

Styron is very sophisticated and erudite; he will break in with a Haydn phrase or a quotation from *Oedipus at Colonus,* to set the unwary on an unnecessary search for a "Waste Land" type of significance.[11] Here, in *The Long March,* the references are of course used with a stark simplicity. The clarity and beauty of the Haydn phrase contrast with the true absurdity of the hot, sticky North Carolina scene. The central victim of its absurdity is Captain Mannix, a friend of Culver's, who persists beyond all but his human endurance to fulfill the Colonel's absurd orders.

> [His persistence] lent to his face . . . an aspect of deep, almost prayerfully passionate concentration—eyes thrown skyward and lips fluttering feverishly in pain—so that if one did not know he was in agony one might imagine that he was a communicant in rapture, offering up breaths of hot desire to the heavens. (*March,* pp. 113-114)

Aside from the evidence this passage offers of Styron's close study of Faulkner's style,[12] it is a statement concerning the world of the absurd. Mannix does not defy its absurdity; he simply goes about to prove that he can meet its terms, and becomes in the end a reduced figure, as a result of his efforts. Perhaps, by way of extenuation, it should be said that the terms are extraordinarily simple. Despite the fact that this world is absurd, there are few problems of communication here. It is not the military world that usually bothers Styron's persons, but the civilian world living in the shadow of a war, a "bomb," and, principally, in a circumstance that permits no easy belief.

3.

It is this combination of appalling and threatening circumstances that makes *Lie Down in Darkness*[13] so sad a novel. Throughout the interior monologue (pp. 335-386) of young Peyton Loftis, the atom bomb just dropped on Hiroshima appears as a menacing minor overtone. This is not a war novel, however; nor is it a novel devoted to diagnoses of civilians hurt by neurosis-inducing fright or guilt. It is, in fact, a "witness novel," that testifies to a special depth of human suffering and struggle. It is, as such, one of the representative novels of the 1950's and 1960's: the postwar novel of anxiety *and* manners, to which American Jewish novels have made so substantial a contribution. There is a point at which the total impact of unhappiness is so great that one has the impression that it is God's will it should be so. But this is not true. The agony is not that of sheer victimization. Superficially, it is set off by a husband and wife who are incompatible and whose sins are visited upon their child.[14] Once again superficially, the novel poses a morality and religion inadequate to the pressure and demands made upon them by the modern world. At any rate, the noises and smells of Port Warwick,[15] Virginia, are sufficiently strong to emphasize the fact that industry has invaded a world accustomed to being governed by a fairly slow, "closed" tradition and manners.

I think it a mistake to assume that *Darkness* is simply a study of "decadence" or "degeneration," two terms that have been too easily applied to both Styron and Faulkner. They do not explain anything. Far from being what Elizabeth Janeway says they are, "hardly conscious enough to be decadent,"[16] the three Loftises are all too alive to the pressures and conditions that continue to get in the way of their understanding each other. The agony of human error is so great that there is no real center of blame. Helen Loftis may at times be thought as the root source; and at times her narrow, religiously excused sentiments toward pleasure and SIN (as she capitalizes it) do appear responsible. But Milton Loftis is deeply at fault, in having taken to drink and adultery too quickly, as though they were nostrums available on the medicine shelf. And, finally, Peyton Loftis, alone in Manhattan, rejected by her husband whom she has quite openly "deceived," is both culpable and pitiful. In short, one comes eventually to the conclusion—as happens often in O'Neill plays—that no one is either totally guilty or blameless; that there is a "fate," terribly and pathetically human, that hovers over the novel.

In his not having settled for easy answers, his refusal simply to settle for "decadence" or "Southern malaise" as an explanation of his Loftises, Styron has struggled toward a great achievement in *Darkness*. Once again, there is a complement of "erudite" references; this time, however, they are largely effective. The epigraph gives us the cue for the title, which is from Sir Thomas Browne's *Urn Burial*:

> . . . since our longest sun sets at right descensions, and makes but winter arches, and therefore it cannot be long before we lie down in darkness, and have our light in ashes . . .

The last words are repeated at the end of Peyton's monologue, as she prepares to commit suicide:

> Perhaps I shall rise at another time, though I lie down in darkness and have my light in ashes. (p. 386)[17]

Lie Down in Darkness, as its title directs it to be, is concerned with human mortality, with the relentless drive of the death wish, which is underscored, of course, by a sense of almost total hopelessness. It is significant that the young Peyton, in the "present scene" of Port Warwick of 1945, is dead; we see her alive only in the past. In fact, we are aware of death in her and working in her in several ways: the coffin itself, of whose contents her father desperately tries to avoid imagining; before that, the body buried in Potter's Field, on Hart's Island, and claimed by her distraught husband of a few months and his friend; before that, death in her body (the womb painfully resists its function in Peyton's several affairs) as she fearfully walks the streets of Manhattan, vainly seeking the forgiveness of her husband, and fighting the cynical view of a mechanical, atomic world. And we may go back, almost to the beginning of her life, when the seeds of death are planted, as she reacts to the sheer hopelessness of her parents' incompatibility and to the almost incestuous tenderness with which her father treats her, by way of overcompensating for the coldness and emptiness of his married life.

Darkness is so constructed that we are forever beholding the fact of death; the coffin holding Peyton's "remains," present before us, poses simply the question "Why did she die?" For, as the epigraph offers us no hope of immortality and bids us prepare for our own death, the corpse of an eighteen-year-old girl is an ever-present *memento mori*.

There are many answers to the questions, and none. Peyton killed herself, or did her father, in his last view of her, frighten her into a pact with death? As she prepares to leave Port Warwick with her husband (as it is, her last time in her birthplace alive) she speaks desperately and angrily of

> "Daddy! He's had so much that was good in him, but it was all wasted. He wasn't man enough to stand up and make decisions and all the rest. Aren't things bad enough in the world without having him crawl back to that idiot? (*Darkness*, p. 317)

The poignancy of these random and angry remarks is not realized until we read the interior monologue preceding the suicide. Peyton has finally had to realize that her father is and will be no protection for her, that she must expose herself to life, alone, which means going, naked, to death.

For *Darkness* is, much of the way, a story of ordinary middleclass incompatibility and adultery: "ordinary," because the description of it is mean, tawdry, and without hope. Neither husband nor wife is heroic in any of it, though for a short time he appears in one of those interludes of fidelity and good intentions. It is also, and in close relationship to its other function, a novel which concerns the modern sensibility's frantic compulsions, its all but helpless drive toward self-destruction. When it is over, Milton Loftis, in his fifties and on the way to the funeral of his only remaining child, rushes into the rain away from his wife and his mistress, acknowledging for the first time *le néant* in all of its emptiness:

> Loftis pulled Helen about so that she faced him and began to choke her. "God damn you!" he yelled, "If I can't have . . . then you . . . nothing!"
> "People!" Carey [the minister] cried. "People! People! He couldn't move.
> "Die, damn you, die!" (*Darkness,* p. 388)
> . . . . .
> The last [Carey] saw of him was his retreating back, amid all the wind and rain, as he hustled on, bounding past wreaths and boxwood and over tombstones, toward the highway.
> Then Helen steadied herself against Carey, and she pressed her head next to the wall, "Peyton," she said. "Oh, God, Peyton. My child. Nothing! Nothing! Nothing! Nothing! (p. 389)

The full impact of this passage can come only after a careful reading of the entire novel. There is truly "Nothing!" left. Milton and Helen Loftis finally face this prospect, Helen ironically in the presence of her minister, whose pitifully futile attempts to bring her the solaces of religion now end in a pathetic figure, quite unable to give her the desperately needed words of God's grace. The stresses and strains are all in the present, as are the ironic meanings of the stench, the noise, the burial-ground, and the Negro revival.[18] Their importance can be sensed, however, only in the past. Through the history of their marriage, and especially in the attractive upper middle-class residential community overlooking the bay, the move toward the hopeless conclusion is inevitable; but its inevitability doesn't always "show." There are times of comparative peace, when both husband and wife seem willing to give in a little.

Nevertheless, three major conditions hover always on the edge of their lives, and make for the pathos of the final hours: Helen's religion (or, her spiteful and even pitiful uses of it); Milton's drinking, which he uses as an easy escape from acknowledging the pathetic sadness of their fate; and Peyton's self-indulgent dependence upon an all but incestuous relationship with her father. Perhaps Styron is saying: these people do not deserve a better fate. Or he may be saying: they are ineluctably fated to end as they do. But beyond any "naturalistic" or "fatalistic" view of them, he sees them as persons engaged in pitifully trying to save themselves, or each other, from a fate they are somehow not able to forestall. As he himself said, in an interview with David Dempsey:

> "I wanted to tell the story of four tragically fated people, one of them [Maudie] the innocent victim of the others. It was important to me that I write about this thing, but I can't tell you why. I didn't conceive it, directly at any rate, as a contemporary statement of any kind. The symbols are there, I suppose, but to me the important thing was the story."[19]

It is, of course, *not* a "contemporary statement," except in the limited sense that industrial ugliness intrudes upon the Loftis world, and the explosion of the Hiroshima bomb sounds menacingly in the distance during Peyton's tragic last day in New York City. The great achievement of *Darkness* is that it is a *universal* situation. There is nothing peculiarly Southern, or even especially characteristic of the "U.S.A." in the novel. It is a bit too much the melodrama to be called a tragedy. Yet the images of a death hovering over life are sufficiently clearly there, to make the whole comparable to the seventeenth century of *Urn Burial,* and of John Donne's sermons.

In short, *Darkness* poses the metaphysical problem of death in a setting in which there is insufficient accommodation for it. The ambiguities of a love and a happiness that seem always beyond reach, for one reason or another; the further perplexities of a man who loves too much, too earnestly, and too vainly: these are novelistic meditations not unlike the poetic and religious meditations typified by the novel's epigraph.

They say a number of things: for one, that we are all doomed; that our lives are but a preparing for death; most importantly, that we somehow (without overtly wishing to, but nevertheless, as if compulsively) help our own way toward self-destruction. Styron is saying that *any* inducement to neurotic behavior, any psychological self-flagellation, is suicidal. The most tragically compelling question at the novel's end is which of the three is the most doomed: Peyton, whose body has been dug up from Potter's Field; Milton, who walks away from her grave crying out "Nothing!" like a middle-class excommunicated King Lear; or Helen, who turns away from the minister of her faith, to repeat the "Nothing!" several times to a blank wall? They are akin in their being doomed, in their having lived a life that somehow has unavoidably led to their doom, in their willing their doom by not acting (perhaps, by not being able to act) to prevent it.

Styron avoids a total surrender to melodrama in several ways. One of these is style. One of the qualities that distinguish writers of Styron's generation from their predecessors of the 1920's is that, for Styron's contemporaries, style actually *does* function to qualify life. Perhaps this is because, most of the time at least, our younger novelists must somehow always "rescue" their work from naturalism and its nihilist metaphysics. They have somehow to improvise their own definitions of evil, their own theological metaphors. So, at crucial points, their characters are moral heroes, or moral clowns, or both.

Saul Bellow's Tommy Wilhelm, weeping desperately at a funeral of someone he has never known alive, at the end of his remarkable story, *Seize the Day* (1956), is an excellent case in point. The fact is that Loftis, no less and no more than his contemporary *personae,* improvises definitions as he invents poses to meet the terrible abysses left in his own society by the abject but somehow comprehensible failure of institutional religion to give protection in extreme crises. These circumstances, it seems to me, make for the kind of tragic failure that we see in this first of Styron's two great novels. Death hovers over the Loftis family from beginning to end; it is through death that we see their lives, as though we too were following the hearse, or waiting for the driver to repair its several mechanical failures, and steadily looking back on the scene of their tragic and impotent lives.

I don't believe that Styron intends the "Daddy Faith" episode at the novel's end to serve the same purpose as does Dilsey's Easter Sunday service in Faulkner's *The Sound and the Fury*. The aesthetic "competence" of Dilsey as a character, and the degree of Faulkner's preparing her for her culminating scene are both more acceptable in terms of the Compson debacle. Besides, the Compson gallery is much more varied. There is very little to go on, for example, when we try to compare Milton Loftis with Quentin Compson's father. Both drink steadily; each is undoubtedly disillusioned with his marriage; the attitude of each has a strong influence on his children. But these are surface resemblances. Styron has earned the right to his own novel.

4.

Set this House on Fire bears a relationship to *Darkness,* as an epic resembles a "tragedy of manners." Neither term quite success-fully defines either novel, but there is an extensiveness of scope and scene in *House* and a largeness of ambition that do not seem relevant to *Darkness.* The suggestiveness of the title is similarly involved in seventeenth-century metaphysics. This time, the source is John Donne's sermon "To the Earle of Carlile, and his Company, at Sion." In Styron's use of it, in his ambitious epigraph, it reads partly as follows:

> . . . God, who, when he could not get into me, by standing, by knocking. . . .hath applied his judgements, and shaked this house, this body, with agues and palsies, and set this house on fire, with fevers and calentures, and frighted the Master of the house, my soule, with horrors, and heavy apprehensions, and so rude an entrance into me. . . [20]

In identifying both his major novels with seventeenth-century texts, Styron is in a sense also identifying them with the twentieth century; for in their contexts, he sees strong resemblances between the two centuries,[21] at least within the limits of certain basic meditations upon "last things."

House can of course be seen superficially as a conflict between the country bumpkin and the millionaire, but this theme dissolves into farce if pushed too hard. It is true that Cass Kinsolving is in the power of Mason Flagg; their names are significantly involved, as is that of Peter Leverett, the narrator of Part One, and the listener of Part Two.[22] There is no doubt that Kinsolving is the hero of the novel, as Flagg is its villain. Both tower over everybody else in the novel, so that the next to final event in Sambuco, Italy (Kinsolving's killing of Flagg by forcing him over the cliff on the approach to a village beyond) is a struggle of giants. The real struggle is not the physical one, but Cass's struggle within himself. Flagg is indispensable to that struggle, of course: as he pushes Cass's weaknesses to the point of ridicule, he also provides the means of release from them.

Cass must be considered the hero of *House;* Peter Leverett says, "It is certainly not myself." (*House,* p. 4) In fact, Leverett is primarily designed to be observer and listener; even his hateful lashing out at Mason Flagg appears to be only an "observation," after all. Leverett is almost "computer-machine" American: "I am white, Protestant, Anglo-Saxon, Virginia-bred, just past thirty,[23] tolerable enough looking though possessing no romantic glint or cast, given to orderly habits, more than commonly inquisitive, and strongly sexed—though

this is a conceit peculiar to all normal young men." (4-5) He is set
up, first, to be attracted (because of an admiration of his apparent
superiority) to Mason Flagg; then, to be repelled by him, as he
slowly gathers in "counter" impressions; then, to be overwhelmed
by Cass's pathetic status; finally, to be committed irrevocably to Cass's
triumph over both Flagg and his own inner weaknesses. Leverett is
also designed to communicate all of these facts without drawing
attention to himself, despite the fact that he grows morally from
step to step of the novel's progress.

Leverett is, in short, a "stamped out" model, a pigmy observing
the struggles of giants. Since he has had no real temptations in his
life, he has had to make neither compromises nor progress. Or, if
there *is* progress in him, it is not interesting. What *is* of interest is
the way Styron maneuvers him in both time and space. Only in
Leverett's past is there a Mason Flagg; Cass's involvement with him
occurs in the Sambuco "present," and this fact is of some importance
to the novel's meaning. The "Thing" against which Cass struggles
didn't start with Flagg, as he says to Peter; it started far back, in
childhood, in youth, in The War, and *in himself*. To call him
"villain" is not to say that he was evil. To Cass, he was "just scum."

> "...Beast, bastard, crook, and viper. But the guilt is not
> his!..." (*House,* p. 249)

Part of this strange "absolution" has to do with the *roman
policier* aspect of *House:* Flagg did not kill Francesca, though he did
rape her and did leave her half-dead; the village half-wit, Saverio,
completed the job. But Cass's killing Flagg *did* take place and is of
the essence. In killing him, Cass destroyed the nastiness inside him:
the meanness which Michel Butor strangely calls "la condition
américaine," as he calls the novel an "allégorie" of this condition and
of "une invitation à la surmonter...."[24] Whether it was "American"
or not, Cass did triumph over a "something within him that had
(in affecting his mien) frightened prostitutes in Paris, driven him to
thoughts of murder and suicide, and led to prodigious feats of
drunkenness, the cost of which, for some weeks lead to a bondage
to the arrogant "scum," Mason Flagg.

If anything, the idea of the millionaire's son, with an overly
indulgent mother, an abundantly fertile imagination,[25] an extra-
ordinary interest in sex (associated with a tendency toward impotence), is a legitimate one. But this fact does not make *House* "une
allégorie de la condition américaine..."[26] The story of Mason Flagg
is one of inventive nastiness; he is like Fitzgerald's Tom Buchanan,
who, having played football at Yale, in middle age "drifted here and

there unrestfully wherever people played polo and were rich together."[27] But while Buchanan is almost sullenly rich, Flagg takes advantage of his position almost creatively, certainly with verve and *esprit*. Peter Leverett refers in one place to him in "the dual role of daytime squire and nighttime nihilist." (*House*, p. 158) It is true that the strategies and the energy that go into the creation and the satisfaction of his whims are prodigious.

That they lead eventually to Flagg's being the Mephistophelean playboy, the archangel of all anti-Christs, is true, and important; because by the time Cass Kinsolving confronts him (despite Cass's disclaimers) he needs a worthy antagonist. For, if we go back, we must remember that the "Thing," this *"quelque chose commeca"* that was destroying Cass's soul and causing him to destroy his body, had started early and grown huge before he finally projected it upon his enemy and, in a traumatic crisis, expelled it in as noisy a catharisis as has been noted for a long time in American fiction.

The crisis is religious in one sense, though it scarcely has a basis in theological symbolism.

> "A man cannot live without a focus," he says to Leverett in South Carolina. "Without some kind of faith, if you want to call it that. I didn't have any more faith than a tomcat. Nothing. Nothing! . . ."
>
> (*House*, p. 54)[28]

In this context, a lack of faith is like a lack of light and air, a secular "dark night of the Soul," of the sort described in the passage of Donne's sermon, used as the novel's epigraph. In Cass's kind of world, God will not "set this house on fire"; the initiative will have to come from Cass himself. And, while the cure seems to be complete, as he tells about it in South Carolina, there is no reason to believe that it might not break out again. It is true, however, that he has "met his match," has expelled his tormentor and killed him. More than that, he has seen the "scum" in himself and killed it; it seems to have disappeared forever over the edge of the cliff near Sambuco.

Part Two of the novel, in which Cass and Leverett "go after" the Sambuco incident together, trying to collaborate on explanations and reasons, carries as its epigraph the last stanza of Theodore Roethke's title poem of the 1953 book, *The Waking*.[29]

> This shaking keeps me steady. I should know.
> What falls away is always. And is near.
> I wake to sleep, and take my waking slow.
> I learn by going where I have to go.

These lines should give us a clue to the "peace" Cass has discovered finally. It is an uneasy peace, for "What falls away is always. And is near." Roethke's own experience, as the evidence of the poems gives it, involved a great dependence upon the father-image, a "falling away" from it, an apparent solution in marriage and in the pleasures of sex, and a crisis of "nothingness."[30] There is no doubt that in both cases the experiencing of *il niente, la nullità,* was traumatic, a major challenge to the heroic self. As the fascist *carabiniere* asks of him,

> "Have you not pictured to yourself the whole horrible vista of eternity?...The absolute blankness,...stretching out for ever and ever, the pit of darkness which you are hurling yourself into, the nothingness, the void, the oblivion?"
> *(House,* p. 196)

In one sense at least, the condition is "américaine." Cass has come from the country near Wilmington, North Carolina, on the Cape Fear River; at sixteen or seventeen, he had come into the city, in the hope of finding sexual experience, and lain with Vernelle Satterfield, whom he'd discovered near the bus station, selling copies of the Jehovah's Witnesses magazine for five cents apiece.

> "...in her little bedroom—she led me in with great piety and dignity, but that bed really *loomed* I'll tell you—she had the goddamdest gallery of Jesuses you ever saw....It was like a regular Jesus cult. It would have put some of those Italians back in the Abruzzi to shame." *(House,* p. 263)

The comic scene has its serious overtones. For Cass, a Protestant Southerner, seems always to have identified his failures with his religious backgrounds. More than that, he sees himself as forever in the role of the poor, ignorant American, trying desperately each time to "prove himself," and failing each time. In the weeks in Paris, with his Catholic wife and his Catholic children, he again suffers (this time, a serious) lapse in confidence. "You know," he tells Leverett, "the old Anglo-Saxon hellfire which we just can't ever get rid of...." (p. 268) Here, trying to justify himself as a painter, he suffers from what he calls "wild Manichean dreams, dreams that told him that God was not even a lie, but worse, that He was weaker even than the evil He created and allowed to reside in the soul of man, that God Himself was doomed, and the landscape of heaven was not gold and singing but a space of terror which stretched in darkness from horizon to horizon...." (pp. 275-76)

There is no doubt that the experience is similar to the Kierkegaardian *Sickness Unto Death.*[31] Cass's "cure" for it consists of wild plunges into excess: drinking, gambling, "the vices" if you will. He is more prodigiously a drunk, with a more Gant-ian appetite than ever Milton Loftis could have had. His experiences of "Nothing!" are grandly climactic, leading into agony dreams, long bouts with the whisky bottle, gambling, and whoring. He even goes the way of the modern scientific humanist, stealing a hundred capsules of a new medicine, which Flagg had himself "lifted" from the PX in Naples, in order to help his friend Michele. (pp. 206-210) But, of course, the act, like others of his life, is scarcely a triumph, and certainly does not lead to a conquest of self.

5.

That conquest must come melodramatically. At least Cass has an antagonist he can recognize; he survives all of the terrors of his *nullità* because of that. Mason Flagg has finally, in *his* excesses, provided Cass with an opportunity to rid himself of his. "Not to believe in some salvation," he says later to Leverett, "to have disbelief rolled over on top of one's head like an un-removable stone yet at times like this . . . to see such splendour and glory writ across the heavens & upon the quiet sand and to see all certitude & sweetness in one's own flesh & seed scampering tireless & timeless on the shore, and then still not believe, is something that sickens me to my heart and center." (*House*, p. 294)[33]

The story of Cass's illness and of his own curing of it has something of the existentialist impact of Faulkner's *A Fable*.[34] Or, it is a dramatization of Faulkner's key phrases in the Stockholm Address of 1950.[35] The fact is that many great artists of the twentieth century have had visions of this Manichean struggle: Catholics, Protestants, and Jews have all had some hand in portraying the agony, and some have suggested—or imagined—a cure. *Set This House on Fire* is notable for its having come really to grips with the problem, and left it after a masterpiece of storytelling; this, Faulkner, in all his earnestness, was not able to do in *A Fable*, though he certainly managed elsewhere. Styron's most recent novel sets the imagination a-going, in the expectation of an American literature of existentialism, as Ihab Hassan has said.[36] But it is perhaps best not to name it that, for fear of weighing it down with labels and classification. The important fact is that Styron has used his talents mightily and to a good effect in this novel. The subject of both it and *Darkness* is the "Nothing!" that both Helen and Milton Loftis cry out as he leaves her and the grave of the girl he has killed by tenderness. It is also Kinsolving's word; but he denies it dramatically, and appears at the end of *House* to have found a way of keeping it from him forever.

NOTES

1. Interview conducted by Peter Matthiessen and George Plimpton, for *Paris Review,* reprinted in *Writers at Work,* ed. Malcolm Cowley (New York: Viking, 1958), p. 273.

2. For what it is worth, I give a partial list of the speculations on Styron's "Southernness": John Aldridge, in the *New York Times Book Review,* September 5, 1951; Malcolm Cowley, "The Faulkner Pattern," *New Republic* 125 (October 8, 1951), 19-20 (Both of these strongly emphasize the Southern tradition); Elizabeth Janeway, in *New Leader,* 35 (January 21, 1952), 25 (she cries "Nonsense" to the idea that *Lie Down in Darkness* is a story, fable, what have you, of decadence in a Southern family); and Harvey Swados, "First Novel," 273 (November, 1951), 453 (who criticizes Styron for "investing his corrupt family with significances").

3. As in *The Long March* (New York, Random House, 1952). Other references to this work are given in the text.

4. The *Paris Review,* 1 (Spring, 1953), 13.

5. They, and other matters emphasized by Styron, point to William Faulkner's Nobel Award Speech in 1950. Styron was, of course, powerfully influenced by Faulkner, but has managed, I think, to bring the influence under control. He once said to David Dempsey about *Lie Down in Darkness*: "Faulkner's [influence] was the hardest to shake off. The early parts of my novel were so imbued with his style that I had to go back and rewrite them completely. . . . "*New York Times Book Review,* September 9, 1951, p. 27.

6. *Set this House on Fire* (New York: Random House, 1960). Other references to this edition are given in the text. See also his remark, in the interview published in *Writers at Work*: events like Hiroshima, he said, "don't alter one bit a writer's fundamental problems, which are Love, Requited and Unrequited, Insult, et cetera." (p. 281)

7. *Life,* 53 (July 20, 1962), 39-42. Faulkner, of course, used this square repeatedly and gave a "mythical history" of almost every

timber and brick, in the long expository passages of *Requiem for a Nun* (1951).

8. In *One and Twenty* (Duke University Press, 1945), pp. 288-90.

9. "The Death-in-Life of Benjamin Reid," *Esquire*, 58 (November, 1962), 142.

10. It is not Styron's first novel, but his second, in time of publication (1952). But it must be considered a minor work.

11. See Michel Butor's "Préface" to *La Proie des flammes*, French translation (by Maurice Coindreau) of *Set This House on Fire* (Paris: Gallimard, 1962), a very interesting series of suggestions concerning the quotation from Sophocles.

12. The style used in describing Mannix generally reminds one of Faulkner's Labove, of *The Hamlet*. The characteristic attitude of deep, almost obsessive concentration, is not unusual in Faulkner's novels.

13. New York and Indianapolis, Bobbs-Merrill, 1951. Other references to this edition (the first) will be given in the text.

14. There are two children, but the cripple, Maudie, starts few speculations and is surely an awkwardly simple "companion" of Helen Loftis's too narrow and too dry Protestantism.

15. The setting of *Darkness*, as well as the birthplace of Peter Leverett, narrator of *Set This House on Fire*. It is probably based upon Newport News, Virginia, a port city where Styron was born in 1925.

16. See the *New Leader* (January 21, 1952), p. 25.

17. This monologue is perhaps one of the most obvious borrowings from Faulkner, specifically from Part Two of *The Sound and the Fury*, an interior monologue which leads to a suicide, which must therefore have been communicated to us from death. But Styron offers us his quite original version of the situation; the resemblance is by no means unflattering to him.

18. The Negro revival, with "Daddy Faith" presiding and Ella Swan attending with her daughter, La Ruth, is once again an "echo" of Faulkner, this time of Part Four of *The Sound and the Fury*, the celebration of Easter in the Negro church, with the Reverend Shegog, a visiting preacher from Saint Louis, officiating. Styron gains an easy contrast by inserting the evangelical event on the edges of the cemetery, and the effects are not nearly so felicitous as those in Faulkner's novels.

19. *New York Times Book Review,* September 9, 1951, p. 27.

20. Epigraph to *House*, n.p. Note that the title of *Darkness*, which must have been a commonplace metaphor of death, is also found here: ". . . then this soule cannot be a smoake, a vapour, nor a bubble, but must lie down in darkness, as long as the Lord of light is light it selfe . . ."

21. There have been other speculations: Michel Butor's "Préface" to the French translation says much about Sophocles' play, *Oedipus at Colonus* (see pp. xi, xviii), as does Andre Bonnichen, in "William Styron et le Second Oedipe," *Etudes*, 315 (October, 1962), 102. This association is of course given encouragement through Styron's having Cass Kinsolving quote from the play (see *House*, pp. 117-18). One American critic links Styron's thought with that of Sören Kierkegaard's *The Sickness unto Death*, and quotes the text to prove it (See "Cass Kinsolving: Kierkegaardian Man of Despair," *Wisconsin Studies in Contemporary Literature*, 3, 1962, pp. 54-66). Another suggests an obscure seventeenth-century document, Henri Estienne's, translated by Richard Carew as *A World of Wonders* in *South Atlantic Quarterly*, 62, 1963, 539-50). John Howard Lawson blames Styron for what he regards as the failure of *House* on his inadequate social perception, his having used Freud to set aside Marx (See *Mainstream,* 13, October, 1960, pp. 9-18). These interpretations have varying usefulness. The wonder is that Styron's approach to life is more "universal" than ideological or regional.

22. Leverett has, inevitably, raised questions of the influence of F. Scott Fitzgerald's Nick Carraway of *The Great Gatsby* (1925). But Leverett is not nearly so well sketched in as Carraway, and Kinsolving is surely no Gatsby. The *idea* of having a narrator, like Conrad's Marlow, question and probe at the same time as he narrates, is of course there; and there is a rough similarity of Part Two to the last section of Faulkner's *Absolom! Absolom!* (1936),

where Shreve McCannon and Quentin Compson try together to reconstruct the legend of Thomas Sutpen.

23. Nick Carraway of *The Great Gatsby* remembers, in the noise of a crucial encounter on a hot July afternoon in 1922 at the Savoy Plaza Hotel, that he has just reached the age of thirty. The fact meant much more to Fitzgerald than it does to Styron.

24. "Préface," to *La Proie de flammes,* p. xi.

25. At one point Flagg points out, to Leverett, the difference between third-rate lying "and a jazzy kind of bullshit extravanganza. . . . meant with no malice at all, but only with the intent to edify and entertain." (*House,* p. 172) This remark has to do with his legendary war experiences in Yugoslavia as an agent behind the lines; he had actually been a draft dodger.

26. Butor, *op. cit.*

27. New York: Scribner's, 1925, p. 7.

28. This is the same "Nothing!" that afflicted both Milton and Helen Loftis in *Darkness.* See above.

29. New York: Doubleday, 1953, p. 120.

30. See my essay, "Theodore Roethke: The Poetic Shape of Death," in *Theodore Roethke: A Tribute,* ed. Arnold Stein (Seattle: University of Washington Press, 1965).

31. See Lewis Lawson, *op. cit.*

32. As Leverett says, seeing him at his worst in Sambuco: "Something held him in torment and in great and desperate need; I never saw anyone I wanted so to get sober." (*House,* p. 201).

33. Here Styron indulges in one of his uncommon "Agrarian" attacks upon the North: "I should have been brought up north in N.Y. suburbs, Scarsdale or somewhere on that order, where I might never have learned the quality of desire of thirst or yearning & would have ended up on Madison Ave. designing deodorant jars, with no knowledge or comprehension of the freezing solitude of the bereft and prodigal son." (*House,* p. 294).

34. New York: Random House, 1954.

35. See *William Faulkner: Three Decades of Criticism*, ed. F.J. Hoffman and Olga W. Vickery (Michigan State University Press, 1960), pp. 347-48.

36. "The Character of Post-War Fiction in America," *English Journal*, 51 (January, 1962), 7.

Israel Potter:*
Metamorphosis of Superman

Ray B. Browne

The most underrated of Herman Melville's novels is *Israel Potter: His Fifty Years of Exile* (1855). The re-written version of what Melville called "a little narrative of. . .adventures, forlornly published on sleazy gray paper. . .now out of print," this novel is vastly changed from the original. Here, as in "Benito Cereno," *Moby-Dick,* and other works that draw heavily on printed sources, Melville telescoped or extended, emphasized or played down sections in order to make his points and develop his themes. Because this work came after the relative failure of *Moby-Dick* and the catastrophic reception of *Pierre,* when Melville's literary and personal fortunes were at their lowest, it is especially significant as an index to the author's thinking during these days.

Simply told, it is the story of a Berkshire mountaineer named Israel Potter. As a young man he wants to marry a certain girl but is frustrated by his father. He runs away from home to seek his fortune. After proving himself on land and sea he returns to discover that his sweetheart has married another man. At the news of the battle of Lexington, Potter answers duty's call. Wounded at Bunker Hill he is hospitalized but returns almost immediately to assist in the fortification of Prospect Hill. Later he is captured by the British and sent to England to be imprisoned. His adventures thereafter are enough to break a dozen men. He escapes his captors and is recaptured. He has chats with King George and comes to respect and even like him. He works with Horne Tooke and other "friends of America." He visits Paris and Benjamin Franklin. He sails with John Paul Jones, participates in the attempt to burn Whitehaven, and in the battle between Jones' *Bon Homme Richard* and the British *Serapis.* He encounters Ethan Allen in prison. Finally escap-

---

*Not presented at the Conference

ing the British officials, he buries himself in London for forty-five years. At the age of eighty, urged by his son whom he has told of the "Fortunate Isles of the Free," Potter returns to America, in time to undergo other disappointments and to die.

In this novel Melville ponders on the matter of human liberty. He had grappled with monster tyranny in his earlier works, in for example, *Redburn, White-Jacket* and *Moby-Dick,* and had baldly stated to Hawthorne his opposition to it. In *Israel Potter* Melville moves the time of his study back to the eighteenth century, the period of revolutions of the common man against oppression, as he is to do later in "Benito Cereno" and *Billy-Budd.*

In this novel Melville demonstrates the triumph of the common man, as he shows it in "Benito Cereno" and *Billy-Budd.* But his technique is quite different. Richard Chase is partly right in saying that Melville's works develop Prometheus' effort to bring fire to the earth. *Israel Potter* shows that supermen and mere men cannot exist apart from one another. All men are the same and therefore must live together. The mixing of the superman and the common man results in a metamorphosis of the former into the latter. By the end of the book the superman of the beginning has disappeared and been replaced by the common man.

That the book deals with supermen becomes evident at the very beginning. Israel was born in the eastern Berkshires, a section of the world as remote as "some terrace in the moon." Here as the eye "sweeps the broad landscape beneath, you seem to be Bootes driving in heaven." In mountain valleys one has "scarcely the feeling of the earth." One realizes that the "very Titans seem to have been at work here," and the people have performed "herculean undertakings." This is the land of giant nature. The eagle soars, the hawk sallies from his crag "like a Rhenish baron of old from his pinnacled castle." Paganism and Christianity are combined. There is a "St. Peter's of these hills," the great purple dome of Taconic, and the "twin summits of Saddleback" are the "two-steepled natural cathedral of Berkshire."

The "original settlers" came into this region because they believed that high land was healthier than low. They were "a tall, athletic, and hardy race, unerring with the axe as the Indian with the tomahawk; at stone-rolling, patient as Sisphus, powerful as Samson" (ch. 4). Potter is of this stock. He is the true mountainman, the backwoodsman, who to Melville always symbolizes a kind of superman. In what is one of his deftest uses of Shakespeare Melville refers to *Anthony and Cleopatra* to make Potter a Caesar in homespun: "he chose rather to plough, than be ploughed" (ch. 3).

The other main characters are supermen also. Sir John Millett, the first Englishman to befriend Potter in England, is a "true Abrahamic gentleman." King George III, with whom Potter has friendly chats in the gardens at Kew, is a superman because "strange and powerful magic resides in [his] crown" (ch. 5). Franklin is a "household Plato" who has a "touch of primeval orientalness" and "the incredible seniority of an antediluvian" (ch. 7). He is "the apostolic serpent and dove," who seems to be "seven score years old," and to whom "supernatural lore must needs pertain" (ch. 7). His style of writing is "only surpassed by the unimprovable sentences of Hobbes of Malmsbury, the paragon of perspicuity" (ch. 8). Jacob, Hobbes, and Franklin are "practical magians in linsey-woolsey" (ch. 8).

John Paul Jones thinks himself a god, and threatens to "rain down on wicked England like fire on Sodom (ch. 10). He is "like David of old" (ch. 15), "an elemental warrior" (ch. 17). His tattooing is "cabalistically terrific as the charmed standard of Satan" (ch. 19). The battle between the *Bon Homme Richard* and the *Serapis* is "akin to the Miltonic contests of archangels" (ch. 19); Potter while clinging on the tip of the yard on the *Richard* "hung like Appollyon" (ch. 19). Ethan Allen, whom Potter sees a captive at Pendennis Castle, is a Green Mountain giant. Daniel Hoffman is certainly correct in saying that Allen was in Melville's day "half-legendary" and folkloristic. He has "leopard-like teeth" (ch. 21). He seems "just broken from the dead leases in David's outlawed cave of Adullam" (ch. 21). With a voice like Stentor's and all heroic figures, he blasts "wasp-waisted" officers backwards "as from before the suddenly burst head of a steam boiler" and snaps their spines (ch. 21). He is a version of an early and idealized Davy Crockett:

> Allen seems to have been a curious combination of a Hercules, a Joe Miller, a Bayard, and a Tom Hyer.... Though born in New England, he exhibited no trace of her character. He was frank, bluff, companionable as a Pagan, convivial, a Roman, hearty as a harvest. His spirit was essentially Western, for the Western spirit is, or will yet be (for no other is, or can be), the true American one.

Melville was to develop Crockett as a symbol of the west more fully in *The Confidence-Man*. In this symbol, this spirit, Melville sees cause for both exaltation and fear. Though it is the only one that can be, there is fear that "intrepid, unprincipled, reckless, predatory, with boundless ambition, civilized in externals but a savage at heart, America is, or may yet be, the Paul Jones of nations" (ch. 19).

Israel Potter is a superman in linsey-woolsey. His role is to demonstrate that as democratic god he can associate with other heroes and reveal the mutual dependence of man and superman. Further, he reveals that his age is that of the last of the demigods. From the beginning of the book Melville shows us the humanization of the supermen through the growth of democracy. In the Berkshires, during the easy times of spring and summer "the heart desires no company but Nature." But in fall and winter, mists and snow make these mountains nearly uninhabitable. December snows drift "to the arm-pits," and "as if an ocean rolled between man and man, inter-communication is often suspended for weeks and weeks." This is the terror of such a life. Even our giant-like ancestors realized that they had to abandon the mountains. "By degrees...they quitted the safety of this sterile elevation, to brave the dangers of richer though lower fields" (ch. 1), leaving untenanted houses and mountain tops showing "an aspect of singular abandonment." Further, there were great stone walls built of rocks of such size that "The very Titans seemed to have been at work on this "herculean" accomplishment now obviously falling into disrepair. This turning to lower ground was inevitable and desirable.

All the later-day supermen in the book are democratic. Franklin, "grown wondrous wise," is a "pocket congress of all humanity" (ch. 8). King George though largely controlled by the institution of which he is a part is personally good-natured and magnanimous, and "acted like a true man" (ch. 14). John Paul Jones is a "citizen and sailor of the universe" (ch. 10). He does not mind having as a "hammockmate a full-blooded Congo" (ch. 11). His arm is covered with tattooing "such as is seen only on thorough-bred savages" (ch. 11), in other words, like Queequeg's, the dignified and democratic cannibal. Jones wears on his face a "look of sagacious, humane meditation...as if pondering upon the chances of the important enterprise: one which, perhaps, might in the sequel affect the weal or woe of nations yet to come" (ch. 12). Ethan Allen hates all that smacks of English aristocracy. Lord Howe is to him a "toad-hearted king's lick-spittle of a scarlet polgroon; the vilest wriggler in God's worm-hole below" (ch. 21).

Potter himself is interested in "such momentous affairs as the freeing of nations" (ch. 10). There is no difference in rank between people. He is in no way awed by the great and wise Franklin, nor by King George; to the latter Potter says, "I have no king," and his natural dignity makes George comment grudgingly, "Very stubborn race, indeed—very-very-very" (ch. 5). Jones and Allen are recognized as only Potter's equals. Further, as Potter says after he has just escaped from the house of the defunct Squire Woodcock and is changing clothes with a scarecrow in a field, there is a "difference between the contents of the pockets of scarecrows and the pockets of well-to-do squires" (ch. 12), but clearly, as the tone indicates, not in the flesh of the two. As Potter had said earlier, "While we revel in broadcloth, let us not forget what we owe to linsey-woolsey" (ch. 3). Some Englishmen who are non-soldiers are to Potter, with obvious contempt in his statement, "a sort of craft aristocracy" (ch. 25). Finally, like Melville commenting on the universality of all kinds of people in his questioning in *Moby-Dick* of who is not a coward, slave, and cannibal, Potter destroys all rank in his query, "Who ain't a nobody?" (ch. 24).

Melville's demonstration of the equality of man is furthered by another way he treats the supermen in the book. That is, his attitude toward them is ambivalent. At the same time he obviously respects and likes them, he can be mischievous, flippant, irreverent.

Melville clearly likes Franklin, for example, yet cannot restrain himself. Melville's humor and irony are so subtle, as they are to be in the later *Confidence-Man*, that they at times go unnoticed. When Potter first enters the Paris apartment of Franklin, we are clearly in the presence of a superman, as we have seen above. Franklin is dressed in a "rich-dressing-gown...curiously embroidered with algebraic figures like a conjuror's robe, and with a skull-cap of black satin on his hive of a head, the man of gravity was seated at a huge claw-footed old table, round as the zodiac" (ch. 7). He is a medieval necromancer. Though the room buzzed with flies, the "sapient inmate sat still and cool...absorbed in some other world of his occupations and thoughts." This is a man whose initial appearance should be dramatic. But Melville parodies the effect. Instead of placing Franklin so that his appearance would be overwhelming, Melville turns him around so that Potter is denied the full effect. Franklin has his back to the visitor and will not turn around: "But when Israel stepped within the chamber, he lost the complete effect of this; for the sage's back, not his face was turned to him." Here the diminution of the superman is neatly accomplished. Melville's technique is the same, though to a lesser degree, as he used in *Typee, Redburn,* and *Moby-Dick* when he burlesques by having people expose their backsides.

Melville cuts Franklin down also by quipping about the old man's obsession with thrift. When Potter arrives in Paris, Franklin hands him some money for his needs, saying that it can be paid back in America. Potter returns it in a few minutes, however, and remarks, " 'No interest, Doctor, I hope' " (ch. 7). Later Franklin economizes on the cost of Potter's stay in the French house by taking out all the extra-cost items such as the Otard, sugar, and colored soap. Potter dryly urges him to be more exhaustive: " 'Oh, you better take the whole furniture, Doctor Franklin. Here, I'll help you drag out the bedstead'." (ch. 9)

The other heroic characters in the book are cut down to human dimensions. King George, though a "magnamimous lion," stammers, as of course he did in life, but he is completely deheroized by being denied his kingship. Potter tells him, " 'Sir, I have no king'." John Paul Jones is reduced by one blunt remark. The great captain is ranting to Franklin and Potter about his prowess on the seas; he remarks, referring to himself in the heroic third person, " 'Paul Jones never was captured'," and demands of Potter, " 'Did your shipmates talk much of me?' " Potter's reply is blunt: " 'I never heard the name before this evening' " (ch. 9). Ethan Allen, though a superman, is like "some baited bull in the ring," a "Patagonian-looking captive," whose "whole marred aspect was that of some wild beast" (ch. 21). Though gallant to the ladies, he has a "bovine forehead" (ch. 21).

Melville's greatest art in dimunition is reserved, however, for God. In bringing God down, Melville to a certain extent and clearly on purpose raises Potter to the stature of a demigod. But more important Melville is stripping God of His superiority and making Him not much superior to mere human beings, surely something not to be worshipped. In this way at least Melville has a quarrel with God, as Thompson has argued. God is whimsical, especially with commoners. Potter is "planted, torn up, transplanted, and dropped again, hither and thither, according as the Supreme Disposer of sailors and soldiers saw fit to appoint" (ch. 13).

Twice Melville cuts God most deeply by use of parody, both times of the Resurrection. When Potter is secreted in the chimney room of Squire Woodcock, which had formerly constituted a "portion of a religious retreat belonging to the Templars" (ch. 12), Melville uses Biblical language to tie in this scene with the Resurrection. In this religious sanctuary Potter waits for release from this "coffin-cell of the Templars" (ch. 12). Squire Woodcock promises to come for the "disentombment" as soon as possible, on the third day at the latest. While waiting, Potter, like countless Christians before him, suffers: "Here, in this very darkness, centuries ago, hearts, human as his, had mildewed in despair; limbs, robust as his own, had stiffened in immovable torpor" (ch. 12). Like their hope in eventual release, his expectations are vain. The scene is reminiscent of the sixteen hours the youthful Ishmael spent in his room waiting for his "resurrection."

Melville parodies Biblical language. " 'This is the morning of the third day,' murmured Israel to himself; 'he said he would at the furthest come to me on the morning of the third day' " (ch. 12). When

Woodcock, the dead god, fails to resurrect Potter on the third day, on the fourth Potter resurrects himself. Significantly he is reborn a Squire. He finds the spring that operates the chimney door and emerges. He discovers that the Squire is dead, and the room hung with funeral drapings.

As Potter emerges from his coffin, "by degrees he began to feel almost as unreal and shadowy as the shade whose part he intended to enact" (ch. 13). Potter becomes Woodcock by dressing in the Squire's clothes. So garbed he emerges from the room, and the servants all believe he is the resurrected Squire. The widow falls into a dead faint at the sight of him. Significantly she falls "crosswise before him," and he, being a god "forced to be immutable in his purpose...solemnly stepping over her prostrate form, marched deliberately on" (ch. 13).

The single overriding theme of this novel is, as Elizabeth Foster says in the introduction to *The Confidence-Man,* the necessity for humanism, of man's faith in the human race in this man-of-war and godless world. This theme is strikingly developed in events which now take place.

Outside the house, "the whole scene magically reproduced to our adventurer the aspect of Bunker Hill, Charles River and Boston town, on the well-remembered night of the 16th of June" (ch. 13), when the first major stroke was made against tyranny in favor of the common man. Now, "acted on as if by enchantment," Potter realizes that he must be reborn as a human being. Suddenly he sees "a man in black standing right in his path...one outstretched arm, with weird intimation pointing towards the deceased Squire's abode." The stranger seems "something more than humanly significant," not a "living man" (ch. 13). But Potter, "the phantom of Squire Woodcock," with something of his "intrepidity returned," firmly marches "straight forward towards the mysterious stranger."

This "mysterious stranger" turns out to be a scarecrow. Potter changes his godly raiment for the sorry, human clothes on the scarecrow, and in so doing introduces one of the most grotesque—and not completely satisfactory—scenes in literature outside of sheer farce.

The morning after Potter has taken on the clothes from the scarecrow, a farm-laborer carrying a pitchfork approaches the spot where the scarecrow formerly stood. Thinking that the scene should not be changed, Potter assumes the position and stance that the scarecrow had had. When the laborer has passed by, Potter runs away as fast as he can. But looking around he sees that the laborer is coming back. Potter then freezes again in the stance of the scarecrow, pointing at the advancing man with his uplifted arm, trying to frighten him. But this implacable human being approaches, puzzled by the apparent supernatural happenings, but determined to get at the truth. Potter now, in trying to escape, attempts to become Satan. "Israel as a last means of practising on the fellow's fears of the supernatural, suddenly doubled up both fists, presenting them savagely towards him at a distance of about twenty paces, at the same time showing his teeth like a skull's, and demoniacally rolling his eyes" (ch. 13). But the man is not frightened. He advances slowly, presents the end of his pitch-fork to Potter's eye, and finally forces the scarecrow to take to his heels. This Satan, this "apparition," is chased away by the laborer and a "dozen laborers" from an adjoining field who join in the rout. Scarecely any stronger statement could be made of man's triumph over the supernatural.

Melville's strongest affirmation of his belief in man not God, and his sharpest travesty of God's creation of man, comes later, when Potter, finished with his wartime adventures, has come to the neighborhood of London and gets a job at a brickyard. Melville immediately makes it clear that this situation must be paralleled with the Biblical account of man's creation. Potter becomes both a buryer and a creator: "Half buried there in the pit, all the time handing those desolate trays [of brick mud], poor Israel seemed some grave-digger, or churchyard man, tucking away dead little innocents in their coffins on one side, and cunningly disinterring them again to resurrectionists stationed on the other" (ch. 22). The Creators—the dozen workers in this section—are whimsical, like God. Obviously influenced by the gravedigger in *Hamlet,* they are indifferent to their vocation, with its "helter-skelter slapping of the dough into the moulds" (ch. 22). These "muddy philsophers" feel that "men and bricks were equally of clay." " 'What signifies who we be—dukes or ditchers?' thought the moulders; 'all is vanity and clay'." Melville extends the comparison between bricks and men: "brick is no bad name for any son of Adam; Eden was but a brickyard; what is a mortal but a few luckless shovelfuls of clay, moulded in a mould, laid out on a sheet to dry, and ere long quickened into his queer caprices by the sun? Are not men built into communities just like bricks into a wall?" (ch. 22). Man "serves" bricks, as "God him, building him up by billions into edifices of his purposes. Man attains not to the nobility of a brick, unless taken in the aggregate" (ch. 22).

In a scene strongly reminiscene of Hawthorne's "Ethan Brand" Melville has Potter sitting before the mouth of the kilns philosophizing while "a dull smoke—a smoke of their torments—went up from their tops" (ch. 23). Melville now philosophizes on how much man must commit himself to life, a question that is present to a greater or lesser extent in all his books, in *Clarel,* and a point on which he severely criticized Ralph Waldo Emerson for his failure to descend from his Olympian heights to mix with the mass of mankind. This question, instead of the one raised by James E. Miller—that the fire equals evil or misfortune—seems more nearly correct.

There are three kinds of bricks taken from the kiln. Those nearest the fire have been broken by the heat. This would seem to be a statement that although heat is beneficial to clay, necessary for the development of bricks, too much can break them. Those bricks furthest from the heat are "pale with the languor of too exclusive an exemption from the burden of the blaze" (ch. 23); here Melville is commenting on those persons who are too detached from life, as he felt Emerson was, to live it fully. Only those bricks which are in the middle are the good ones. Not broken by life's poverty and adversities, not detached and therefore indifferent, but truly and completely and democratically committed, they are the best bricks for the wall of humanity.

The religious implications of the scene as a continuation of the preceding one are clear: "These kilns were a sort of temporary temples constructed in the yard, each brick being set against its neighbor almost with the care taken by the mason" (ch. 23). But the bricks last longer than the temples, for once the bricks—men— are formed, down come the temples "in a tumbled ruin," and the bricks are sent off to mix with and serve humanity.

Melville's moral, his leveling of God and man and the democratic mass, is made explicit at the end of this chapter. Paralleling the fate of the American Israel with that of his Biblical namesake, now "bondsman in the English Egypt," Melville concludes that men are all the same regardless of time or nation in which they live: " 'What signifies who we be, or where we are, or what we do?' Slap-dash! 'Kings, as clowns are codgers—who ain't a nobody?' Splash! 'All is vanity and clay' " (ch. 23).

Melville's feeling that men are the same throughout time and space does not extend to the belief that all countries are the same. He will modify this feeling in *Clarel.* Now, however, as it had been throughout most of his earlier works, America is the hope of humanity, "the Fortunate Isles of the Free." England represents the opposite. Potter quits his job at the brick yards and goes to London, "entering, like the king, from Windsor." But though he can enter a city from the same side as the king, not every man in London is yet a king. Significantly, Potter enters on the Fifth of November, Guy Fawkes day, when a man tried to destroy one symbol of English institutions, the Houses of Parliament. To Potter London represents "that hereditary crowd—gulf-stream of humanity—which, for continuous centuries, has never ceased pouring, like an endless shoal of herring, over London Bridge" (ch. 24). Here as in *Clarel*, Potter joins the stream of humanity.

But London Bridge, over which the stream of humanity flows, epitomizes the evil of anachronistically institutionalized England. The Southwark entrance has been the place through the ages on which "the withered heads and smoked quarters of traitors, stuck on pikes" have tyrannized the people and kept them in their place. The scene thunders with the same cry of outrage as that at the end of "Benito Cereno," as well as elsewhere in Melville's works, when Babo's head piked above the street is the white man's ultimate in self-degradation.

In London, where he wanders for forty years, Israel knows "that being of this race, felicity could never be his lot" (ch. 24). It is not. Melville drags Israel through every possible adversity, "wrangling with rats for prizes in the sewers," "crawling into an abandoned doorless house... where his hosts were three dead men, one pendant" (ch. 25), fathering eleven children only to bury ten, jostling with thousands for bare subsistence, warming himself and his remaining son "over a handful of reignited cinders (which the night before might have warmed some lord)," (ch. 25), words and scene paralleling closely the leftover food being fed the poor in "Rich Man's Crumbs." Finally Potter flees England and returns to America, largely because his son "felt added longing to escape his entailed misery" (ch. 25).

Potter's return and fate in America rounds out Melville's theme. Back in this country, on the Fourth of July he discovers that most of the country's gratitude consists in raising monuments, as the one on Bunker-Hill. A purse is raised for him, however, and he, "the bescarred bearer of a cross," returns with his son to the mountains of his youth. There all traces of the Potters have disappeared. Inquiring from a stranger who is ploughing, Potter discovers that the man is in fact plowing up the last remains of the Potter old homestead. This man reports that the Potters have "gone West." In an agony of remembrance of his lost life Potter says to the laborer, "Plough away, friend."

In this sentence, Melville reintroduces one of the main themes of the book. This is a reawakening of his earlier statement when like a plebeian Caesar he would rather plow than be plowed. Now he is willing to stand aside and allow the plowing by others. But the statement is not one of desperation. Though Potter has been denied a pension by "certain caprices of law," though "his scars proved his only medals," though his name faded "out of memory," and though "he died the same day that the oldest oak on his native hills was blown down," the book does not end in despair. Rather, as in *Hamlet* and *Caesar* there is hope in the fact that Potter leaves a son behind him.

Further, there is some satisfaction in the fact that man can endure the hardships that Potter suffered for eighty years. There is hope in sheer animal endurance. Most important of all, however, is the obvious moral of the book, that men must stick together. Here, as in *The Confidence-Man,* which Melville is to publish two years later, is the author's statement of the need for humanism joining all men—high and low, rich and poor—into a wall against adversity.

Finally, a word should be said about Melville's style in this book. It has none of the rhetoric that sometimes blemishes *Moby-Dick* and often mars *Pierre.* Instead the style is fast, direct and restrained. When necessary Melville gallops through or around material but never trips the reader. Having purged himself of most of his surfeiting of literary allusions and mannerisms, he here can paraphrase the Bible or Shakespeare with great dexterity, as we have seen. Furthermore there is a whiplike prose here which forecasts its finer use in Melville's next book, *The Confidence-Man.* Yet through all, there is a sure handed poetic tone that reveals how confident Melville felt in his use of the material, as the following section from the fight between the *Bon Homme Richard* and the *Serapis* reveals:

> Not long after, an invisible hand came and set down a great yellow lamp in the east. The hand reached up unseen from below the horizon, and set the lamp down right on the rim of the horizon, as on a threshold; as much as to say, Gentlemen warriors, permit me a little to light up this rather gloomy looking subject. The lamp was the round harvest moon; the one solitary footlight of the scene. (ch. 19)

All in all, this book about the wandering American Israel must be placed among the top half dozen of Melville's works.

Charlie, a Little Fellow

James Sandoe

Comedy is, of course, style not subject: the stuffs that make *Coriolanus* make *The Misanthrope*. Hauptmann and Brecht bring widely disparate manners to comparable matter.

Inflection is the heart of comic style and it may involve the puncture of pretensions by a barbed phrase or by a banana peel. Aristophanes used both with relish. Lately, that ancient and honourable weapon, the slapstick, has fallen into disrepute as being too gross for our refined age. The vogue of "pop" art may do something to restore it although I wonder how many of its fans cleave to the sturdy comment of the custard pie merely *per se*.

The coming of the custard pie occurred early in 1913. No one remembers the precise date, which is a pity, for it is a date of considerable significance in the history of the cinema. But the circumstances are well-known. It happened that Ben Turpin, whose walrus moustache and insignificant cross eyes were merely the outward decoration of a refined and resourceful comedian, was ordered by Mack Sennett to thrust his head through a door.

"You're not funny," Mack Sennett objected.

"Shall I uncross my eyes," Ben Turpin asked, unhelpfully.

"No, just be funny. Do your damndest to be funny."

Ben Turpin tried. He glared, he opened his mouth, he closed his mouth, he wiggled his walrus moustache, but he was a signal failure. In desperation he rolled his crossed eyes, but the director only groaned. They worked until late afternoon, their tempers fraying. Suddenly from out of nowhere a custard pie sailed over the camera to land squarely on Ben Turpin's face. The camera crew and everyone on the set howled. It was funny enough when Ben Turpin was smacked by the custard pie, but it was funnier still when he attempted to unstick the thing from his face and blinked pitifully through the mess.

"Who sent the custard pie," Mack Sennett asked.

99

"I, with my little pie," Mabel Normand answered. "I threw the pie."
The subtle refinements inherent in pie-throwing remained to be explored."[1]

There is nothing inherently funny in a custard pie: the fun comes, if it comes, in the skill with which it is thrown into a situation at someone in need of deflation. The banana peel that fells a little old lady and breaks her hip is a very different banana peel from the one that upsets the scornful gentleman in the top hat and plants him on his well-rounded rear.

The prologue of William Congreve's comedy, *The Way of the World* (1700) says of the play:

> Some plot we think he has, and some new thought,
> Some humour too, no farce—but that's a fault.[2]

In fact, there *is* farce, in the succession of variously weaving drunks who inhabit much of the fourth act, and in the false refinements and tenderness of Waitwell's sweating courtship of Lady Wishfort. His exhausted retrospect of the effort sums itself up in his judgment of her: "Oh, she is the antidote to desire!"

But Congreve's elegance expresses itself, like Watteau's, in careful flicks of words, set like jewels in careful, symmetrical sentences. While some of it is visual fun, nearly all of it is verbal fun - the antithesis of Chaplin's, but demanding of itself an equal deftness and requiring of the actor a delicate precision of inflection to express the meaning. Congreve demands a great deal of an audience, Congreve assumes an audience of more or at least of different sophistication than ours, and Congreve depends enormously upon the actor to catch and toss on his subtlest intention.

Early in the first act, as Mirabell and Fainall converse, and after Witwoud, Petulant and Lady Wishfort (each bearing a name indicative of the character behind it) have been introduced by name, Mirabell recalls his irritation at having been badly treated the night before when visiting Millamant:

> *Fainall.* Prithee, why so reserved? Something has put you out of humor.
> *Mirabell.* Not at all; I happen to be grave today, and you are gay; that's all.
> *Fainall.* Confess, Millament and you quarreled last night, after I left you; my fair cousin has some humors that would tempt the patience of a stoic. What, some coxcomb came in, and was well received by her, while you were by.
> *Mirabell.* Witwoud and Petulant, and what was worse, her aunt, your wife's mother, my evil genius; or, to sum up all in

her own name, my old Lady Wishfort came in.

Fainall. Oh, there it is then! She has a lasting passion for you, and with reason. What, then my wife was there?

Mirabell. Yes, and Mrs. Marwood and three or four more, whom I never saw before. Seeing me, they all put on their grave faces, whispered one another; then complained aloud of the vapors, and after fell into a profound silence.

Fainall. They had a mind to be rid of you.

Mirabell. For which reason I resolved not to stir. At last the good old lady broke through her painful taciturnity, with an invective against long visits. I would not have understood her, but Millamant joining in the argument, I rose and with a constrained smile told her, I thought nothing was so easy as to know when a visit began to be troublesome. She reddened and I withdrew, without expecting her reply.

Fainall. You were to blame to resent what she spoke only in compliance with her aunt.

Mirabell. She is more mistress of herself than to be under necessity of such a resignation.

Fainall. What? though half her fortune depends upon her marrying with my lady's approbation?

Mirabell. I was then in such a humor, that I should have been better pleased if she had been less discreet.

Fainall. Now I remember, I wonder not they were weary of you. Last night was one of their cabal-nights; they have 'em three times a week, and meet by turns at one another's apartments, where they come together like the coroner's inquest, to sit upon the murdered reputations of the week. You and I are excluded; and it was once proposed that all the male sex should be excepted; but somebody moved that, to avoid scandal, there might be one man of the community; upon which motion Witwoud and Petulant were enrolled members.

Now risibilities vary and no laugh-meter can calibrate them more than approximately. Indeed, the laughter that is summed up in a delighted smile defies meters as much as an all-out yack dizzies them. Some of the most deeply appreciative laughter makes no more noise than a small, melting hmm (the beginning of one of those memorable Lynn Fontanne laughs). But in this passage and particularly in the final speech from Fainall, the audience which laughed appreciatively at the ladies likened to a coroner's inquest, quite missed Fainall's wry if accurate judgment of Witwoud and Petulant as just half a man apiece.

The same thing is true of audiences watching Chaplin: he is at once too generous and too fast for us. We catch the large points and often miss the little ones, those ornamantations of laughter which augment the effect. In this connection it should be said that Chaplin has a superlative sense of where to start and an even more superlative sense of where to stop—and that is always carefully short of what an audience wants. His astuteness in discovering how far a gag can be carried is never carried (in my experience) to the point of milking it dry. In *The Pawnshop*, for instance, he shows some of the possibilities of a ladder (as a slapstick) but his use of it is not repetitive but deliciously an exercise in theme and variations, a virtuosity of likeness with crucial differences.

Chaplin's capacity to deploy a slapstick is ultimate. In *Easy Street*, it takes many forms. One of them is obvious, the billy-club with which he corrects the scoffer outside the police station. He has already exercised it adroitly to correct the police captain. There it has taken us off guard. Not that we know something of its capacities there is a lovely anticipatory lift in watching it swing a little, a little more and then in a splendid, precise bop, quell the uncouth satirist. The billy club may not be the traditional "device [to quote Webster-Merriam] made of two flat pieces of wood, sometimes used in farce by one actor in striking another in such a way as from the loud noise to make it appear that the blow was a severe one." But it is as much a slapstick as the gaslight, the stove and the needle—on which Charlie sits inadvertently but usefully, late in the film.

As an exercise of fancy I would ask you to imagine how Jerry Lewis would have deployed the same properties. Mr. Lewis, obviously talented, has been widely popular in spite of a grave lack of discipline and of discretion. He sweats as if comedy throve upon it; he confuses insistence with adroitness and noise with fun; and he seems to assume that the agonies of a rubber face will reduce an audience to helpless laughter. He is, regrettably, a clod, not a comedian, and this is a sad loss to comedy.

Charlie is associated most strongly with his character, the tramp, for all that in early films and late ones he essayed other characters. Of the others there is the drunken dandy of *One A.M.* and you may be lucky enough to be able to recall Adenoid Hynkle, the great dictator (1940); Monsieur Verdoux (1947), the cool multiple murderer; or Calvero, the aging music hall star of *Limelight* (1952).

The tramp seems to have begun from a need to improvise for Mack Sennett who, as Chaplin recalls it, said "Put on a comedy make-up. Anything will do."

> I had no idea what make-up to put on. I did not like my getup as the press reporter. However, on the way to the wardrobe I thought I would dress in baggy pants, big shoes, a cane and a derby hat. I wanted everything a contradiction: the pants baggy, the coat tight, the hat small and the shoes large. I was undecided whether to look old or young, but remembering

Sennett had expected me to be a much older man, I added the small mustachs, which, I reasoned, would add age without hiding my expression.

I had no idea of the character. But the moment I was dressed, the clothes and the makeup made me feel the person he was.[3]

Earlier, he had written about the symbolism of his costume:

His little moustache? That is a symbol of vanity. His skimpy coat, his trousers so ridiculously baggy and shapeless? They are the caricature of our eccentricity, our stupidities, our clumsiness. . . . The idea of the walking-stick was perhaps my happiest inspiration, for the cane was what made me speedily known. Moreover, I developed business with it to such a point that it took on a comic character of its own. Often, I found it hooked round someone's leg, or catching him by the shoulder, and in these ways I got a laugh from the public while I was myself scarcely aware of the gesture. I don't think I had fully understood in the beginning how much, among millions of individuals, a walking stick puts a label marked 'dandy' on a man. So that when I waddled onto the stage with my little walking stick and a serious air, I gave the impression of an attempt at dignity, which was exactly my aim."[4]

Of the character of the tramp he writes:

In the Keystone days [working for Sennett, who had, in spite of nervous scruples, more than wit enough to let Chaplin begin writing and directing his own films as well as acting them] the tramp had been freer and less confined to plot. His brain was seldom active then—only his instincts, which were concerned with the basic essentials: food, warmth and shelter. But with each succeeding comedy the tramp was growing more complex. Sentiment was beginning to percolate through the character. This became a problem because he was bound by the limits of slapstick. This may sound pretentious, but slapstick demands a most exacting psychology.

The solution came when I thought of the tramp as a sort of Pierrot. With this conception I was freer to express and embelish the comedy with touches of sentiment. But logically it was difficult to get a beautiful girl interested in a tramp. This has always been a problem in my films. In *The Gold Rush* the girl's interest in the tramp started by her playing a joke on him, which later moves her to pity, which he mistakes for love. The girl in *City Lights* is blind. In this relationship he is romantic and wonderful to her until her sight is restored.[5]

None of the three films under consideration here shows the encroachment of sensibility upon the pure assault of comedy. In none of them are we called upon to engage more than the complex of our risibility. Nowhere in these films is there any hint—as there is in some of their fellows from the same period: *The Vagabound,* for one, and *The Immigrant*—of the sadness of the clown which makes the ending of *City Lights* a deeply sobering and tearful, matter. Or makes the conclusion of *The Great Dictator* an urgent plea for understanding and for brotherhood among men which still seems to invite (or obtain) an astonishing amount of complaint even from Chaplin's allies.[6]

Risibilities, not sensibilities, are his concern in these films, all drawn from his busy days at Mutual (1916-17): their mode is slapstick managed with that carefully concealed discipline that is the ultimate in camouflage.

If you have ever been fortunate enough to see Chaplin in rehearsal your assumptions about his perfectionism will have been perfectly supported. I once had the good luck to see a succession of rehearsal "takes" through which he was striving to perfect a gag: dapper and drunken, he wove into a bowling alley, tripped, fell, was spun around by the whack of a bowling ball, got somehow (effortlessly, if still tipsy) to his feet and wove delicately off.

How much preparation went into this sequence before he was willing to trust it to trial filming, I couldn't guess. But he has always been at once a perfectionist and a cautious millionaire; so it seems certain that these successive "takes" were hopeful trials on film after much studio rehearsal. The watching was fascinating, take after take, each showing some change to polish the notion, sharpen it towards its objective. Eventually the dapper drunk was pulled in by an eager terrier who added to the perils of tipsiness and made for keener tension and a faster pace. Take followed take, each grasping for the one that would do. But not one of the lot, even with refinements, ever met Chaplin's demands upon himself: the sequence stayed in the archives, never incorporated into a film.

Relying at this point entirely upon pantomime (with occasional captions, few of which are vital and some of which are witty) Chaplin depended at the same time upon exceptional bodily adroitness and a dancer's grace. From first to last *Easy Street* is choreographed: Chaplin may be the principal dancer but he has infected the whole company with his direction and his sense of rhythm. The hulking bully is as light on his feet as the miniature cop while the neighborhood inhabitants advance and retreat in neatly arranged order or disorder.

No sequence shows surer or more delicate dance direction than the one beginning with Charlie's fatuous flat-footed progress into Easy street, his great shoes flapping tidily right and left and his assurance at an apogee. He discovers the bully with alert alarm and changes his strategy. He makes a contemplative tour of the block—the heavy bully close at his heels all the way and equally dextrous. His carefully concealed indifference becomes more and more precisely panic—the bully still and more closely at heel, as formidably heavy as ever but just as light footed, too: as a sequence it is precisely *pas de deux*.

Chaplin's choreography was the subject of one of his great contemporaries' envious scorn:

> "Perhaps the best testimonial to Chaplin's greatness is the fact that [W. C.] Fields was incapable of watching him perform for more than a few minutes. The virtuosity of the little fellow's pantomime caused Fields to suffer horribly. One evening, a few years before Fields' death, he was persuaded to attend a showing of early Chaplin two-reelers. At a point in the action where Chaplin suffocated a 300-pound villain by pulling a gas street lamp down over his head, the laughter rose in a deafening crescendo, and Fields was heard to cough desperately.
>
> "Hot in here," he muttered to his companion . . . I need air." Fields left the theatre and waited outside in his Lincoln. Later, asked what he thought of Chaplin's work, he said, "The son of a bitch is a ballet dancer."
>
> "He's pretty funny, don't you think?" his companion went on doggedly.
>
> "He's the best ballet dancer that ever lived," said Fields, "and if I get a good chance I'll kill him with my bare hands."[7]

Fields was a very good if a jealous judge: his reputation was first made as a juggler, famous on any continent he chose to engage himself upon. And his dissmissive summary of Charlie's skill is, as Taylor says, an ultimate testimonial, not from an observing critic but from a critical fellow player.

As a performer Chaplin has been from a very early point responsible not just for Charlie but for all the rest of the proceedings: script, cast, direction, music, cutting—the works. Even Shakespeare had no such free hand nor so absolute a responsibility.

Movies are something that most of us take pretty much for granted, having been used to them all of our lives. Yet most of us never look very closely at what we see. True, we can remember a plot, more or less, recall the stars, identify a supporting player, talk about a "theme," and a good many of us, not knowing how to be articulate about that sort of technical and artistic work, speak enthusiastically about "the wonderful photography." (It may have been wonderful but what we may have responded to is not the fact that the camera was in focus but the fact that it was, by careful calculation, *out* of focus). We are as often striving to say that the director's original angle of shot was strikingly apposite or that his cutting, juxtaposing this image and that, made a point or touched a nerve in a memorable way.

The sophisticates among us have a vocabulary and they will often invoke a director rather than an actor. They will speak in technical terminology of long shot or close up and, as sensitively as a sound music listener, recall the phrasing of themes that have affected the rest of us without our very specific awareness.

Chaplin's use of camera is as simple as Eisenstein's is complex. Chaplin's fancy is alert but in film terms it would never find occasion to employ the complexities of montage as, say, they were used in the infinitely skillful "Odessa Steps" sequence of Potemkin, through which one is crushed by a cumulation of images purposefully juxtaposed.

Easy Street (1917) shows us how a tramp, wandering into a mission meeting, is reformed and applies for a position on the harassed local police force. He is assigned to a very tough neighborhood dominated by a bully. He meets and defeats the bully as well as a set of anarchists and is able, finally, to walk down Easy Street observing its exemplary order.

Nothing about any of this is inherently funny. It sounds like stuff for Horatio Alger. What can Chaplin do with it to make us laugh? What are the emphases that make for comedy: Surprise? Disparity? Rhythm? Repetition—or, more properly, theme and variations? Exaggeration? Some jarring view of authority or respectability? It sounds like unlikely fun.

When watching the film, to be alert for these things:

1. Make certain that it is being shown at the proper speed for silent films or you will get a distortion of pace.[8]

2. Structure: It is arranged in seven episodes (a) the mission, (b) Easy Street and the police station (the film cuts back and forth between them) to the first quelling of the bully, (c) the filching female —who turns out to be the bully's girl, (d) the benevolent visit to the large but poor family, broken by (e) the bully's return to Easy Street which involves a splendid chase sequence expanding from the apartment to the street and then racing through the neighborhood, (f) the incursion of a villainous troupe of anarchists (?) who kidnap the heroine, quell the tramp, and have to be quelled themselves, (g) epilogue: Love, backed by force/Forgiveness sweet/Brings peace and light/To Easy Street.

   a. Mission: the hortatory preacher (Alfred Austin, later one of the policemen), the pretty organist (Edna Purviance), the pudgy assistant (James T. Kelley), the congregation: an unshaven drunk, a plump woman with a baby (Charlotte Mineau), others less distinctive.

Gags: Charlie establishing his illiteracy, the circulation of the collection box, the problem of the damp baby, the sonorities of the sermon, the attempts at conversion. (Two uses of the close-up: a quick flash of the girl's face and one of the tramp's.) Return of the collection box.

b. Easy Street/Police station: there are very simple camera positions and the actors work within them. Note the sequence in which Charlie falters before the police station, moving back and forth in a space of eight or ten feet. The cutting back and forth from the tumults of Easy Street to the police station is simple but serviceable and from chaos the figure of the bully (Eric Campbell) begins to dominate.

Charlie's police uniform is as absurd a fit as his tramp's clothes have been and the perch of his helmet as useful as the perch of his derby, with the advantage, which will emerge, of having a front and a back. The billy club replaces the cane— which you will see deployed in *The Pawnshop*—and is used adroitly as an instrument for admonition, first on the police captain—where it catches us off guard—and then on a scoffer outside the police station—where we can anticipate it.

The meeting between the little cop and the bully is wonderfully careful art. The bully is in the foreground, resting on his laurels. Down the block toward him comes Charlie, all assurance, his feet in the enormous shoes working precisely. (Through the film those feet are expressive, perhaps most of all when stairs have to be managed in a desperate chase.) The walk up and down the block, the bully at his heels, is, as I have suggested earlier, an example of careful choreography and is followed by a succession of attempts to call a policeman in the course of which the earpiece becomes a telescope, a musical instrument, anything but what it is. A sudden attempt to quell the bully is succeeded by others—the bully obliging— which prove his impregnability. Charlie's position is as unenviable as Odysseus' in the cave of Polyphemus. In what follows the large effects are obvious, but watch for Charlie's delicate, diagnostic taking of the bully's pulse. In every print of the film I have seen the final gag suffers from a loss of footage: triumphant but unwary, Charlie lights a match and the gas blows up. Indeed, throughout the film, as often as the tramp reaches a level of self-satisfaction, something happens to interrupt it or cut it short.

c. The filching female has begun running as Charlie catches up with her, examines, remonstrates, collapses in sympathy. Chaplin's face, always expressive, manages the whole gamut.

d. The benevolent visit: It is a crowded scene: Charlie and the diminutive father in the foreground, the large, defeated wife and the mission worker in the background with a litter of children on the floor. Charlie's incredulity leads past interrogation to admiration: he pins his police badge on the father, measures food as if it were drapery and scatters it as if the children were chickens.

But things are happening simultaneously: in the police station the bully is recovering and we cut between the two sequences. The one moving camera shot in the film begins with the bully's handcuffs and looks up at his face. (Campbell's eye make-up is cheerfully exaggerated.)

Kafka in "The Metamorphosis" indicates with delicate understatement how Gregor's room must have looked and smelt after weeks of occupancy by a cockroach. Here, on entering the poor family's attic hovel, Charlie sniffs and, in consternation, lifts up his sole to see what offal he has brought in unwittingly. This is another of those "ornaments" which we are likely to miss, this time particularly miss because the camera does not swoop in to note the nervousness. We have to see the small note in the larger score of uproar which attacks our eyes. It is a quick and delicate inflection, so deft and so tiny that anyone could be excused for missing it. But in adding up Charlie's arithmetic, it needs counting in since the complexities and richnesses of his comedy are so incessant. It is the bops one tends to count and measure, the culminations. Any procedure which overlooks the ornamentations hasn't yet adjusted its eyes.

e. The bully's return to Easy Street interrupts the benevolent visit and Charlie, springing to duty, adjusts to the situation, given some trouble by the low doorway of the attic apartment. He marches with brisk composure across the street and discovers that his problem is the bully again. The expanding chase begins: around a bed, around a room, upstairs, downstairs, up the block, around the neighborhood in absolute breathlessness. It concludes with an iron range, but not until Charlie has picked up and rejected as insufficient a small chamber pot.

f. Villains abduct the heroine abruptly. Charlie emerges, triumphant again, keeps the villains at bay briefly and then they bop him on the head and lug him off to throw him into a cellar where the girl is being pursued by a dope addict around a breakaway table. His needle (poised early and in a close-up) galvanizes Charlie into a wild efficiency in which he takes on the whole gang, managing a smashing victory at the end of which, of course, his triumph is a little dented.

g. The epilogue plays games with change and with manners. The mission is now at the end of Easy Street and people are streaming to it dutifully: the bully in a very tight suit, swinging an umbrella nicely, his tamed shrew of a wife on his arm. His reformation is underscored by a remembrance that the gentleman does not walk on the inside. Then Chaplin makes Charlie equally forgetful and the course is run.

There are more things than these to be observed in this tight little film in which I still find things I have overlooked after half a hundred viewings. It is a prodigious little exercise.

One A.M. (1916) is a sole performance assisted by a great many properties, culminating in a massive warfare between a drunken dandy and a malevolent murphy bed. Rugs snarl and bite, coat hangers fail, tables spin away when he reaches for a drink, stairs defy him, a mad pendulum challenges him at a doorway and the infinite beastliness of Things makes a jungle of domesticity.

Robert Payne, reminding us that the film has nothing to do with the image of Charlie, the tramp, adds that "Here, for the first time, Chaplin the clown was photographed" (p. 142-3) adding that it is the most fastidious of Chaplin's comedies.

The Pawnshop (1916) is Charlie again, working for a portly pawnbroker (Henry Bergman) with a pretty daughter (Edna Purviance). He bickers with a fellow clerk (John Rand) but not until he has put his derby fastidiously in a bird cage and dusted his cane with care. The rivalry expresses itself in fisticuffs and feet-cuffs, survives a summary dismissal, and resumes, assisted by a ladder which is put to other perilous uses as Charlie polishes the brass balls in front of the shop. He teeters and we all teeter, anxious with empathy. His fall is as inevitable as his recovery is quick. His first concern is the watch he carries—and has compared solemnly with a wall calendar on arrival (late) for work.

A sequence in the kitchen where the girl is baking involves dozens of matters, large and small, from the kitten in the dough to Charlie's elegant dishwashing with the assistance of a clotheswringer, employed with absolute and meticulous solemnity. If we have no custard pie we do have dough, diversely deployed as a weapon, a Hawaiian lei and even as a pie crust.

Payne observes that "The prodigious verse of these scenes is frightening, but there is more to come. It is all spontaneous, quick and darting as a bird's wing. The drab world has become a dance. He throws aside all the advantages which come to him from his comic costume; we are no longer aware of the comic costume, only the dancing. The deft beauty of his clowning illuminates the space he dances in." (p. 147).

Thereafter he engages with a series of customers including one luckless fellow who brings an alarm clock in to pawn. The demolition that follows is a wonderfully ingenious procedure carried out with great seriousness, meticulous and various while Charlie changes from doctor to jeweller and only very lately to pawnbroker, rejecting the chaos he has created with such care. Unlike Keaton, Chaplin is rarely deadpan, but in this sequence it is the very careful control of a diversity of characters that expresses the comedy.

We have a touch of melodrama for the finish: a huge if sneaky fellow (Eric Campbell, the bully from *Easy Street*, deploying that bulk with enormous elegance, a dastardly dandy) holds up the pawnshop and is about to escape with the loot when Charlie, in a victory as rapid as that in *Easy Street,* emerges from a trunk, fells the robber, embraces the girl and winks at us all in a single, uninterrupted swoop.

I began this paper by observing that treatment, not subject, was the point. Then I invoked the word "inflection" which may very well have troubled you. By inflection I mean a line soundly bent for perfect expressiveness or a movement calculated to the same end. At tryouts for a play one hears beginners read Shakespeare's verse as if it were prose and read it without any apparent grasp of character, situation, or inflection within the situation.

I have no ambition to explain what comedy is: centuries of critics have uttered theories, all of which are relevant and not one of which (from Aristotle to Freud) is very deeply effective. Trying to explain comedy is like trying to pick up quicksilver from linoleum, an effort I am simply not clever enough to attempt. Bergson bent his French elegance to the task and emerged with a trace of quicksilver in his palm. So did Meredith. But they both assumed that comedy was an elegant dame rather than a sort of Protean bitch with variety more infinite than Cleopatra's.

In inflection is the artistry that knows when to insist, when to dismiss, when to accent, when to understate. And Chaplin is supremely an artist in his inflection.

NOTES

1. Robert Payne, *The Great Charlie* (London: Pan Books, 1957), p. 91-92. Of the many books about Chaplin as "Charlie" this seems to me the best. Mr. Payne, carefully not concerned with biography of the actor, is concerned with the biography of the character. His book has been published under several titles, including *The Great God Pan*. This edition has a foreword by G. W. Stonier, who as "William Whitebait" wrote distinguished film criticism for *The New Statesman*, including a number of luminous essays on Chaplin's films.

Theodore Huff's *Charlie Chaplin* (New York, 1951) is of interest and has helpful documentation. Gilbert Seldes' various essays on Chaplin are among the earliest tributes and can be read usefully in conjunction with George Jean Nathan's scattered comments which, oftener than not, are designed to dismiss the allegation that Chaplin is a "genius".

Peter Cotes' *The Little Fellow* (presently available in paperback: New York: The Citadel Press, 1965), written in collaboration with Thelma Niklaus, insists rather heavily upon the tragic mask behind the comic one but it, too, has some useful observations and documentation.

No book about Chaplin is more central than *My Autobiography* (New York; Simon and Schuster, 1964, also available in a Pocket Books edition) but it, like many actors' autobiographies, is much more concerned with remembering how I went to the Duchess' for tea than how I evolved a film. Its earlier chapters are a brilliant and painful evocation of a wretched boyhood in London. Thereafter Chaplin is characteristically reticent about his private life, forthright about his political opinions, and while often enough harassed, externally and internally, happily not the Pagliacci his admirers have striven to make him.

Chaplin's life and work have resulted in an enormous number of books and an infinitude of articles and reviews, international and thus far without even a very good selective guide so far as I know.

His earliest films are available, in part, to private buyers and in both 8mm and 16mm gauge at moderate cost. The source I use is Blackhawk Films, Davenport, Iowa, which can supply as well films by such of his contemporaries as Laurel & Hardy, Buster Keaton, and W. C. Fields.

2. William Congreve, *The Way of the World,* ed. Kathleen M. Lynch (Lincoln: University of Nebraska Press, 1965). This admirable edition is a part of the Regents Restoration Drama Series; general

editor: John Loftis. I would hope that you are all aware of it; if not, mend your wits when you need to consult a text in this area. Further quotations are from the same edition in its Bison Book paperback edition.

3. *My Autobiography* (Pocket Books edition) p. 143.

4. Cotes (Citadel edition) p. 163.

5. *My Autobiography*, (Pocket Books edition) p. 224.

6. Cotes reprints this (Citadel Edition), p. 168-169, and I, for one, preferring comedy "pure," am a pushover for it.

7. Robert Lewis Taylor: *W. C. Fields; His Follies and His Fortunes.* (New York, New American Library, 1949) p. 7-8. The wonderful Fields, if in a more constricted way, was as unusual an artist as Chaplin. Imperious and approximately impossible, he bearded production lions in their offices and emerged with contracts of exceptional width. I think he was not nominally director of any of the films he wrote under sundry symptomatic names (including Mahatma Kane Jeeves, which you can work into 'My hat, my cane—Jeeves' if you like that sort of work as much as I do) but there is ample reason to believe that he supervised the consequences far more absolutely than the brilliant Orson Welles was ever allowed to.

8. "Silent films" have tended to be a sort of "pop art" joke and enthusiasm which is made "funnier" by running them at excessive speed so that everything happens twice as fast as life. Tony Richardson in *Tom Jones* used this device knowingly and amusingly in the night-chase sequence (and with harpsichord accompaniment) but he did it with what I seem to be calling "inflection" and not, as the enthusiasts do, because it's funny to see people moving faster than people can.

The silent picture makers knew very well when speeded action was effective and used it to that end, Chaplin among them. But to run a whole film at a forced speed is slightly less intelligent than running bottled Shakespeare in an hour— TWO PLAYS AN AFTERNOON! SEE THE CLASSICS QUICKLY!

The New Western: or, The Return of the Vanishing American

Leslie A. Fiedler

Nearly fifty years ago, D. H. Lawrence wrote in one of the series of essays that was to become, after much revision, *Studies in Classic American Literature:* "assuredly the dead Indians have their place in the souls of present day Americans, but whether they are at peace there is another question...It is presumable, however, that at length the souls of the dead red man will be one with the soul of the living white man." "Then," he wrote prophetically at a distance of five decades, "we shall have a new race"; and suddenly his "then" is our "now"—or, at least, many of the writers who move us most begin to speak as if what he foresaw were already a fact. Toward the end of Allen Ginsberg's hilarious little poem. "America," for instance, the voice of a Jewish Walt Whitman from Paterson, New Jersey, mocking the fear of Russia that vexes the land, becomes suddenly the grunt of a stage Indian:

> The Russia wants to eat us alive. The Russia's power
> mad. She wants to take our cars from out our *garages.*
> Her want to grab Chicago. Her needs a Red Reader's Digest.
> Her wants our auto plants in Siberia. Him big
> bureaucracy running our filling stations.
> That no good. Ugh. Him make Indians learn read...

And at almost the same moment, Sebastian Dangerfield, J. P. Donleavy's *alter ego,* in that joyous Irish-American extension of the methods of Joyce, *The Ginger Man,* is yelling at the top of his fool voice, "Did you know I'm part Mohawk? *Whoo hoo!*" It scarcely seems to matter, descendants of East European Jews or Dublin Irish, at home and abroad, everyone who feels himself in any sense an American, feels the stirring in him of a second soul, the soul of the red man—about which, not so very long ago, only one expatriate

Englishman, "kindled," as he liked to boast, "by Fenimore Cooper," had nerve enough to talk. And some such writers have begun to write books in which the Indian character, what we called only yesterday (with a security and condescension we can no longer even imagine) the Vanishing American, has disconcertingly reappeared. But books with Indians are, as any small boy could tell you, "Westerns"—and "Westerns" we were sure, up to a decade ago, had vanished along with the Indian into a region where no "serious reader" ventured: the world of pulp magazines, comic books, Class B movies, and innumerable second-rate T.V. series, not even interesting as Camp. And how certain we used to be—in that irrecoverable recent past—that the distinction between high literature and popular culture was final and beyond appeal.

But in the last several years, beginning somewhere around 1960, John Barth and Thomas Berger and Ken Kesey and David Markson and Peter Matthiessen and James Leo Herlihy and Leonard Cohen, as well as the inspired script writers of *Cat Ballou* (to adduce only the names which stay on the top of my mind) have been creating a New Western, a form which not so much redeems the pop-Western as exploits it with irreverence and pleasure, in contempt of the serious reader and his expectations. And in doing so they have not only raised certainly general questions about the relationship between "high" and "low" art, but also two specific ones about the particular genre in question: first, what is the Western anyhow, in its classic or traditional form; and second, what precisely is new about the New Western?

To begin answering the first of these questions, we need only notice a fact too obvious, perhaps, to have been properly observed or understood, the fact that geography in the United States is mythological. From the earliest times, at any rate, American writers have tended to define their own country—and, much of our literature has, consequently, tended to define itself—topologically, as it were, in terms of the four cardinal directions: mythicized North, South, East and West. And correspondingly there have always been four kinds of American books: Northerns, Southerns, Easterns and Westerns—though only the last has, for reasons which should become clear as our discussion proceeds, been customarily called by its name. I do not mean to suggest, of course, that all American books fit into one or another of these geographical categories, or even some combination of them; merely that much of our most distinguished literature is thus mythologically oriented, and can be fully comprehended only in the light of this.

The Northern tends to be tight, grey, low-keyed, underplayed—avoiding melodrama where possible, sometimes, it would seem, at all costs. Typically its scene is domestic, an isolated household set in a hostile environment. The landscape is mythicized New England, "stern and rockbound", the weather deep winter: a total milieu appropriate to the excesses of puritanism: "Here where the wind is always north-north-east,/ And children learn to walk on frozen toes.../ Passion is here a soilure of the wits,/ We're told, and Love a cross for them to bear..." In the field of the novel, the Northern is represented, in general, by books I do not much relish, since there is not much savor in them, books which—in the time of the Culture Religion—could easily be thought of as *belles lettres,* fit only for readers in search of loftier satisfactions than pleasure. The *other* novels of Harriet Beecher Stowe (what she wrote when the demon which dictated *Uncle Tom's Cabin* deserted her) are a good instance of the type, as is most of William Dean Howells, a little of Henry James, and, super-eminently, Edith Wharton's *Ethan Frome:* a dismal lot, on the whole.

The Scarlet Letter is an apparent exception to these observations; but it seems to me a *pre-* Northern really, describing the mythological origins of the world which wholly contains the later, true Northern. Actually, the Northern works better in verse than prose, in the narrative poems of Robert Frost, "The Witch of Coos", for example; in much of Edward Arlington Robinson, from whose sonnet on New England I quoted above; and most recently, in the work of Robert Lowell. But one of its classics is that prose-poem in the form of a Journal, Henry David Thoreau's *Walden,* which defines once and for all the archetypal essence of the Northern: the struggle of the transplanted lonely WASP in the midst of, or, better, *against* the American wilderness—in the course of which, he becomes transformed into the Yankee.

The Southern, though its name is not quite so standardly used as that of the Western, is at least as well-known, perhaps too familiar to need definition. Certainly, it is the most successful of all the topological sub-genre of the novel in America: as triumphant on the highbrow level—from, say, Edgar Allen Poe through William Faulkner to Truman Capote or Flannery O'Connor—as on that of mass entertainment—from another side of that same Poe to Thomas Dixon's *The Clansman* (which suggested to D. W. Griffith the plot of *The Birth of a Nation*) or Margaret Mitchell's *Gone With the Wind* (the movie version of which leads a life nearly immortal). The Southern has always challenged the distinction between High and Pop Art, since not merely Poe, its founder, but such latter-day successors of his as Faulkner and Capote have thrived in the two presumably sundered worlds of critical esteem and mass approval.

Perhaps this is because the Southern, as opposed to the Northern, does not avoid but seeks melodrama: a series of bloody events, sexual by implication at least, played out against a background of miasmal swamps, live oak, Spanish moss, and the decaying plantation house so dear to the hearts of movie-makers. Indeed, until there were ruined plantations—which is to say, until the Civil War, defeat and Reconstruction—there could be no true Southern (Poe, being ante-bellum, had to imagine the doomed mansions appropriate to his horrors in a mythical Europe); since the mode of the Southern is Gothic, American Gothic, and the Gothic requires a haunted house at its center. But it demands also a symbolic darkness to cloak its action, a "blackness of darkness" which in the Old World was associated with the remnants of Feudalism and especially the dark-cowled ministers and "Black Nobility" of the Church.

What the Church and feudal aristocracy were for European Gothic, the Negro became for the American variety: "the Black," as he is mythologically called, being identified by that name with the nightmare terror which the writer of Southerns seeks to evoke; with the deepest guilts and fears of transplanted Europeans in a slave-holding community, or more properly, in a community which remembers having sent its sons to die in a vain effort to sustain slavery. But projecting those guilts and fears out upon the Blacks, draining himself of all his vital darkness, as it were, the European in the South condemns himself to a kink of mythological anemia, becomes "Whitey."

Without the Negro, in any case, there is no true Southern; and whoever treated the Negro in our fiction—until urbanization changed everything—tended to write a Southern, whether he thought of himself as doing so, or not; unless, of course, like Mark Twain in *Huckleberry Finn* (think of it side by side with *Pudd'nhead Wilson,* which is quite another matter) he turned his Negro protagonist into a Noble Savage, i.e., an Indian in Blackface. Only where Jim is really a "nigger," i.e., at the very beginning and end of the novel where he plays the comic darky, or at certain points on the raft where he "camps" the role, addressing Huck as his "young master," does *Huckleberry Finn* become anything like a Southern; most of the way it is something quite other which we still have not defined. And occasionally it even threatens to become an Eastern, or a parody of one, when the Duke and the Dauphin bring their European pretension aboard the raft; for the Eastern deals with the American confronting Europe, and cultural pretension is an essential to it as tourism.

Customarily, the Eastern treats the return of the American (who only knows then for sure that he *is* an American) to the Old World, his Old Home, the place of origin of his old self, that original Adam, whom the New World presumably made a New Man. Its season is most appropriately Spring, when the ice of New England symbolically breaks, and all things seem—for a little while—possible; and, as is appropriate to that erotic time of year, it deals often with love (*The Roman Spring of Mrs. Stone* is the protypical title of one Eastern, the single novel of Tennessee Williams, who turned from his mythological South when he briefly forsook drama): the flirtation of the American—usually female—with the European—most often male. Sometimes, as in Henry James's *The Ambassadors*, the sexual-mythological roles are reversed, or, as in James Baldwin's *Giovanni's Room* both are males; though one suspects Baldwin's Giovanni of being a Negro in disguise, and the book consequently a Southern in disguise. In any case, the distribution of sexes makes little difference in the Eastern; the encounter of European and American is doomed to frustration in any case. In part, this is so because the American turns out to be impelled by motives not so much truly erotic as merely anti-anti-erotic; and in part, because, being not an emigre or a cosmopolitan but only a tourist (and the Eastern is the form which defines the American precisely as a "tourist"), he—or, if you like, she—has to go home.

It is Henry James (who may have sent his Lambert Strethers home, but who never returned to stay himself) whom we think of as the High Priest of the Cult of the Eastern, or even as its Founder; though Nathaniel Hawthorne, in *The Marble Faun,* and James Fenimore Cooper before him, in *Homeward Bound* were there first. But James began his career by asserting a claim to the form in *The American,* a claim which came to seem more and exclusive as he produced example after example (turning his hand to an occasional Northern like *The Bostonians,* as a breather) until he could write no more. And with James—not so much originally, as after his revival in the twenties—the Eastern became associated with that Culture Religion, so virulent in the United States between the two World Wars.

Basic to that worship of High Art was the dogma that there are some books (in the field of the novel, chiefly James himself), an appreciation of which distinguishes the elect from the vulgar, the sensitive from the gross; and that those books can be known im-

mediately because (a) they are set in Europe, (b) they mention—
often so casually that only the cognoscenti know without the aid of
footnotes—other works of art, and (c) they are written by expatriates.
Obviously, most of the poetry of T. S. Eliot and much of Ezra Pound
("Tourist" of Eastern poetry *par excellence)* fall into this category;
as does that of their so-long unsuspected counterpart in the mid-
nineteenth century—bound to them by many affinities besides a
common love for Dante and a preference for being "abroad"—Henry
Wadsworth Longfellow.

Not all Easterns, however, belong in intention or in retrospect to
the realm of High Art; if any book which deals with the reaction of
the American abroad (via tourism or dreams) in the genre, Mark
Twain was one of its most assiduous practitioners, all the way from
Innocents Abroad to *A Connecticut Yankee in King Arthur's Court.*
And in our own century, we have had Scott Fitzgerald's *Tender is
the Night,* a border-line case, perhaps; as well as most of the novels
of Hemingway, who thought of himself, surely, more as an emulator
of Twain than James. But not everything is what it seems to a super-
ficial scrutiny; and looking hard at Hemingway's *The Sun Also Rises*
and *For Whom the Bell Tolls,* we discover that certain characters
whom he presents as Spanish peasants look mighty like Montana or
Upper Michigan Indians—and that, consequently, he is actually
writing if not quite Westerns, at least crypto-Westerns, since it is the
presence of the Indian which defines the mythological West.

Not the confrontation with the alien landscape (by itself this
produces only the Northern) is the heart of the Western, but the
encounter with the Indian; that utter stranger, for whom our New
World is an Old Home—that descendant of neither Shem nor
Japheth, nor even, like the Negro imported to subdue the wild
land, Ham. No grandchild of Noah, he escapes completely the
mythologies we brought with us from Europe, demands a new one of
his own. Perhaps he was only a beast of the wildwood, the first
discoverers of America reassured themselves, not human at all; and
at the end of the fifteenth century, Princes of the Church gravely
discussed whether, being descended from Adam, the Indian indeed
had a soul like our own. It was a question by no means settled once
and for all when the Church answered "yes"; for, as we have seen,
at the beginning of our own century, Lawrence amended that answer
to "yes, but—" Yes, but *not* like our own, except as our own have the
potentiality of becoming like his.

And how, in the five hundred years between, the Indian in his
ultimate otherness has teased and baffled the imagination of genera-

tion after generation of European voyagers and settlers. How they have tried to assimilate him to more familiar human types, to their own mythologic stock-in-trade. The name "Indian" itself memorializes the first misguided effort of Columbus to assure himself that he was in those other, those *East* Indies, after all, and confronting nothing but types known since Marco Polo, like the inhabitants of Cipango or Cathay. And after that delusion had collapsed, after the invention as opposed to the mere discovery of America, there were new explainers-away eager to identify the Red Men with the Semites, the Lost Tribes of Israel. From those Apostles to the Indians in the seventeenth century, penetrating the wilderness to bring the Old Testament back to those to whom it belonged; through Fenimore Cooper in the early nineteenth, recounting the adventures of just such a deluded missionary in the form of Patson Amen in *Oak Openings* (to whom the bewildered redskins object that being Indians, they can never be *lost*); to the later Mormons, incorporating the wrongheaded myth in their essential mythology; and the rancher of *Cat Ballou* baffled at the Indian who refuses to answer his greeting of *"Shalom!"*—the tradition has never died. But the Indian, though as stubborn and persistent a witness as the Jews, refuses to become anything so familiar as a Jew.

Everything else which belongs to the Western scene has long since been assimilated: the prairies sub-divided and landscaped; the mountains staked off as hunting preserves and national parks; fabulous beasts, like the grizzlies and the buffalo, killed or fenced in to make tourist attractions; even the mythological season of the Western, that non-existent interval between summer and fall called "Indian Summer," has become just another part of the white year. Only the Indian survives, however ghetto-ized, debased and debauched, to remind us with his alien stare of the new kind of space in which the baffled refugees from Europe first found him (an unhumanized vastness), and the new kind of time through which, despite all our efforts, he still moves (a historyless antiquity). It is for this reason that tales set in the West seem to us not quite Westerns, unfulfilled occasions for myth rather than myth itself, when no Indian—"stern and imperturbable warrior" or lovely, complaisant squaw, it scarcely matters—appears in them.

The Western story in archetypal form is then a fiction dealing with the confrontation in the wilderness of a transplanted WASP and a radically alien other, an Indian—leading either to an alteration, a metamorphosis of the WASP into something neither White nor Red (sometimes by adoption, sometimes by sheer emulation, but *never* by actual miscegenation); or else to the annihilation of the Indian (sometimes by castration-conversion or penning off into a ghetto, sometimes by sheer murder). In either case, the tensions of the encounter are resolved by elimination of one of the mythological partners—by ritual or symbolic means in the first instance, by physical force in the second. When the first method is used, possibilities are opened up for another kind of Western, a secondary Western dealing with the adventures of that New Man, the American *tertium quid;* but when the second is employed—our homegrown Final Solution—the Western disappears as a living form, for the West has, in effect, been made into an East.

But into what exactly is the transplanted European converted by the Western encounter, when he resists resolving it by genocide? It is easy enough to name the aspects of Americans defined by the three other forms; the Northern, in which we become Yankees; the Southern, in which we are turned into Whitey; the Eastern, in which we are revealed as Tourists. But the transformation effected in the Western evades easy definition. Thinking of Natty Bumppo (that first not-quite-White man of our literature, for all of his boasts about having "no cross in my blood") and his descendants, we are tempted to say that it is the woodsman which the ex-European becomes beside his Red companion—the hunter, the trapper, the frontiersman, the pioneer, at last, the cowboy; or maybe even he is only next-to-last, for after him comes, the hippy, the beatnik—one more wild man in highheeled boots and blue jeans.

It is tempting, at this point, to take the dilemma as the answer; and to settle for saying that, since this new kind of man came into existence only with the West, he is best called simply "the Westerner." But we know, too (and if we forget it for one moment, there is the title of Henry James's early book about a barbarian from San Francisco actually named Newman, to remind us) that at the moment, when, looking into the eyes of the Indian, the European becomes as Westerner, he becomes also "The American." Before white man had set foot on American soil, the whole continent had already been dreamed by Europe as the West—or, at least, though unknown and unsuspected, it filled the mythological space in which European fantasy had located such mythological Wests as Atlantis, *Tir-nan-oq,* the Earthly Paradise itself: visionary worlds beyond the wave or under the wave, lands of the dead and those who rise from the dead. And once the Atlantic had been crossed, every part of the continent was successively denominated "the West," as wave after wave of invading Europeans pushed forward past the natural barriers, the Appalachians, the Mississippi, the Rockies.

Vermont or Maine may be eternally the North, and Georgia forever the South; while New York City, straddling the harbor from
which tourists sail continually to the Old World can hardly be
thought of as anything other than the East. But where, geographi-
cally, is the elusive West? First of all, it was Virginia, then Kentucky,
Louisiana, Ohio, Missouri, the Oregon Territory etc. etc., always
just beyond the horizon, or just this side, where we confront *on their
own grounds* the aboriginal possessors of the continent. And now
that we have run out of new territory to mythologize, now that the
Indians are everywhere wards of the White nation, confined to
enclaves in a world securely ours, where can we re-establish the
West? The earth, it turns out, is mythologically as well as geographi-
cally round, and the lands across the Pacific will not do—since on
the rim of the second ocean, West becomes East, our whole vast land
merely (as Columbus dreamed, and Whitman nostalgically remembered at the opening of the Panama Canal) a Passage to India.
Maybe the Moon will serve our purposes, or Mars; since up and out
may be an equivalent to the Way West—as we already begin to suspect, calling some of the literature of space adventure "space operas"
on the model of "horse operas," which is to say, Westerns. But unless
"stern and imperturbable" Martians await us, or lovely and complaisant lady Lunatics (as certain brands of science fiction try to imagine),
whom we can assimilate to our own myths of the Indian, Outer
Space will seem not an extension of our America, the America
which shocked and changed Europe, but *another* America, which
may shock and change us.

On our shores, the myth of the West which had possessed the
European imagination up to the time of Dante, the myth of the
unpeopled world, *il mondo senza gente,* was transformed and
naturalized into one of a world inhabited by hostile aliens—a myth
so profoundly implanted in us that, in spite of scientific testimony,
we insist on imagining the New Worlds we now approach inhabited
by natives, "savages," benign or threatening. We have defined the
unknown for too long in terms of home-made mythologies, created
out of our meeting with and response to the Indians, to abandon
them without a struggle. They have proved sufficiently adaptable to
describe our relations with Negroes and Polynesians, all colored
peoples in fact (Twain's Nigger Jim and Melville's Queequeg are
blood brothers, after all, to Cooper's Chingachgook), and we dream
of taking them with us into a future, not quite so unforeseeable as it
sometimes seems, if only they will work there, too.

Three Indian myths are especially dear to us, informing the major
works of our literature and our deepest sense of ourselves: the Myth

of Pocahontas and Captain John Smith; the Myth of the Trapper Alexander Henry and His Indian comrade, Wawatam; the myth of Hannah Dustan and her escape from Indian Captivity. I have written about all three of these in one way or another before; and I intend some day to treat them at much greater length, but for my present purposes it is necessary only to say that in the original sources of all three (mythologized chronicles older than any American novels, or, indeed, the very notion of an American novelist) the major Indian personae of the great Western *epos* have already been invented: the redeeming Indian Maiden, convert and traitor to her own people, in Pocahontas; the threatening Indian father, stone axe in hand, in Powhatan; the Noble Savage, who comes out of the woods inexplicably as in a dream, in Wawatam; the skulking Bad Indian, in the anonymous captor and would-be "Master" of Hannah Dustan.

And beside them there exist, too—long before Cooper—their White counterparts: the bully and exterminator, proud of his craft and sexual prowess (of Pocahontas, he boasts that he could have had of her "what he willed"), in Captain John Smith; the refugee from the world of civilization, seeking a help meet for him in the unsubdued wilderness, in Alexander Henry; the avenging WASP mother of us all, ten bleeding scalps at her feet, in Hannah Dustan. Of Alexander Henry's *Adventures* alone, Henry David Thoreau wrote toward the beginning of his own career: "It contains scenery and rough sketching of men and incidents enough to inspire poets for many years...It reads like the argument to a great poem on the primitive state of the country and its inhabitants..." But the "great poem" was somehow never quite written....

The American Utopian Anti-Novel*

Virgil L. Lokke

1.

The American utopian novel, which flourished so vigorously in the last quarter of the nineteenth century, has been interpreted as an expression of "escapist" tendencies—of reformist drives which no longer found outlet in political channels or in the foundation of utopian communities. The ubiquitous "closing frontier" has been offered as an explanation of the resort to literary flights in time and space. The evidence from the novels and the testimonies of the authors, however, indicate that the majority of these writers had embarrassingly naive practical reformist intentions, and in resorting to "literature," these reformers were acting—given their assumptions concerning the nature of the novel—in the most pragmatic manner possible. The anti-utopians, who followed in the wake of Edward Bellamy's spectacularly successful *Looking Backward* (1888) also accepted the utopian convictions concerning the social role of the novel and rushed into print to counteract what they regarded as dangerously persuasive propaganda. Both regarded the novel as an instrument of social control. With the majority of utopians, the reform technique was that of preparing society for change through a propaganda barrage in which the novel would play a central role. Publishing houses sprang up in New York, Chicago, Omaha, Topeka, Cleveland, and San Francisco, which specialized in reformist and "educational" fiction bearing such names as the Utopia Company, Utopia Publishing Company, and The Equity Publishing Company.

---

*Not presented at the Conference

One Chicago house alone, the Charles H. Kerr Company, published at least five utopian romances; Kerr's advertising reflects enthusiastic commitment to the novel as the vehicle for mass education.

The "literary" reformers were nearly universal in their insistence that the community must be persuaded of the necessity of change and that action can be taken only when the public mind is prepared. Henry Olerich's warning in his preface to *A Cityless and Countryless World* (1892) is characteristic of the frame of mind in which most of the utopians presented their solutions:

> Now let me state right here that I do not wish to be understood that the masses are suited, as they are at present constituted to...become members of...this social and economic system...outlined in this work; but the aim of the work is to fit that vast multitude who are still unfit for it by having them mentally assimilate some of the facts expressed and suggested in it, for let us not forget that man-made institutions are, as a whole, always nearly suited to the mental capacity of the masses. ...Improve the mind by unfolding it, and the human-made institutions will improve to correspond.[1]

The purposes of the utopists are fearfully simple and painfully sincere—to convince the reader that the present society is undesirable and to demonstrate through example and reason that economic suffering can be eliminated and that a good society is within human grasp. The novels are in purpose as escapist as any text book in comparative economics of the day. All the writers make assumptions concerning strategies of mass education and manipulation of public opinion. Most feel that the facts are all in possession—the plans have been drawn—and all that stands between human distress and peacefully constructive lives is ignorance. The bridge then is the novel, for the novel is a highly popular vehicle based on readily accessible formulas which any writer can master with relative ease. These widely shared assumptions concerning the nature of the novel are described by Francis Marion Crawford in *The Novel: What It Is* (1893) where he explains among other things that the purpose of the novel is public amusement and that it must deal largely with love. The crude and direct expropriation of the novel reflects the disdain, if not contempt, for autonomous art of any kind among these reformers—it was, in short, a means of reaching feminine and weaker minds incapable of responding to direct discourse.

The Tennessean, Albert Chavannes, author of a score of books on psychology, "mentation," and social evolution, expresses the prevailing attitude of the utopian novelist in his introduction to *In Brighter Climes: A Realistic Novel* (1895):

> I apologize for trying to write a novel at all....
> The only reason I have to offer is that I am a man with a hobby, which at the present time happens to be a more or less correct belief that our social institutions are not quite equal to what they might be, and that if this same belief could be driven into the heads of the average citizen, it would result in a quickening of the efforts now made for improvement, and be an important factor in reform work.
> Under this impression I have already written two books in true reform style, where by arguments ponderous and reasonings cogent, I have tried to instill my belief into my fellow citizens. But these books have not met with the success their good intention deserved, and I have decided to try the old expedient and write a novel with a purpose. I have *sugar coated* the pill and offer it once more to the public, fondly hoping that in its new guise it will meet with a more ready acceptance.[2]

In *The Future Commonwealth* (1892), which was written in support of the Bellamy thesis, Chavannes declares:

> In my picture I have not drawn on my imagination but have carefully studied the line of possible and probable progress.[3]

Illustrative also is the comment Bradford Peck makes in the introduction to *The World a Department Store* (1900). Peck's story was meant to point out the values of "cooperative" principles.

> This book is not intended as a literary effort, but as a word from one business man to others who know the cares of business life, and written so a youth could understand it.[4]

Reverend Charles Lund in a commendatory introduction to the book testifies:

> Mr. Peck, the writer of the book and organizer of the combination, is no visionist, but a practical business man of thirty-five years standing, President of the B. Peck Company of Lewiston, Maine, the largest department store in New England outside of Boston, and vice president of the Joliet Dry Goods Company, Joliet, Illinois. His ideas are the result of close study and practical experience in human affairs and have evolved from his belief that the "conservation of energy" is the keynote to the business of life in the future.[5]

Peck was practical in his literary intentions to the point that he expected to finance the experiment with the money he received from the sale of his utopian romance, which significantly enough takes place only five years from the date of writing. Various editions were offered for sale. To the person offering the largest sum would go issue number one, and for five dollars one could receive the book and have his name engrossed upon the roll of founders.

Peck was not alone in his expectation of almost immediate realization of his social objectives. H. L. Everett's book, *The People's Program* (1892), expects action to start in the following year. The book was dedicated to T. V. Powderly and Samuel Gompers, "the world's greatest labor leaders," and offers "to give to the cause of the workingmen in America one half of the profits of this story." Everett suggests further that "the labor unions should cultivate the literary method of increasing the numbers of their friends and members."[6]

Two other utopian romances also predict almost immediate results, namely, *Solaris Farm* by Milan C. Edson and Frederick U. Adams' *President John Smith* (1897). Edson's story, written in 1900, takes place in the year 1905. Another preachment on the cooperative thesis, it is insistent in contending its practicality. Adams, an assenting voice in the stream of Bellamy-inspired Nationalist theories, begins his story in the year the book appears; he traces developments up through the year 1900 during which time assassinations, dictatorial regimes, and class wars play across the scene, the final denouement occurring with the establishment of a Nationalist society.

William Garrison, in the preface to *The Story of My Dictatorship* (1894), a single-tax utopia with an English locale, analyzes what seems to be the basic assumptions of most of the writers: the increased efficiency of the social, political, economic, or religious treatise when disguised by fable. He explains:

> Many people will read an allegory who would shrink from a treatise. If John Bunyan had neglected to clothe his ideas with the alluring garments of a story, it is doubtful whether Pilgrim would have made much progress in his own generation, to say nothing of his unimpeded march through the centuries...the concrete is easier to grasp than the abstract, and one who finds a sermon on courage tiresome glows with enthusiasm over the mythical hero who embodies and reveals it in brave deeds.[7]

Another utopia of the single-tax, Byron S. Welcome's *From Earth's Center* (1894), is blurbed by the *Boston Herald* as

> An interesting romance that will be read by millions who find *Progress and Poverty* too obtuse, and will interest students who wish to trace the effects of the single tax reform on social institutions of all kinds.[8]

The Diothas, or A Far Look Ahead (1893), by James Macnie, excuses itself by the simple comment that the present tendency is to "look forward to the future rather than to admire the past."[9]

It is more difficult to establish the purpose of John Jacob Astor's fantasia, *Journey to Other Worlds* (1894), beyond the fact that he too feels a distrust of the past and respect for the future. He writes:

> How much more interesting it would be if, instead of reiterating our past achievements, the magazines and literature of the period should devote their consideration to what we do not know.[10]

He adds: "Next to religion we have most to expect from science."[10] In his novel, however, Astor places his real confidence in science and technology.

The incentive which seems to motivate Ignatius Donnelly in *Caesar's Column* (1890) may be found in the passage he quotes from Goethe:

> The true poet is only a masked father confessor, whose special function it is to exhibit what is dangerous in sentiment and pernicious in action by a vivid picture of their consequence.[11]

To effect this literary purpose, he dwells at length on the bloody class struggles and attendant destruction in most graphic terms. By pointing to what he assumes is the logical outcome unless change is brought about, he urges his readers to reject the present civilization.

Other novels are frankly and simply written in support, elaboration, or in contradiction of Bellamy's *Looking Backward,* using his plot, his characters, and his thesis as a springboard from which to launch their project. They are for the most part so anxious to get into the political and economic discussion that they fail to do more than occasionally hint at the existence of fable. Among the novels of this latter type may be listed Schindler's *Young West* (1894), the anonymous *A. D. 2050* (1890), Vinton's *Looking Further Backward* (1890), Michaelis' *Looking Further Forward* (1890), and Wilbrandt's *Mr. East's Experiences in Mr. Bellamy's World* (1891).

Most of the utopian writers, as has been shown, reject the present state of society. Their mode of rejection follows a specific and well established pattern, that is to say, they utilize a transportation in time and more rarely a transportation in space to permit a description of the type of society which they would find satisfactory. What is more important, they are almost wholly concerned with the method of transition from the old to the new society. Many lure the reader by contrasting the old society to the utopian form. Some, like Donnelly, wish to force change by threat of an impending class war. All feel their stories to be practical instruments for social reform. Their faith in the efficiency of the method of teaching through story is not confined to economics. Its practicality is so strongly felt by Alcanoan O. Grigsby that he is prompted to treat all knowledge in this form:

Nequa: How is it that your entire people have such a clear understanding of every economic, social, and ethical problem?

Oqua: These lessons have all been treated in the shape of allegories and historical romances to make them attractive.[12]

2.

Excluding Howells' *A Traveler From Altruria* (1894) and Bellamy's *Looking Backward* (1888) from the list, the utopian novels of the eighties and nineties are transparently sub-literary as might well be expected in light of announced intentions and the writers' conceptions of the novel. Beyond the fact that the authors use the word "story" or "romance" in their titles, there is only the feeblest indication of concern with aesthetic or structural problems. Plot, characterization, scene are attended to at convenient and inobtrusive intervals and are never permitted to delay the presentation of the political, economic, or ethical thesis. The plot generally involves no more than a transportation in time of a naive observer, an encounter with a sage (patronizing and pompous) who describes the new world, compares it with the old, and wonders at nineteenth century stupidity. What little story progression is offered follows the boy meets girl, love at first sight formula. Characterizations are universally flat and unprogressive, and there are almost no heroes in utopia.

American utopian novels divide readily into two groups: those directly based on *Looking Backward,* which utilize the same or a slight variant of the Bellamy machinery and those which attempt an original plot. Prominent in the total flood of utopian productions are those directly inspired by *Looking Backward.* Richard Michaelis was one of the first rising to the challenge with a portrayal of what he saw as destructively communistic in the nationalistic program of Bellamy. His book, *Looking Further Forward* (1890), is one of the many climbing on the Bellamy bandwagon by establishing kinship of title. He establishes a precedent to be soon followed by A. D. Vinton and others of carrying on the story where Bellamy stopped. Michaelis writes, "I propose to continue Bellamy's story demonstrating what would be the logical conclusion of his story."[13] Lifting characters and all from the book he wishes to criticize, he portrays the inequality and dissatisfaction arising from Bellamy's practice of awarding honorary distinction to those outstanding in public service.

Arthur D. Vinton published a similar book in the same year using the companion title *Looking Further Backward.* Vinton, a graduate of Columbia Law School, was not a literary novice. He held for some time an assistant editorship of the *North American Review*. His story begins in Boston twenty-three years after the time of the events in *Looking Backward*. In Bellamy's novel Julian West was given a position as Professor of Medieval History. Vinton's book is organized as a series of lectures delivered by Professor Won Lung Li, a Chinese successor to Julian West. In order to show just how refusal on the part of the Nationalist society to arm for war brought the downfall of the state, Li quotes extensively from a manuscript found in Julian West's possession at the time of his death in the Battle of Lake Erie. We learn first of West's growing apprehension as he watches China conquer the nationalistic states in Asia and Europe one by one and how America is overwhelmed because of the inefficiency of a government unprepared for war and fearful of concentrating power in any central authority. He tells of the courageous stands and of the heroic deeds of West in his futile resistance. At the close of the story we find the Chinese in control of both seaboards. Some hope is to be seen for the gradual recovery of American independence in the militaristic preparations and changed governmental organization in the yet unconquered Middle West. Vinton writes civilized prose, his treatment of the escape of the aging Dr. Leete is told with a certain deftness, and at times he gives the dead Julian West more life than he ever possessed in *Looking Backward*. We are even spared a picture of blood and rape-drunk Chinese conquerors. Vinton portrays them on the whole as intelligently urban.[14]

The anonymous *A. D. 2050*, by a Former Resident of the Hub, is the third book of the year 1890 contradicting Bellamy's ideal portrait. The author suggests that Julian West had not thoroughly investigated the situation because upon arrival he had "fallen into the hands of Dr. Leete, cooperative or communistic boomer of his day."[15] The story opens with the main character falling asleep and awakening fifty years after the establishment of Bellamy's nationalistic society. A description follows of rioting and bloodshed which is spreading contagiously throughout the land. New York is portrayed as the last stronghold of society and private capitalism. Finding New York, too, a doomed city, Captain John Jones, a wealthy and far-sighted capitalist, organizes an unoccupied island of some 60,000 square miles in territory. From this point the narrative is largely concerned with a statement of the constitution and plan of operation for the new state. It should be added that the state concentrates for a time on the building of a navy and army through which the rest of the world is gradually "brought to its senses."

The preface of J. W. Roberts' *Looking Within* (1893) suggests at once the argument and method of treatment. A printed letter dated Renewed America, January 1, 2027, reads

> Inhaling the inspiring breath of the new life which invigorates the nation so lately struggling in the toils of a lingering death, and cheered by the resurrection of all industries from the grave in which they were utterly buried, we hail the dawn of a new era of progress....[16]

This book, an answer to Bellamy's *Looking Backward,* employs basically the same structure. James North, refused in marriage, calls upon the services of a chemist, who is able to suspend animation for an indefinite period of time. As was the case with Julian West, North is put to sleep in a sealed room. He awakes in 1927 to find America fighting a class war. Airplanes, portentously enough, play an important part in the struggle. Most of the blame for the present conditions is placed upon *Looking Backward,* which is described as follows:

> *Looking Backward* has been the bane of this nation....It breeds a notion in the minds of thousands that somehow the government will be compelled by agitation to do for them what God, nature, and society demand they shall do for themselves. ...Multitudes who never saw the book have received its teachings second-hand, and been poisoned by them.... Like the upas tree, it is fair to behold, but all who come within its shade are doomed. Its poison is more insidious than that of a rattlesnake, and it does not give warning of its bite until the deadly fangs have struck the fatal blow....[17]

Disgusted with the whole situation, James North decides to go to sleep again. This time he intends to sleep only for five years but makes the mistake of taking the wrong bottle and awakens in the year 2000. He meets an old gentleman who explains that while social conditions appear to be satisfactory, the state is in reality "rotten" and "hideously deformed" within. There are, for example, "ten thousand drunkards in Boston." The foreign element is seen as particularly obnoxious. To the optimistic Dr. Barton of Bellamy's world Vinton poses as a foil the "thoroughly posted" and "realistic" Dr. Butler. All is not hopeless, however, for signs of the future indicate that the paternalistic state is doomed. By the year 2027 Julian North can proudly proclaim, "Paternalism is Dead."

In addition to being a typographical curiosity (Publishers' note: We beg to call the attention of our patrons to the colored margins which will become universal in the near future.... The margins may be had in blue, green, or yellow.), Solomon Schindler's *Young West* (1894) reveals that not all the literary imitators of Bellamy were using his structure to project an antagonistic thesis. This book in direct continuation of *Looking Backward* is the story of Julian West's son, Young West. Mr. Schindler's offers a purported autobiography of Young West, the son of Edith and Julian West. It deals at length with the educational experiences of West, carrying him through college and the citizenship proceedings. The story tells of his love affair which results in marriage; how he is able to save his country from ruin in disastrous days of crop failure, drought, and destructive tornadoes; and how he is finally elected president of the Nationalist world.

The moral is to be found in a nostalgic note penned by his father, Julian. The elder West feels completely out of key with his present surrounding, and the narrative concludes with a reminder that we cannot jump into a new world but must rather grow into it:

> The present only is ours. The social reformer must never try to hasten the natural and national development of conditions. He may show the way; he may prophesy what will happen; he may argue the justice of a measure, or denounce the justice of an established way; he may prepare the mind of the people for the coming change, but beyond that he must not go.[18]

Several novels neither directly critical nor commendatory of the Bellamy thesis also employed some of his basic fictional devices. *The Story of My Dictatorship* (1894) by L. H. Behrens, first of the single-tax panegyrics, opens with the falling asleep of the central character who awakens in England. Parliament, holding an open-air meeting, is discussing ways and means of achieving true democracy and of repairing the inefficient economic system. Absolutely no progress is being made. A bystander shouts impatiently, "That's very simple," and he is immediately elected "Lord Protector, or rather, Dictator." From this point the story is an elaboration of the problem-solving efficiency of the single-tax theory of Henry George. In the hero's journey through England of the indefinite future, he meets the Loafer, the Shopkeeper, the Socialist, the Capitalist, the Laborer, the Lover, and the Preacher, who are convinced one by one of the logical necessity of the single-tax. After his work is done, he is reluctant to resign because he has grown used to the exercise of power, but he is expelled by the main force of the principle he had generated. He is awakened by the words of his wife: "Get up, my dear, get up; you must be quite stiff, sleeping all night on that hard chair." This book, as the preface suggests, owes more to *Pilgrim's Progress* than to *Looking Backward*. Notable also is the parody of the "Socratic method."

One fictional device employed by Bellamy both in *Looking Backward* and *Equality* which found favor in following books was the parable. Many readers, who have long forgotten the tenuous arguments of "Private Capital stolen from the Public Fund," will remember the "Parable of the Watertank" in *Equality* and Bellamy's effective and still interesting "Parable of the Stage Coach" in *Looking Backwards*. Albert Adams Merrill's *The Great Awakening* (1899), which offers to solve the world's problem by a program of currency revision, includes "A Parable of the Clock Maker" obviously in imitation of Bellamy. A slight variant of the usual way of projection into the future is offered by Merrill. In this case, a soul, an intelligence used to nineteenth century conditions, finds itself reincarnated in the body of an inhabitant of the twenty-second century. Through surgical accident the soul enters the body of Richard Pangloss while an operation to cure his insanity is in progress. He is taken in custody by Professor Harding (a man with all the character traits of Bellamy's Dr. Leete, i.e., highly educated and thoroughly grounded in the economics of the time).

During a series of bicycle rides, automobile rides, and airplane trips in the company of the constantly talking Professor Harding, Pangloss manages to learn all about the present society. Special attention is given to historical development through which we learn of a group of pioneer money reformers establishing a highly successful society in Africa. The historian speaks of a Messiah of Money Reform, Thomas H. Blackburn, who was born reminiscently enough in Springfield, Illinois, and who became president. Because of his unrelenting devotion to the cause of money reform he is assassinated. A revolution follows in which the devoted but misguided people throw off the yoke of eastern financeers. After the revolution in 2021, society becomes as near perfect as it can ever be.

Bradford Peck in *The World a Department Store* (1900) uses the almost standard method of having his character fall asleep, this time to awake after only five years. At a banquet in the hero's honor, opportunity is given for a speaker to trace the history of the accidents of progress from private capitalism to a cooperative state. A friend introduces him to a woman, and the description of the new world is elaborated while the two are eating in a cooperative restaurant, attending a cooperative theater, and riding about in a horseless carriage. The story concludes with a double marriage and a trip to Niagara Falls.

Those plot structures which owe very little, if anything, to Bellamy's *Looking Backward*, include a variety of story patterns keyed to the pitch of the dime novel of the period. Although Bellamy's plan for transportation into the future seems to be one of the most commonly imitated elements of his plot, some other techniques are employed to bring the reader into the utopian world.

Probably the most bizarre of all springboards into the future was that employed by the most prolific of all utopian writers, Frank Rosewater, in his book, *96, A Romance of the Future* (1894). Writing from Omaha, Nebraska, at the time when the West took its Populism most seriously, Rosewater advocates with some attempt at subtlety a program variously styled as Centrism, Proprietarism, or Atlism, all of which are, in essence, manipulations in mediums of exchange.

The story begins in 1893. Dr. Giniwig is elaborating a theory of time to a wealthy young patient, Ross, who is troubled by a blotch which constantly confronts his eyes. The blotch, Ross explains, has been bothering him ever since he received a telegram from his Chicago firm that his business has collapsed. Dr. Giniwig burns the blotch with a match and proceeds to explain his belief concerning time. By the method of a specially compounded shampoo, Giniwig contends that it is thoroughly possible to be transported in time either forward or backward. This explanation is carried off with a great deal of pseudo-scientific hocus pocus. The scene of the story changes to the year 1850, and we find ourselves lost in the heart of the African jungle with a party of eighteen men and women, who finally stumble down into an amphitheatre completely surrounded by a chain of mountains.

Rosewater again picks up the narrative of Dr. Giniwig and Ross. Recovering from a shampoo treatment, they find themselves in a balloon which has broken its moorings. After weeks of floating, they wake up in the time-juggled state of Lukka. There Ross, through interest in the beautiful Arda, becomes involved in fighting for social justice against a well-intrenched aristocracy of wealth. Eventual defeat of this system comes not through the machinations of Ross but through the breakdown of eastern Lukka's economic system which in turn brings about a revolution. This revolution is portrayed in the most vividly bloodthirsty terms at Rosewater's disposal. When the gates of prison containing Lukka's thousands of wage slaves burst open, they spew forth a mob of greater ferocity than Dickens' revolutionaries—they spare no living soul—the very hero responsible for inciting them to action by a poetic recitative is torn asunder and the city is left in smoldering ruins.

Important for our consideration is the way in which the economic downfall of Tsor is effected. Rosewater creates a western Lukka which had for long supplied eastern Lukka with raw material and had during this same period been held in subjection by the financiers of the East. This western state secedes from the union, agreeing to pay its indebtedness only in terms of labor and labor products. The smug eastern Lukkans did not recognize their dependence on western raw material. Freed from the burden of an "unjust" system of exchange, western Lukka becomes a true utopia, and democracy in terms of equality prevails. When eastern Lukka falls, the utopia of Tismoul takes over and begins the necessary process of reconstruction.

Here is an attempt, crude as it is, on the part of the utopian novel to preach its story allegorically. Although some patience might be necessary to uncover the intended meaning for such esoteric names as Zuzo, Zrog, and Urg, there can be little question in our minds as to the actual identity of the western state, with its capital Tismoul and its minister of Finance, Aggra. Nor is there any confusion concerning the identity of the eastern Tsor, which worshipped a golden idol named Zmun. Rosewater doubted his reader's intelligence because he blunts his allegory by having a scientist of Lukka employ a time machine which tells the history of America during the period 1891-1930. Here the Free Labor Party of the West with its monetary reforms is able to bring about the necessary changes to avoid the fate of Tsor. Be it sufficient to any that here is God's plenty in the literary sensational; for the story runs the gamut of melodramatic cliche with stolen love, innocence defiled, plotting and counterplotting by gangs of thugs, murder, attempted seduction, poisonings, suicides figuring at every turn of the plot. The long final chapter on American history containing the purely didactic comes almost as comic relief.

Ignatius Donnelly's *Caesar's Column* (1891)[19] should be linked with and possibly even labelled as a predecessor to Rosewater's *A Romance of Utopia*. Donnelly's novel offers a plot of complications and (minus its populist thesis) could easily have been from the pen of any true "romantic" writer of the period. Intrigues, plots, counterplots, secret murders, secret societies, the wronged innocent in the hands of the heartless villain, nick-of-time escapes, and last-minute rescues play across Donnelly's picturesque backdrop.

Although the locale is different (in this case New York City) and the method of projection into the future less singular (beginning without further ado in the twentieth century), the story has several accidents of plot and character which reappear in Rosewater's story. In *A Romance of Utopia,* a young girl is sold to the wealthy and evil aristocrat, Prince Urg. Donnelly has Estella Washington, a descendant of George, sold to Prince Cabano, a wealthy and evil aristocrat. Both girls escape "the fate worse than death" through the jealous intervention of a previous favorite in the household. Both princes are Jews. The coincidence of plot may be interpreted as a stereotype of the melodramatic. The latter indicates the anti-semitic sentiment common to the Populist and most reform parties of the West during the nineties. It is by no coincidence that the two Westerners make their most evil character Jewish. Donnelly's argument and his bias are obivous as he writes:

> But his father, who grew exceedingly rich and ambitious, purchased a princedom in Italy for a large sum, and the government being hard up for money, conferred the title of Prince with the estate . . . Yes . . . the aristocracy of the world is now almost altogether of Hebrew origin . . . They are the great money getters of the world. They rose from dealers in old clothes and peddlers of hates to merchants, to bankers. . . .[20]

As if to cinch his case against the Jewish race, Donnelly makes one of the leaders of the conspiratorial brotherhood a Jew as well. In the end, this radical Jew, who has helped to bring on the revolution, turns traitor and absconds with millions from the public treasure.[21] Donnelly also shows, as did several utopian novelists before him, a strong distrust for "foreigners" with the exception of the Scandinavian immigrants, who, naturally enough for a man writing from Minnesota, are portrayed as sound, worthy citizens.

The stories which envision their utopian society as realized in the present or in the immediate future are Henry L. Everett's *The People's Program* (1892), Frederick U. Adams' *President John Smith* (1897), and Milan C. Edson's *Solaris Farm* (1900). Everett's book is a truly impressive record of eclectic confusion. No literary crudity or logical contradiction seems to escape him. We follow the adventures of a young American social reformer, Streeter, who, while a student in Germany, becomes interested in helping the working man. With the aid of Minnie Ryerson, an American living abroad, he forms a student organization called the Geometric League. Its first success is the elimination of the "barbaric practice of duelling." Streeter, out for bigger game than Minnie, attempts to win the hand of Princess Victoria. The students' union becomes international, and pressure is brought to bear upon Kaiser Wilhelm to institute social reform. An international labor conference is called, and many important international reforms are instituted. The scene changes to England where further reforms are effected after Princess Victoria tells Streeter she can be only a sister to him. Spain serves as the center of a vast student Chautauqua, and Streeter's ideas are spread to all portions of the globe. Principal among these are the eight-hour day and the adoption of an international language. The Chinese, he explains were pleased to adopt the new tongue because of the difficulty of learning their own. The final scene is laid in America where Streeter is now president of the Student International. A vast labor corporation is established in the West where a program compounded of revivalism and "variation from specialization" is put into practice. The laborer's errant religious attitude is corrected by revivalist Sankey, and workers are made happy by diversified employment during their lifteime.

As a concession to the socialists, public ownership of railways and public utilities is advised. Some suggestion as to the composite nature of his program may be gained from Everett's concluding paragraph:

> The plans which were attaining realization for the amelioration of mankind were not the suggestions of Edward Bellamy; they were not precisely the purposes of socialists; they were evolved from the productive brain of George Streeter, and were enlarging the happiness of humanity infinitely more than all the programs of socialist reformers and labor parties. In fact, they achieved for the world improvements which the socialists like better than their own plans.[22]

President John Smith (1897) by Frederick Upham Adams makes a single protagonist responsible, in the main, for the good society which is established. This narrative traces the development of an increasingly corrupt government through a capitalist inspired war with Germany, an ensuing panic and financial depression, and a temporary dictatorship under an erratic and grotesque figure, George Francis Train, who comes to power by playing on popular gullibility and anti-semetic sentiments. The story is resolved by electing to the presidency the mildly socialistic John Smith, whose policies, it should be added, are intended to follow the line of Bellamy's Nationalistic program.

Milan C. Edson's *Solaris Farm* (1900), another cooperative utopia, begins five years in the future. The story opens with the portrayal of the plight of the farmer. Fillmore Flagg, a hero with all the heroic virtues, meets Fern Fenwick, a wealthy heroine, interested in solving the farmer's problems. Fillmore finds that Fern is spiritually guided by her dead parents, who speak to the young people daily through a large golden trumpet specially adapted for such conversation. Aided by such wise direction, they found a cooperative farm so successful in operation that it merits adoption by the rest of the United States. By turning over the trumpet to the noble soul of Fern's father, Fennimore Fenwick, Edson is afforded excuse to indulge in long didactic soliloquies concerning the nature of progress, the needs of the race, the curse of competition, the value of proper environmental conditions for motherhood, pre-natal education, and stirpiculture. His instructive message is a mixture including the theories of Elmer Gates,[23] Henry George, Edward Bellamy, Lawrence Gronlund, M. Godin, Herbert Spencer, and Emerson, which is finally called "Socialism of the most progressive type." Style and method of characterization common to the *genre*, literary utopia, are illustrated in the following description of Edson's hero, Fillmore Flagg:

> Fillmore Flagg was fully six feet in height, though his compact well-rounded figure made him seem less tall; his straight, muscular limbs were in harmony with his deep chest and symmetrical shoulders. His rather large but beautifully turned neck and throat rose straight from the spinal column, firmly supporting a noble head, everywhere evenly and smoothly developed. His thick, soft brown hair, worn rather short, was inclined to curl, giving the outlines of the head a still more heroic size. . . . Later we shall learn to know him better by his genial temperament, mental and moral characteristics.[24]

John Jacob Astor's fantastic *Journey to Other Worlds* (1894), like Rosewater's novel, involves a transportation both in time and space. Astor carries his reader through a project for straightening the world's axis (The Terrestial Axis Straightening Company, a common stock one hundred dollars per share) which is to bring a universally temperate climate to Mars and Jupiter, the home of the dead earthlings including retired Presbyterian ministers. The movement derives from exciting hunting expeditions on Jupiter in which pterodactyls, "man eating lilies with voices like sweet trombones," giant insects, and reptiles are joyously slaughtered. Professor Bearwarden, head of the interplanetary expedition, is enthusiastic about two things: the excellent hunting prospects in a land not already "shot out" and the possibilities for industrial development.

Several lengthy chapters are devoted to the pronouncements of the spirit of a Presbyterian minister, who explains that a scientific program and the increased production of material goods are only the means of fulfilling God's interest wherein man is intended to progress from the animal to the spiritual form. Ayrault, the wealthy young vice president of the Terrestial Axis Straightening Company, university man and scientist, returns from his tour of the Universe, and marries a Vassar graduate to afford excuse for stopping the narrative.

The majority of utopias project their ideal society into the future. A few take their journeys both into space and time. We have left to consider the expedient of bringing to the present a visitor from a society far advanced from our own. Such is the technique employed by Amos Fiske in *Beyond the Bourne* (1891). He uses the device of the discovered manuscript left by a mysterious stranger. The story relates the experiences of a grief-stricken man who has just lost a wife, mother, father, sister, and brother-in-law. Life does not seem worth living. In this mood, he is in a train wreck. While on the surgeon's table he enters the spirit world where he converses with all the members of his family. In heaven we discover that the soul continues to develop. Sinners have a long process to endure; the saintly have a shorter road to perfect glory. A sage who has been in heaven for 2000 years explains to the hero the nature of progress and the constant evolution from the material to spiritual. An excursion takes them to another planet, where the sage explains that the state of comparative perfection there has been attained by growth and development of the individual character, by education and voluntary cooperation and not by communism or socialism or any other device of public regulation. When the surgeon repairs the damaged body, the heavenly visitor is forced to return to the mortal world much against his will.

The second utopia of the single tax, Byron S. Welcome's *From the Earth's Center* (1894), again resorts to the contrivance of the stranger with a manuscript as does the later cooperative utopia, *Nequa* (1900), of Alcanoan O. Grigsby. The true author is recognized as Ralph *Spencer*, who with three others, Frank Hutchens, *Ricardo* Fleming, and *Owen* Radcliff, sets out to investigate the theory advanced by Captain John Symmes, which held that the earth was made up of two hollow concentric spheres with openings at both poles. The men sail into the inside world, which is described and compared to America of the nineties. Reminiscent of Julian West's Edith is the highly intelligent Celia Lathrop, who amazingly is a fifth cousin to Ralph Spencer. Centralia, it should be explained, is populated by descendants of *Josey Quesney*, who left America upon being refused permission to marry the girl of his choice, and *Mlle. Turgot*, who organized a rescue expedition composed of English women. The inner world is made comparable to the outer in all geographic respects, having a Europe, Asia, Africa, etc. We follow Ralph through the country where he learns the revolutionary possibility implicit in the single-tax thesis, reaching as it does into the religious, economic, cultural, and educational life of a country. Ralph has a little difficulty in approaching Celia, an enfranchised and highly educated woman, but he succeeds and their marriage brings down the curtain.

Grigsby's *Nequa* is in several respects similar to Welcome's narrative. Once more we have the story opened by the stranger with the manuscript, the expedition setting out to test the accuracy of Symmes' theory of the concentric spheres and the discovery of a polar opening into an inside world. Grigsby also indulges in a good deal of weighted naming. The pleasure resort is located on Lake Bybliss. The Cocytos is an important river leading to Kroy, fallen city of the capitalist world. Bona Dea is the matron of the very important maternity hospital which specializes in providing proper pre-natal environment for embryonic Altruria. Most of the utopians have mentioned the influence of woman as being wholly for the good, but Grigsby proceeds the farthest in this direction, making his society practically a matriarchate. Pointing backward to Bellamy is the "Parable of the Long Bridge and the Short Bridge," which is used to insinuate the value of consumer and producer cooperatives. Much credit is given to the fact that the people through the educational experience of a class war which finally destroys the old capitalist world are prepared for a return to the golden rule and the true teachings of their prophet Krystus. Hopefully, Grigsby had tongue in cheek when he permits one of the worldings to speculate thus:

> MacNair has a theory . . . that the psychic conditions in a concave world tend directly towards concentrated effort and cooperation, because the heads of the people all point toward each other and converge at a common center, while in the outer world they point outward, each in a direction of its own, tending directly toward individualism and the development of every selfish instinct.[25]

Unless the unintentional is included, this is the *sole* suggestion of humor in all the American utopian literature examined.

The fable of *Nequa* is quite substantially developed including as it does the story of Cassie Van Ness, who loves the courageous, honorable Raphael Ganoe. A designing guardian tricks her into an illegal marriage to obtain her inheritance. Ganoe, believing the marriage is real, seeks forgetfulness in adventure on the high seas. He is master of the ship headed for polar explorations on which Cassie ships, dressed as a boy. During the Arctic explorations, which result in the discovery of the opening into the central world, Grigsby sustains an interesting narrative. Some artistry, leavened by the God-awful, is shown in the concluding episode. Cassie volunteers to make an airplane trip to the outer world alone. As she leaves, she discards her mannish dress in favor of her old dress and reveals herself to Ganoe. He cries, "Cassie, Cassie, come back." We are left to imagine that somehow she is able to return.

Henry Olerich, writing from his farm near Holstein, Iowa, introduces something new in the way of utopias in his *A Cityless and Countryless World* (1893). A visitor from Mars, canvassing Herbert Spencer's *Synthetic Philosophy*, calls upon the Uwin home. Finding the Uwins an intelligent family, he reveals his identity and proceeds to explain the nature of his utopian home in Mars. Rather crudely drawn are the type characters: Mr. Uwin of philosophical bent, Mrs. Uwin of the open mind, Rev. Uwin of the conservative religious mind, and daughter Violet of the open heart. These characters manage to ask the right questions while Midith, the man from Mars, proceeds to explain the advantages of philosophical anarchism. The story, full of measurements of buildings and diagrams of cities, analyzes the Martian social structure in great detail.

Consideration of Chavannes' *In Brighter Climes, A Realistic Novel* (1895) has been postponed because this book is an attempt to adapt the so-called "realistic" technique to the utopian novel. What realism means to Chavannes may be briefly illustrated. The plot concerns Charles Morrill, unemployed through the caprice of private capitalism. Upon receipt of a letter from an officer in the Nationalist Society in Spencer, Socioland, Morrill decides to make the trip with his wife. On shipboard he meets three men representing three attitudes toward religion. A discussion takes place between a Catholic priest, a Protestant minister, and Mr. Proctor, merchant, scholar, and philosopher. The latter readily points out the "stupidity" of all formal religion. Morrill enters Socioland and goes to work. A detailed description of everyday life follows. Mary, his wife, has an affair; Charles has an affair. The novelty wears off. Charles comes back to his wife and all is forgiven. They settle down to important problems of economic and social reform. The characters in this novel milk cows, build houses, wash dishes, and change diapers. As the book closes, the people are showing a tendency to try a completely communistic experiment in favor of the cooperative program they have been following. Realism for Chavannes then means documenting the commonplace and daring to argue openly in favor of free love, communism, and atheism. But for him realism has nothing to do with the form or structure of his novel, which in essence is no different from the romantic. All that is involved is a shift in permissible content.

Excluding Chavannes and Howells, the American utopians felt they were using a romantic vehicle for their messages. Literary connections with the past may well exist; that is, some may have formulated their notions of romance through contact with such English writers as Bulwer-Lytton, Scott, and Dickens, all of whom are mentioned favorably by these writers. Some of the propagandists seem to have drawn on Poe, Harriet Beecher Stowe, or Cooper's imitators represented by Professor Ingraham, whose *The Prince of the House of David* was read in thousands of American homes. Again their concept of popular literature may be indebted to the dime novels which enjoyed such fantastic success. Perhaps the heavy use of the plot providential or character description through enumeration has literary origins. But there is stronger evidence both in overt statement and in practice that their notion of literary art was directly inflected by oral conventions of the pulpit, the lecture platform, and the stage. The impression is left that the writers thought of themselves as lecturers and assumed that the book was a replica of the tent, auditorium, or church. Dialogues frequently impress the reader as exchanges between speaker and audience. The hortatory, the histrionic postures, the strenuously elevated diction, the exaggerated tone, the employment of anaphora, the parable, the hard line allegory, the repetitive illustration—all suggest an oral tradition. The response of the contemporary reader is not merely that he is reading bad literature but that it is "bad" in a peculiar way, for there is a strangeness evoked by the dissonance one experiences in watching the first talkies or the direct filming of a play or a beauty-talent show on TV. Conditioned expectancies concerning the relation of form and content have been violated unintentionally, and the reader experiences a revealing insensitivity, as Marshall McLuhan has taught us, to the modalities of the sermon, the stage, and the book. What these writers responded to in literature was that which most closely paralleled the lecture-sermon, and their aesthetic had been gained largely at the feet of the local minister.

3.

"In utopia our poets have a great deal to say about clouds and novelists use them for spice in literature."

Alcanoan O. Grigsby, *Nequa*

American utopian fiction operates within a particular theory of mass communication involving a notion of the mass, the elite, and the intermediaries. It makes assumptions about mass psychology and embodies a strategy for implanting information. It implies a hierarchy of human response ranging from the heights of the vatic and spiritual to the depths of laughter. A laugh can not, for example, bear information or "truth." Laughter only distracts and leaves the auditor in a passive benighted state. One reaches the masses through their susceptibility to descriptions of courtship, a series of events including numerous detours in which man and woman are finally brought properly to bed or almost. Through this susceptibility, this hole in the hard head of mass man, difficult and important messages can be delivered. More accurately, the theory depends upon the mass female; for the uneducated male is regarded as being incapable of direct response to literary suggestion. Woman, no matter how bleak her state of actual ignorance, possesses instinctively a capacity to respond to love in fiction, that is, the spiritualized love to be found there. It is a natural gift which man, unless blessed by the accident of a partially feminine nature, must acquire through strenuous artificial development.

Woman, then, holds the key. Because of her sensitivity, she can be educated quickly and painlessly. The flow of events in the romance need no longer be stalled by the usual elaborate delays (differences assumed to be real or assumed to be assumed of wealth, intelligence, or taste and other elaborately constructed barriers), but rather by blocks of instructive content; the consumer, the female, is now a creature who upon finishing the novel possesses knowledge, spirituality, and power. Mass man may then be led, not kicking and screaming in class war, but quietly and eagerly through the bedroom door into utopia.

Within nineteenth century society, the men who possess spiritual sensitivity are assigned to a hierarchy of roles—they are the elite. At the very top are the preachers and teachers, usually academic historians. Slightly below appear the novelists and poets whose function it is to mediate between the female audience and the elite. Their merit is measured by the degree to which they have earned the right to mount the pulpit or chautauqua lecture platform openly, freed from all auctorial disguise, to enlighten their partially elevated audiences concerning the hope of the future.

All utopians reflect an ill-concealed disdain for fiction, for the novel or "romance" is neither serious nor thoughtful. Thus the writer fulfills his role only in so far as he subverts the frivolous format by important spiritual, political, and scientific knowledge into the "speeches" of his characters. In a sense the utopians seem dedicated to the destruction of not only imaginative literature but in effect all art, at least as an independent value. Intentions, concerns, techniques of the utopian novelist—all operate in sharp contradiction against the uniquely "literary."

Lawrence Gronlund's widely read *The Cooperative Common-wealth*, a straight-forward statement of utopian socialist goals, describes the attitude toward literature and the arts among the American utopian novelists: the function of the aesthetic modes is to gain uniformity of opinion. Literature, painting, sculpture, and drama exist to provide consensus in political, economic, ethical, and religious domains. Gronlund asserts,

> The anarchy of opinion in this transitory age is an enormous evil. Unity of belief is the normal condition of the human intellect; it is just as natural for healthy men to think and believe alike, as it is for healthy men to see alike.[26]

Art, properly, has only public goals. Private visions, coterie art is bad. He adds:

> When one harmonious sentiment thrills through the whole of Society, we may expect a revival of the aesthetic sense of ancient Greece. This Gilded Age with its so-called "promoters of the arts" creates prostitutes of art, who exercise it, not for love of it, but to "make" money by it.[27]

Of all the arts, Gronlund has most concern for the stage:

> It can be made the mightiest educational instrument. In particular, manners and address [elocution] can be learned to perfection in the theatre, and only there.[28]

Art must be communal; at best it provides Matthew Arnold's "spectacle of a cultured people:"

> So in the Cooperative Commonwealth where *care* is forever banished art will once more belong in the midst of the people because of its eminently educational importance.[29]

Much has been written about the American utopian novels, and in many treatments the assumption is made that there exist successful models of the *genre*. Bellamy and Howells are cited as writers who bridged the inherent difficulties, giving us both literature and intelligent direction for the future. They are, after all, the most literate of the utopians, and it might be suspected that neither would insist on the simplistic separation of form and content reflected in their imitators and inferiors. However, the lesser lights are only stating in cruder ways the convictions of their mentors. Much has been written about Bellamy as a skillful literary artist. We are led further to understand that Bellamy inherited his skill from such masters as Tolstoy, Hugo, and Dickens. The question is asked, Why do we remember Bellamy in our time? Why is it that *Looking Backward* has never been out of print since the date of its publication in 1888? The answer given by Joseph Schiffman in his preface to the Modern Library edition is "consummate literary craftsmanship." Note however what Schiffman points to as supporting evidence:

> Bellamy was a superb rhetorician: his analogy of the stage coach . . . is as effective as any in Plato; his homiletics and his parable of the rosebush recall the art of Jesus who "taught them many things by parables"; his skillful handling of the Socratic method of argument lends an air of reason to a subject traditionally acrimonious. . .; his use of tragic irony in the enemy of society scene. . .indicts the callousness of his age; his rare blend of personification and parody in the spectre of uncertainty scene . . . is hauntingly emphatic. . . .[30]

What is said here has almost nothing to do with the art of fiction and everything to do with pulpit oratory—a "superb rhetorician" may well be a miserable novelist.

Within *Looking Backward* itself Bellamy expresses his notion of the literature of the future. Out of the past the utopians single out Dickens as the prime favorite, ". . . not because his literary genius was highest, but because his heart beat for the poor. . . . No man of his time did so much as he to turn men's minds to the wrong and wretchedness of the old order of things, and open their eyes to the necessity of the great change. . . ."[31] As for Bellamy's novelists of the twenty-first century, we have examples in Berrian, who has written several masterpieces including *Past and Present, In the Beginning, Penthesilia,* and *Ruth Elton.* The first two are imaginary re-writes of *Looking Backward; Penthesilia* besides drawing upon the sleep theme of *Looking Backward* is described as a

> romance . . . in which there is love galore, but love unfretted by artificial barriers created by the difference of station or possessions, owning no other law but that of the heart. The reading of *Penthesilia* was of more value than almost any amount of explanation would have been in giving me something like a general impression of the social aspect of the twentieth century.[32]

Ruth Elton, another romance by Berrian, has as its plot a story of the responsibility of women in society in whom "the keys of the future are confided."[33] Women must seek out and mate with industrious and dedicated men. It is their moral responsibility to reject loafers and shirkers. Such a feeling in woman amounts to a "religious consecration . . . a cult."[34] Awash in the sea of nineteenth

century femininity, Bellamy offers Aedology (pre-natal education—
the aggressive head-start program of his time), stirpiculture (moral
eugenics), and The Faith that Makes Faithful (ectoplasmic sexual
communion) as the wave of the future. Bellamy and his fellow
utopians are worshippers of Bona Dea. When he thinks of art, he
sees ". . . standing out from the front of the building, a majestic
life-size group of statuary, the central figure of which was a female
ideal of Plenty, with her cornucopia."[35]

All art is educational, elevating, naively utilitarian, and democratic. The theater, for example, is to function as public spectacle;
its standards are established by vote.

> In art . . .., as in literature, the people are the sole judges. They
> vote upon the acceptance of statues and paintings . . ., and their
> favorable verdict carries with it the artist's remission from
> other tasks . . . to devote himself to his vocation.[36]

Music in Bellamy's utopia is provided by a kind of MUZAK. One
awakens to a lively Turkish reveille and is softly soothed to sleep by
a nineteenth century version of "Moon River." Such pleasant and
functional background music, available twenty-four hours a day,
anticipates the "classical supermarket" of our time.

> "Of course we all sing nowadays as a matter of course in
> the training of the voice [elocutionists all in utopia], and
> some learn to play instruments for their private amusement;
> but the professional music is so much grander and more per-
> fect than any performance of ours, and so easily commanded
> whenever we wish to hear it, that we don't think of calling our
> singing or playing music at all. All the really fine singers and
> players are in the musical service, and the rest of us hold our
> peace."[37]

Bellamy had obviously heard too many "little old piano[s] . . .that
had tin pans in [them] . . .and too many young ladies sing 'The Last
Link is Broken' or play 'The Battle of Prague' "[38] to wish home
talent on the future. Beyond this, his scarcely concealed contempt for
popular taste in the arts reveals the uneasy hypocrisy of the overt
statements which assign final judgments in the arts to the populace.
William Dean Howells and most other utopians are equally supine
and pusilanimous on the issue of art and the masses.[39] What is, of
course, deeply involved here is the whole ambiguous relationship of
the intellectual and the public, particularly that of the reformer or
ideologue whose performance is traditionally saturated with public
praise of and private contempt for the audience. The paradoxical

burden which the propagandist bears is transparent in Bellamy's description of his own intentions in the writing of *Looking Backward:*

> The object . . . is to assist persons who, while desiring to gain a more definite idea of the social contrasts between the nineteenth and twentieth centuries, are daunted by the formal aspect of the histories which treat the subject. Warned by a teacher's experience that learning is accounted a weariness to the flesh, the author has sought to alleviate the instructive quality of the book . . . by casting it in the form of a romantic narrative, which he would be glad to fancy not wholly devoid of interest in its own account.[40]

Something else is involved in the quoted passage other than the politely patronizing stance *vis a vis* the novel and the audience, that is, the assumption that history can be made easy. The historians in utopia, in *Looking Backward* and in most of the novels, all hate the past. Their function, a somewhat curious role for the historian, is to destroy it or to selectively simplify it so the audience will learn to hate it. At best these utopian historians will select figures and events for eulogy, martyrs—prescient men whose advice was ignored—and events which really belong in the future. These pragmatic, neo-Hegelian historians, are interested not in history but rather in the uses of the past, and unless some ideological propagandistic function can be discovered, the past can be safely ignored. Again this ought not to weigh against the utopians since most of American historical writing follows the basic pattern, even among our most sophisticated practitioners. Followers of the credo include Bancroft, Beard, Robinson, Parrington, Read, and Arthur M. Schlesinger, Jr.[41]

One further aspect of American thought reflected in the American utopian novel is that which may be given the rather pretentious label, The Gospel of the Collapsed Distinction, a habitual preference for the synthetic over the analytic. The definition of intelligence as the ability to see differences where others see only similarity is almost instinctively rejected. Those who press hard for sharp distinctions are frequently categorized as Jesuitical spoilsports. Contradictions and paradoxes tend not to be resolved or responded to for the hard challenge they present but rather homogenized in unitarian brotherhood. The American utopian novel bears a heavy freight of such synthetic bliss, as is fully apparent in the summarized novels of the previous section of the paper. However one quick straightforward example of this bent of mind occurs in Gronlund's *The Cooperative Commonwealth:* "Spencer's later philosophy is really socialist."[42]

Neither *A Traveler from Altruria* nor *Through the Eye of the Needle* is a utopian novel, at least not a hard line example. Both are, however, "escapist" in the most transparent sense of the word, for they are almost completely devoid of reformist intent. Howells himself had been through the door and was already in utopia, thoroughly domesticated. Nothing is really at stake in these novels, except perhaps the timorous twitching of the author's literary conscience. Mr. Twelvemough is forced to wonder on occasion whether he ought to be committed to something. Perhaps there is commitment, for at times one does suspect that what is really being written here is an instructional manual on How To Talk Politely About Socialism. As a believer in "smiling America," Howells is unable to invest his characters with the intensity of conviction. The strongest emotion revealed is in the aggressive petulance of a half smile. It is merely a record of fearfully civilized conversation in the parlor—gentle vapors, wishless reverie, distanced and abstracted preachment. The stance is that of the present-day minister who is willing to "entertain" some pretty advanced ideas on race relations, economic reform, and the death of God, revealing the sincere hypocrisy of the uncommitted. Finger doodling on their antimacassars, Mr. Homos and his friends "aver," "refer," "smile indulgently," "suppose," "venture," "concede," "mildly protest," and "beg each other's pardon." It's all writing about talk.

It is not however that Howells did not know where to introduce propaganda if he did entertain serious reformist intention. He knew his audience well and is capable of unbelievable flattery, partially because as a resident utopian he too has bought the idea of the transforming power of woman. How else explain the notorious passage in *Criticism and Fiction:*

> . . . The novel in our civilization now always addresses a mixed company, and . . . the vast majority of the company are ladies, and . . . very many, if not most, of these ladies are young girls. . . .[43]

Let us not, Howells continues, cut ourselves

> . . . off from the pleasure—and it is a very high and sweet one— of appealing to these vivid, responsive intelligences, which are none the less brilliant and admirable because they are innocent.[44]

Contrasted with this respectful attitude toward the female reader is Howells' opinion of the relation between the author and the mass man. An author, he explains, ". . . is in the world to make beauty and truth evident to his fellow-men, who are as a rule incredibly stupid and ignorant of both. . . ."[45] Howells clearly had the theoretical formula for mass manipulation well in mind. He just was not really interested in changing the economic order. A much deeper conviction is a faith in the Power of Positive Grammar. How else in American society of the late nineteenth century could anyone know that he was spiritual, cultured, and intelligent, that he too had a piece of the feminine soul? One must perforce learn to talk like a book; this is the difficult road that mass man must climb to the mountain top. Howells had already made the trip.

In his literary criticism, Howells writes much about the need for using American native speech in the novel. But his own handling of dialectal speech always comes off as fictive pastoral, a self-congratulatory squeezing of his literacy. He was, he admits, a very poor speaker and could thankfully acknowledge that he had never learned to talk. In at least one distracted moment, Howells must have convinced himself that *A Traveler from Altruria* was a true utopian novel and not a conversational rule book, that it really was appropriate to the oral modes of Bellamy and his imitators, involving the replication of the preacher, the pulpit, and the flock:

> "What do you think of my preaching yesterday in church here," Howells asked his wife; "Their 'supply' didn't come and the crowd got round and pleaded with me so to speak or read, that I raced over to Barnbury, got the *Trav. from Altruria*, and gave 'em a good dose of socialism. They liked it so well that they all shook hands and thankt me. Marthy reported later that it was the greatest hit ever known in K. P. [Kittery Point][46]

And well it might have been.

* * * * * *

The microcosm of late nineteenth century literary utopia provides a fascinating text for explication. Most of its subterranean meanings lie unexplored. Spelunking expeditions may, however, provide clues to the highly complex relations of aesthetic, sexual, political, and religious responses of the period. Attention to the aesthetics of their media, their modes of discourse, and their sexual economics may, for example, help us to a better understanding of still only crudely guessed at interactions of politics and imagination. What is, for example, to be made of the following text from utopia:

> . . . In front of one of these elegant structures [Utopia-Hilton] we observed a plant . . . a triumph in the science of cultivation . . . [it] resembled the banana plant, only much larger and more magnificent. The leaves grow up from the ground and are frequently fifty feet long, bending over in a curve, with their tips nearly touching the ground. The stem of the leaf is a dark

blue, and of a beautiful silky texture, while the bell-shaped flowers, hanging in graceful clusters around a shapely central pedestal often thirty feet high, are of a rich carmine, shading off to a soft orange in the center. The petals are ten inches in diameter and twelve inches long, and blossom with the greatest profusion. The plant is kept perfectly clean with a spray of water, is evergreen and always in bloom. When it becomes dull in color, a coat of specially prepared varnish is applied; and it is as fresh as ever.[47]

Obviously there is much more to be said about the *genre* than that it contains anticipations of the telephone, radio, television, air-conditioning, supersonic airplanes, atomic energy, aluminum and glass skyscrapers, the two-hour working day, credit cards, instant divorce, smog elimination, disease and pest control, extended life span through Geritol, a privacy-free society in which every member carries a governmental mini-corder around his neck. . . . and, of course, interplanetary travel. Such facts ought only to be the beginning points for an exciting game of "sprouts," analogical in a sense to that pleasant and instructive topological game. Perhaps it is still possible that American Studies can escape the moribundity covertly assigned to the field in the brilliantly arch scholarly *politesse* of Sigmund Skard in his essay in *Norvegica Americana*.

NOTES

1. Henry A. Olerich, *A Cityless and Countryless World* (Holstein, Iowa, 1893), p. 8.

2. Albert Chavannes, *In Brighter Climes: A Realistic Novel* (Knoxville, Tennessee, 1897), p. 1.

3. Albert Chavannes, *The Future Commonwealth* (New York, 1892), p. 1

4. Bradford Peck, *The World a Department Store* (Lewiston, Maine, 1900), p. 1.

5. *Ibid.*, p. 12.

6. H. L. Everett, *The People's Program* (New York, 1892), p. v.

7. Anon., *The Story of My Dictatorship* (New York, 1894), p. iii.

8. Byron S. Welcome, *From Earth's Center* (Chicago, 1895), title page.

9. James Macnie, *The Diothas, or, A Far Look Ahead* (New York, 1893), Preface.

10. John Jacob Astor, *A Journey to Other Worlds* (New York, 1894), p. iv.

11. *Ibid.*

12. Alcanoan O. Grigsby, *Nequa* (Topeka, Kansas, 1900), p. 52.

13. Richard Michaelis, *Looking Further Forward* (New York, 1890), p. vi.

14. *Looking Further Backward* is of extra-curricular interest because of the prophetic way Vinton treats the rise of a form of government (in this case Nationalism) to an almost universal acceptance and its ultimate internal decay fostered by an unwillingness to recognize the existence of forces of opposition. He further explains the subtle operation of this solely opposing monarchial form through a well developed bureau of intelligence. It is not too difficult to suggest a contemporary spokesman for the following:

> Our statesmen were convinced that sooner or later an appeal to arms would be necessary to preserve our own system of government, and it was then that China began to prepare for war. . . .

> In one generation China had been transformed into a vast camp where every able-bodied man is a soldier or a sailor, armed and equipped with the most recent weapons of war. Our surface and submarine navies are the finest that have ever yet been seen. . . .
> Our aim was in reality a defensive war undertaken by China to crush out the Nationalist theory of government. (Arthur D. Vinton, *Looking Further Backward,* Albany, New York, 1890, pp. 32-35.)

15. Anon., *A. D. 2050* (San Francisco, 1890), Preface.

16. J. W. Roberts, *Looking Within* (New York, 1893), p. 1.

17. *Ibid.,* p. 64.

18. Solomon Schindler, *Young West* (Boston, 1894), p. 282.

19. Although Parrington points to the book as the only Utopian romance in which is found a portrayal of a class war, at least six of the listed authors can be cited as treating the topic: Anonymous author of *A. D. 2050,* Michaelis, Vinton, Roberts, Merrill, Adams, and Rosewater.

20. Ignatius Donnelly, *Caesar's Column* (Chicago, 1890), p. 36.

21. The Populist controlled Vanguard Press of Indianapolis published one of the most violent anti-semitic documents of the decade. A quotation from O. D. Jones' *The Tocsin of Alarm* (1892) will prove illustrative:

> For sixteen centuries the Jew waged a losing fight with the Christian Church for his favorite practice of usury. Today all is changed—his victory, his ascendancy is complete. He made the issue squarely with the Nazarene, and as it stands today he is absolutely victorious. Yes, gentlemen of the plutocratic clergy and church press, you need not wince; now it is Jewdom and debt. The intelligent "common people" of whom it is written, "they heard Jesus gladly," plainly behold you, playing in the hands of your Jew usury masters; you deceive no one any longer but yourselves. "He that is not for us is against us." Where are you the "devourers of widow's houses," "The whited sepulcher full of widow's bones?" We do not say where you are; but we beg leave to inform you, you will very soon be compelled to get on one side or the other of this struggle between "the common people" and the English-American-Jew aristocrat and plutocrat. And in the end the Jew and his plutocratic allies are going to the wall, in this struggle as sure as the Nazarene ever trode the earth, looked into the faces of men and inspired them with the gospel of temporal, as well as eternal salvation.

22. Everett, *The People's Program*, p. 207.

23. Elmer Gates was a psychologist of some repute in his day. From his laboratory at Chevy Chase, Maryland, came forth theories similar to those of E. S. Pers of today. He also boomed the idea of pre-natal education.

24. Milan C. Edson, *Solaris Farm* (Washington, D. C., 1900), p. 2.

25. Grigsby, *Nequa*, p. 169.

26. Laurence Gronlund, *The Cooperative Commonwealth* (Boston, 1884), p. 232.

27. *Ibid.*, p. 233.

28. *Ibid.*

29. *Ibid.*

30. Edward Bellamy, *Looking Backward* (New York, 1959), p. xiii.

31. *Ibid.*, pp. 147-148.

32. *Ibid.*, p. 166.

33. *Ibid.*, 258.

34. *Ibid.*

35. *Ibid.*, p. 103.

36. *Ibid.*, p. 160.

37. *Ibid.*, p. 112.

38. Mark Twain, *The Adventures of Huckleberry Finn* (New York, 1949), p. 104.

39. Note Howells' humiliation as he waffles around in his essay "The What and How in Art." The unfairness of such judgment lies only in singling out Howells for what has been an almost commonplace practice in American literary criticism.

40. Bellamy, p. 12.

41. For a longer list and truly impressive analysis of the commitment of the American historical fraternity to a rather simplistic notion of the uses of history, see "The American Past: Is it Still Usable?" by R. R. Pole, *Journal of American Studies*, I (April, 1967), 63-78.

42. Gronlund, p. 256.

43. William Dean Howells, From "Criticism and Fiction," *American Heritage*, Vol. Two, ed. Leon Howard, Louis B. Wright, and Carl Bode (Boston, 1955), pp. 415-416.

44. *Ibid.*, p. 416.

45. William Dean Howells, "The What and the How in Art," *Literary Criticism in America,* ed. Albert D. Van Nostrand (New York, 1957), p. 183.

46. William Dean Howells, *Traveler from Altruria* (New Jersey, 1962), p. 143.

47. Welcome, p. 30.

Economics and Race in Jazz

Leslie B. Rout, Jr.

The history of jazz reveals a melangé of paradoxes. The music earned its unwelcome appellation because white Americans tried to discredit a white band copying what they had heard Negroes play in the red-light district of New Orleans.[1] The club owner where the band was playing resourcefully outwitted the opposition and profited handsomely. In contrast, the early Negro composers of America's only native music were either skinned alive or shabbily treated by white men, who sensed both the composers' need for ready cash and the music's financial prospects.[2]

Proof of this contention is not difficult to display. For example, W. C. Handy sold his "Memphis Blues" to publisher T. C. Bennet for $100.[3] The former gentleman's major creation, the "St. Louis Blues," has probably undergone more renditions than "White Christmas." Handy therefore should have died rolling in royalties. He did not. In New Orleans, Negro street bands adopted an old French *quadrille* to ragtime and called it "Praline," or "Jack Carey." A white group, the "Original Dixieland Band," recorded the tune as "Tiger Rag" in 1917 and gathered in the premiums.[4] Scott Joplin, thought by some to have originated ragtime, sold his "Maple Leaf Rag" to John Stark's publishing house for $50 plus royalties, admittedly good terms for the year 1901. With the proceeds from this one tune, black Mr. Joplin bought a thirteen room house; white Mr. Stark built and equipped a printing plant. Subsequently Stark published ten other Joplin rags and became wealthy; Joplin soon lost his home and died broke.[5]

Negro musicians began migrating from New Orleans about 1910 and by 1912-13 they had spread the ragtime gospel to New York and Chicago.[6] The music did not take hold until two white bands—the Original Dixieland Band in New York and the New Orleans Rhythm Kings in Chicago—skyrocketed into prominence. In 1917, the Origi-

154

nal Dixieland Band became the first jazz aggregation ever to record; no Negro musician was to be allowed this opportunity until 1921. The black man's recording debut was hardly financially auspicious; over the years the musicians involved collected $4 in royalties.[7] An informal but durable pattern was already emerging: (1) Black men might make the jazz innovations but white jazz performers would necessarily introduce the product to the public. (2) The Negro would incubate the product and iron out the problems while the whites would supply the polish, the packaging, and net most of the receipts. Admittedly, artists of every epoch have suffered despoilation at the hands of clever manipulators, but few have been as systematically victimized as the Negro jazzman.

America's only indigenous musical form was born in the Storyville district of New Orleans where a "Louisiana Purchase" could be made every night. In subsequent years, it flourished in the gutter because polite society looked the other way. Then F. Scott Fitzgerald coined the term "Jazz Age," and the 1920's claimed ex-bawdy house music as its own. The trouble was that the public generally heard diluted pablum served up by Tin Pan Alley tunesmiths. Music to dance to it was; jazz it was not.

By 1922, Paul Whiteman, controller of twenty-eight East Coast orchestras, had zoomed to the forefront of American popular music.[8] On February 12, 1924, at Aeolion Hall in New York, Whiteman and an East Side youth named George Gershwin, performed "Rhapsody in Blue." The former gentleman had deliberately opened the program with "Livery Stable Blues"—an Old New Orleans tune—in order to show how crude jazz had been before Whiteman. When the audience applauded the bandleader was momentarily non-plussed: "I had for a moment the panicky feeling that they hadn't realized the attempt at burlesque—that they were ignorantly applauding the thing (i.e., *Livery Stable Blues*) on its merits..." From the vantage point of two generations we might say that the joke was on Whiteman. "Rhapsody in Blue" demonstrated that Gershwin had visited a few speakeasies or listened attentively to a few records. His composition embodied "bluesy" reed inflections—for example, the clarinet introduction—and snatches of syncopation but improvisation was conspicuously absent. Such details, however, were unimportant. Jazz had become respectable by virtue of its marriage to classical forms and publicists crowned Whiteman its king. Unfortunately for the latter, "Symphonic Jazz" proved to be a short-lived hybrid. Actually, the Aeolion Hall incident and Whiteman's reign as jazz potentate proved advantageous in the long run. With jazz a semi-respectable music, real jazzmen found more work and record companies made more jazz records.[10]

The jazz scene of the 1920's was dominated by Fletcher Henderson, Duke Ellington, and Louis Armstrong and such whites as "Bix" Beiderbecke and Frankie Traumbauer. Since jazz musicians of different races normally did not work or record together their meetings were usually limited to informal "jam sessions."[11] As had previously been the case the Negro was the jazz pacemaker. The Fletcher Henderson band gradually developed rudiments of a new jazz style and sported tremendous soloists. Paul Whiteman and Ferde Grofé visited Harlem's *Cotton Club* in 1927, listened to Duke Ellington's orchestra for a week, and "finally admitted that they couldn't steal even two bars of the amazing music."[12]

Artistic success was no barometer of economic prosperity or social conditions. Erskine Tate, one of the more successful Negro band leaders of the period, has recalled the 1920's as hardly a golden era for sepia jazzmen.[13] Mr. Tate vividly related the economic impediments under which Negroes labored in Chicago until Al Capone, hardly an exemplary member of polite society, raised the color bar.[14] Most intriguing was the ex-bandleader's commentary on social conditions. After completing a six month engagement at the *Arsonia Cafe,* the club owner told Tate:

> . . . let me tell you something. Anytime you want to play at this club, you're welcome because you have a bunch of gentlemen in your band.[15]

The meaning of "gentlemen"? The spry old man chuckled ruefully: "He meant that we stayed away from the white women."[16] Experiences such as these plus the obvious disproportion in the division of the proceeds deriving from musical activities only reinforced the black jazzman's belief that white society was determined to brutalize him while stealing the fruits his race had nurtured.[17]

Jazz activity languished during the Depression and both white and Negro artists headed for Europe. The doldrums ended in 1935. A new jazz style, "swing," became the rallying force for the youth of the era, and Benny Goodman became its pied piper. Actually the basis of swing had been worked out as early as 1927-28 by the Fletcher Henderson orchestra.[18] The latter's aggregation was excellent—but it was not white. A compromise of sorts resulted: Goodman became "King of Swing"—outside of Harlem and the other Negro ghettos— and Fletcher Henderson became his chief arranger.[19]

White bands led by Artie Shaw, Tommy Dorsey, and Glenn Miller soon joined Goodman as leading gentry in the swing hierarchy. The new black powerhouse battalions included Chick Webb, Jimmy Lunceford, Earl Hines, Lucky Millinder, and Count Basie. While the critics agreed that the Basie band was the greatest swing orchestra bar none, Marshall Stearns, in his history of jazz, took stock of the other side of the coin:

> Some twenty or so big colored bands, with Ellington and Basie at their head, were probably playing better jazz than the white bands ... and earning about half as much.

It may be argued that the success of the white bands made recognition of the sepia swingmen possible, but such a defense only emphasizes the fact that for the public the success of swing was intrinsically connected with the skin color of the performers.

Perhaps the most inflammatory aspect of the business of black jazzmen was the question of recording publicity and promotion. In 1932, Fletcher Henderson recorded "New King Porter Stomp" (*OKEH*-41565). In July, 1935, the Goodman band re-recorded the Henderson arrangement (*VICTOR*-25090). Jazz critics almost universally preferred the Henderson record, but the Goodman disc outsold the Henderson version almost one thousand to one.[21] In 1937, Count Basie recorded "One O'clock Jump," but when Goodman recorded his version in 1938 it sold a million copies.[22] Tommy Dorsey found a gold mine in Pine Top Smith's "Boogie Woogie," while Glenn Miller's version of Erskine Hawkins' "Tuxedo Junction" brought him the lion's share of the swag. Commenting dolefully on the tendency of white bands to get rich on later renditions of songs originally recorded by Negro jazz artists, Stearns wrote, "The same pattern was pretty general throughout the swing era."[23]

Black swingmasters of the thirties were more cognizant of economic factors than their brethren of previous eras for their appetites had been whetted by the few crumbs tossed their way. At the same time they felt themselves unable to overcome the phalanx of clubowners, bookers, disc jockeys, record companies, and publicity agents who determined the product directed toward the public. To the eternal credit of Benny Goodman and Artie Shaw in particular, white bandleaders demonstrated a much less biased attitude than white musicians of previous epochs.[24] The lowering of the color bar was seen as a major step forward by whites but paradoxically it probably increased Negro discontent. From the black man's viewpoint, his employment only demonstrated how terribly white orchestras needed Negroes! Such a need was considered proof of the superiority of Negro jazzmen and made the question of economic retribution doubly acute. Benny Harris, a trumpet player in Chick Webb's band during the 1930's, was asked whether Negro musicians felt they had been short-changed during the swing era. His reply revealed years of suppressed wrath:

> In those days, you'd have been an idiot to express a feeling like that. . . . Ask yourself if we received credit: Why do you think Fletcher Henderson was writing for Goodman?"[25]

If the Negro wished to change his socio-economic status in jazz, the best method was to initiate a new jazz revolution. The time was appropriate, for by 1941 swing had reached its maturity. Youth still pledged allegiance to the Goodmans, Shaws, and Millers, but the musicians were already searching for further innovations. During the winter of 1940-41, a handful of sepia jazzmen began working out the basis for a new form. Whimsically they hoped to make the new jazz too complex for white musicians to reproduce, thus guaranteeing both the long sought recognition of achievement and a corner on the profits that might accrue.[26]

What became known as "re-bop," "be-bop," and finally "bop" developed essentially from jam sessions and experiments conducted at *Minton's Playhouse*, a club in Harlem.[27] The recording ban of 1942-44 prevented the public from becoming cognizant of the burgeoning rebellion, but its chief apostles, John Birks "Dizzy" Gillespie (trumpet) and Charlie "Yardbird" Parker (alto saxophone) soon converted a hard core of militant musicians. The first be-bop combo (led jointly by Gillespie and Oscar Pettiford) began working in New York during the winter of 1944.

The public and many musicians were totally unprepared for the nuances of be-bop, and their appreciation was not enhanced by the cold demeanor its disciples displayed while performing.[28] Of major importance, however, was that for the first time a jazz movement was not only originated by black jazzmen but trumpeter Gillespie was sold to the public as its high priest. White musicians aspiring to play bop slavishly copied Gillespie's affectations in clothing and the musical characteristics of various Negro bopsters.

Alas, the acclaim of critics, musicians, jazz afficionados, and public recognition of Gillespie as the premier bopper could not be transformed into coin of the realm. In 1947, Billy Shaw left MCA in order to give Gillespie a real publicity build-up but the campaign produced negligible results. The scourge of the 1946-1949 period was the all-white Stan Kenton band. Dubbing his musical repertoire "progressive jazz,"[29] Kenton saw his orchestra become the first in jazz history to reach an annual gross of $1,000,000 in 1948. Meanwhile, Gillespie's disbandment in June, 1950, signalled the end of the be-bop crusade. Musicians white and black continued to play bop but the music lost the separate status it had enjoyed since 1944-45. Contemporary jazz activity was practically eclipsed by a veritable renaissance of the swing and Dixieland style. Disgusted, disillusioned, and pauperized, many white musicians joined dance-bands while some black musicians embraced Mohammedanism.[30]

Before passing from the jazz scene as a separate movement, be-bop gave birth to one illustrious progeny, "cool jazz." The source of this style lay essentially in the efforts of a small group of New York jazzmen who made a series of recordings for Capital Records in 1949-50.[31] The distinctive sound of both the soloists and the group's arrangements caught on as the "cool sound." European jazzmen were quick to embrace it but it was a Stan Kenton alumnus, Milton "Shorty" Rogers, whose employment of the style proved most decisive. Settling in the Los Angeles area in 1950, Rogers found the West Coast quite receptive to "cool" jazz interpretations. Some New York area musicians went West looking for work. Publicists took note of the rapidly expanding jazz activity in Los Angeles and environs and labelled it "West Coast jazz."[32]

Los Angeles-based jazzmen often denied that a separate jazz movement existed on the West Coast and the tag in no way described the multiplicity of jazz styles—many of which were not "cool" at all—being played in the land of sun, smog, and freeways. On the other hand, encouraging the public to believe that an intrinsically different music was being produced helped to make West Coast jazz a financial smash. The popularity of California jazzmen reached its apogee in 1954 when Dave Brubeck became the first jazz figure to appear on the cover of *Time* since pre-World War II days.[33]

The sudden ascendancy of California-based jazzmen failed to endear them to their East Coast counterparts. The latter consistently trumpeted their own superiority and denigrated California jazz stylings and its makers as "Bopsieland."[34] Such dyspeptic disdain may have provided emotional release but it failed to interrupt the frequent trek of Brubeck, Rogers, and associates, to the banks of their choice.

Black jazz-makers were especially quick to note that West Coast groups consisted almost entirely of white musicians. The financial success of these groups and the paucity of dark faces among their integrants all suggested a continuing conspiracy to rob the Negro of his birthright. The ascendancy of West Coast jazz marked the emergence of a new phenomenon probably envisaged partly as a defense mechanism: Enter "Crow-Jim."[35]

Popular tastes change and 1955 witnessed the initiation of a dramatic reversal of form. Old-fashioned be-bop returned to favor, but with new twists: First, the rhythmic intensity of the music increased noticeably—sometimes to the point of freneticism. Secondly, partisans of the revival maintained that West Coasters had over-cerebralized jazz by allowing foreign—that is, classical—forms to predominate. Jazz was to be purified and returned to its "roots." And what were these origins? The Negro Baptist and Spiritualist churches of the South, which were the incubators of the musical elements later forged into jazz. The economic and psychological effects of such a premise are clear: Sepia jazzmen, the obvious recipients of this heritage, played with "soul";[36] white jazzmen might imitate, but only by living in a presumably Negroid environment could they hope to obtain what Negroes allegedly possessed instinctively or learned from childhood. The net result was that first in New York and then all over the country, there appeared slashing, highly-charged, overwhelmingly Negro combos playing what was called "hard bop," or "soul jazz."[37]

The success of the be-bop revival during the 1955-60 period had far-reaching results. West Coast jazzmen discarded their previous stylings and demonstrated their allegiance to hard bop. More important, the theoretical bases of the neo-bop movement seemed generally accepted by a good many white musicians.[38] An increasing number of Negro musicians began to bask in the spotlight of popular appeal and for the first time a considerable number made truly large sums of money. By 1960, Negro leadership in the jazz field had been established as never before.[39] Yet, the arrival of the black man in a preeminent position in jazz carried with it some unfortunate aspects. Crow-Jim remained a potent factor in jazz relationships and aspiring whites soon discovered that for advancement in the field a copious supply of Negro blood was by no means a handicap.[40]

The year 1959 ushered in the first major revolution in jazz since the be-bop explosion. A bearded saxophonist named Ornette Coleman arrived in New York from Los Angeles. Coleman huffed and puffed, and stirred up winds of change which have not yet ceased to blow. Cometh now "free jazz," or what its advocates call the "new thing."[41] Like all previous jazz innovations the most militant advocates were primarily young musicians and a handful of jazz critics. The music was sometimes provocative, usually harsh, and for most listeners difficult to follow. Controversy over the relative merits of free jazz has continued to permeate the contemporary jazz scene. Most new thing performers, while increasingly interested in the economics of the jazz field, still see themselves essentially as artists. There exists, however, a small number of left-wing free jazz artists who in addition consider their music as a kind of socio-political weapon.[42] Indeed, the socio-political views expounded by this segment of new thing advocates has caused nearly as much acrimonious debate as the music itself.

One of the most articulate and vehement of the left wingers is Archie Shepp, tenor saxophonist:

> Jazz is the product of the whites, the ofay—too often my enemy. It is the progeny of the blacks—my men. By this I mean: You (i.e., whites) own the music and we make it. You own us in whole chunks of flesh.... I play about the death of me by you. I exult in the life of me in spite of you.... That's what the *avant-garde* is all about.[44]

Is that segment of the *avant-garde* that Shepp represents a jazz-man's *SDS-SNCC?* Are they subtle racists preaching the destruction of white society by some anticipated Afro-Asian coalition? These questions are of more than passing interest because Shepp and his associates have received an inordinate amount of publicity in the jazz press and their influence in the field is far in excess of their actual numbers.[45]

It is well to bear in mind that musicians, like other artists, are sometimes incurable idealists in their view of socio-political problems. Influenced (and who has not been?) by the civil rights movement of the 1950's and 60's, the left-wing avant-guardists believe that the black revolution taking shape in America is "good." Similarly, leftist political revolutions in Asia, Africa, and South America are also "good." Free Jazz is thus the expression of the sentiments believed embodied in these revolutions. The left wingers villify the American "power structure" which they see as the great impediment to human freedom. In particular, they view themselves as oppressed and believe that the club owners, representatives of the possessors of power, are united in an effort to make them bow and scrape.

While one may praise the courage and honesty of these outraged young men, their beliefs and practices are hardly consistent. Parties who do not appreciate free jazz, or who do appreciate the music but not the socio-political views of the left wing are generally dismissed as bigots. Crow-Jim remains a mute point: Shepp and his friends may hire white jazzmen but they infer that skin color somehow limits the potential of the whites.[46] This same clique of new thing jazzmen deplore the attitude of nightclub owners and intimate that a vast conspiracy has been formed to keep their music away from the people whom they insist have not had a chance to appreciate it. Unfortunately, neither they nor free jazz fans have done anything to establish a haven where their music can always be heard. For avant-gardists all over the country of whatever political persuasion the past years have not been easy. Only a handful of liquor dispensaries in New York, Chicago, San Francisco, and Detroit provide any kind of free jazz exposure and the album sales of its performers have not been outstanding. To date, free jazz has been even less of a financial success than be-bop and the future does not appear promising.

After thoughtful consideration of the suppositions of left-wing avant-gardists, it is the suspicion of this writer that much of their polemicizing has an even more distinctive economic overtone than they are prepared to admit. For example, pianist Cecil Taylor noted that after working for seven straight weeks for the first time in several years he underwent "metamorphosis."[47] To interviewer Nat Hentoff, Taylor declared:

> "I expect that within the next five years. I should be making what a good chamber musician gets and that will be quite a change."[48]

These are hardly the words of a hardened revolutionary! Even LeRoi Jones, who has called for the destruction of the white race,[49] took stock of the sad economic prospects for left-wing avant-gardists and intimated that he believed Caucasians might perform this beneficial act:

> Great White liberals of the World, give these young men a job or at least some money, until they learn, and all other black people learn that they must finally support themselves.[50]

The Shepps and the Taylors are embittered, but it would be interesting to review their socio-political views if and when they obtain the affluence and recognition of a Miles Davis, a Duke Ellington, or a Thelonius Monk.

* * * * *

In the 50 years since 1910 jazz has become respectable. Some of its artists, first the whites and finally the blacks, have received significant financial remuneration from their chosen field of endeavor. Since he has now arrived, the role of the Negro as jazz progenitor and pioneer is no longer a major issue. If one may employ the past to reflect the future, we can expect that each new jazz revolution will produce musical militants intent upon change and economic recognition of the success they hope to achieve. As a result, each new revolution will demand more of the listener. In addition, the prevailing racial tensions in the nation will continue to make themselves felt in jazz, producing sporadic manifestations of Jim-Crow or Crow-Jim sentiments.

As stated originally, jazz history is a melangé of paradoxes. In the next two decades, jazz will have to solve some inconsistencies with which it so far has failed to cope:

1. The increasing respectability of the jazz vocation plus the financial success enjoyed by a few of its performers have caused more and more young men to enter the field. Supposedly there is always room for the truly gifted musician but the extremely limited number of places to perform has caused the field to become glutted. Relief will come only if large traveling orchestras again come into vogue; this prospect does not appear promising.

2. Eventually jazz will receive some kind of regular subsidy from either the federal government or some kind of cultural foundation. Jazzmen have often complained of their failure to attract financing of this sort, but before effective action can be taken, answers will have to be provided to the following questions: On what basis will the musicians be picked who will receive the subsidy? Should such assistance be limited to one style of jazz rather than another? Through what agency should the funds be channeled? To date, organizational difficulties of this kind have rarely received the jazzman's attention.[51]

3. Admittedly, jazz and jazzmen have suffered grievously because of an unsympathetic communications media generally interested in the bizarre and sensationalist aspects of the music. If the music-makers hope to improve their image, they will have to unite in order to exercise more control over the manner in which they are presented to the public at large. The trouble is, jazzmen have consistently refused to organize on anything except the most elementary levels. Few will admit it, but freedom from organizational responsibility has long been considered one of the vocation's stellar attractions.

If propitious answers are provided for the problems outlined, the lot of the jazzman by 1990 should be considerably brighter. On the other hand, given their intrinsic individualism, jazzmen will probably always be looking over their shoulders gauging the shape of the economic shadow they are casting.

NOTES

1. Marshall Stearns, *The Story of Jazz* (New York, 1962), 4th Printing, p. 154; Rex Harris, *Jazz* (London, 1956), 4th Printing, p. 72; Stephen Longstreet, *The Real Jazz—Old and New* (Baton Rouge, 1956), p. 150; and Robert Goffin, *Jazz* (New York, 1944), p. 64. All agree on the origin of the word "jazz." Spelled "Jass," the term was used to designate heterosexual relations in houses of prostitution. The term was applied to Tom Brown's Dixieland Band as a form of derision by union pickets, because the Brown aggregation was non-union.

   The proprietor of the club where Brown was playing (*Lamb's Cafe*) took advantage in the interest drummed up (apparently, people were curious as to the kind of music played in whorehouses) and advertised the ensemble as "Tom Brown's Dixieland Jass Band." The word "jass" (later corrupted to "jazz") apparently was never used by the New Orleans musicians.

2. Rudi Blesh and Harriet Jones, *They All Played Ragtime* (New York, 1950), p. 64. For a study on how badly Negro composers were swindled, see Alain Locke, *The Negro and His Music,* The Associates in Negro Folk Education (Washington, D.C., 1936), p. 61.

3. *Ibid.,* p. 76.

4. Stearns, p. 74. The cornet player of the Original Dixieland Band, Nick La Rocca, claimed the authorship of "Tiger Rag."

5. Blesh-Jones, pp. 52, 116-117.

6. Goffin, p. 55-56; Nat Hentoff and Albert McCarthy, eds. *New Perspectives on the History of Jazz*—(New York, 1959), p. 140-141. A Negro band, Louis Mitchell's "Southern Symphony Quintet" had opened in the Flatiron building in New York in 1912. It continued to perform in various Manhattan cafes and restaurants until 1917. Prominent jazzmen, "Jelly Roll" Morton and Tony Jackson (pianists) began performing in Chicago in 1911-12.

7. Rex Harris, p. 93. Kid Ory's Sextet made six sides for the now defunct *Sunshine* label. Stephen Longstreet, (p. 73) disagrees, and claims that King Oliver's jazz band was the first Negro band recorded in 1922.

8. Abel Green and Joe Laurie, Jr., *Show Biz from Vaudeville to Video* (New York, 1951), p. 317. That year, Whiteman grossed $1,000,000.

9. Paul Whiteman and Mary M. McBride, *Jazz* (New York, 1925), p. 94.

10. Stearns, p. 168. "Colored people would form a line twice around the block when the latest record of Bessie [Smith] or Ma [Rainey]...came in...nobody asked for Paul Whiteman; I doubt if they ever heard of him."

11. Bary Ulanov. *A History of Jazz in America* (New York, 1964), 5th Printing, pp. 108-109. A "Jam Session" referred to informal playing (i.e., not for money) by musicians generally under relaxed circumstances. "Jamming" was usually possible only at clubs which hired Negro musicians. It became customary for white jazz musicians to go up to Harlem after the downtown halls closed, or out to the southside in Chicago, in order to play with and/or learn from Negro musicians. The Harlem clubs especially, did not cater to a Negro clientele. Negroes were admitted to the fashionable Harlem speakeasies only if they were celebrities.

12. Nat Hentoff and Nat Shapiro, *Hear Me Talkin' to Ya* (New York, 1955), p. 235.

13. For a history of Erskine Tate's jazz activities in Chicago, see Orrin Keepnews and Bill Graver Jr., *A Pictorial History of Jazz* (New York, 1962), 5th Printing, pp. 39 and 50. Among the major jazz figures to have played in Tate's band during the 1920's were Louis Armstrong, Cab Calloway, Eddie South, Fats Waller, and Earl Hines.

14. Personal Interview, Erskine Tate, Chicago, Illinois, February 5, 1967. Mr. Tate related that until 1928-29, Negro bands were confined to a "strip" along State Street, roughly between 31st and 47th Streets. Not until Al Capone interceded, did Negro orchestras get the opportunity to play the numerous cafes and speakeasies on Chicago's West Madison Street.

15. *Ibid.*

16. *Ibid.*

17. See Nat Hentoff, "Jazz and Race," *Commonweal*, LXXXI, 15 (January 8, 1965), 482. The author quotes Duke Ellington: "I tried to convince Fletcher Henderson that we ought to call what we are doing 'Negro Music.' Then we'd have something to hang onto...."

18. The story of how Fletcher Henderson and Don Redmon worked out the jazz style known as "swing" is related in Goffin, pp. 91-92. Ulanov, p. 184, gives an equal share of the credit to Duke Ellington.

What was "swing"? The best definition possible would be an analysis of the music's technical aspects; it is on this basis that definition is attempted. In addition to improvised solos, there was a steady reiteration of two and four bar phrases (eventually called "riffs") between brass and reed sections. These phrases were usually scored to sound like spontaneous solo bursts, and replaced the collective improvisation idea that had been basic to Dixieland jazz. Ordinarily, "swing" orchestras included at least thirteen musicians while Dixieland aggregations where rarely larger than six or seven men.

19. Benny Green, *Jazz: The Reluctant Art* (New York, 1963), p. 66. As early as 1934, Goodman had thirty-four Fletcher Henderson arrangements in his repertoire. These were new to white musicians and the general public, but five or more years old to Henderson. Mr. Green is quite succinct: "The Goodman Band . . . was the best that was exploitable on a national scale."

20. Stearns, p. 220.

21. *Ibid,* p. 209, and Ulanov, p. 189.

22. Stearns, p. 213.

23. *Ibid.,* p. 209.

24. Ulanov, pp. 189-190, Rex Harris, p. 184, and Goffin, p. 163. Goodman hired Teddy Wilson, a Negro pianist, in 1936. The "King of Swing" had numerous trials with bookers, club and hotel owners, but later in the year he also hired Lionel Hampton (vibraphonist). In 1939, Goodman hired Charlie Christian (guitar) and his 1940 orchestra included Christian, Cootie Williams (trumpet), and Sid Catlett (drums).

Shaw became the first white bandleader to hire a Negro vocalist (Billie Holliday, 1938), and in 1941, he also hired Oran "Hot Lips" Page (trumpet).

25. *Metronome,* LXXVIII, 11 (October, 1961), 20. Harris stressed the fact that Negro jazzmen resented the huge profits made by white bands but felt that any vigorous protest would have resulted in boycott or backlash.

26. *Time,* LXXX, 16 (November 19, 1962), 59. Pianist Mary Lou Williams quoted Thelonius Monk, one of the progenitors of be-bop, as saying: "We're going to create something they (i.e., whites) can't steal because they can't play it." Nat Hentoff, "Jazz and Jim Crow", *Commonweal,* LXXIII, 26 (March 24, 1961), 657, ridiculed the idea: "I suspect that these tales of the birth of modern jazz as a secret society are almost entirely apocryphal." Don DeMichael, editor of *Downbeat* Magazine (Interview,

Chicago, Illinois, February 17, 1967) noted that Dizzy Gillespie had told him a story similar to the comments made by Mary Lou Williams to the *Time* reporter. DeMichael dismissed the idea of some continuing conspiracy. Considering that the musicians would employ westernized tools and means (i.e., saxophones, chords, traditional notation) to communicate their ideas, it was really only a question of time before the whites caught on.

27. Hentoff and Shapiro, p. 340, and Stearns, p. 222. Be-bop employed radical chord conceptions (augmented ninths and flatted fifths). Harmonically, be-bop represented a veritable flight into chromaticism.

    Rhythmically, the concept changed almost entirely. The bass was no longer thumped but plucked and in some instances bowed. Drummers kept time on their cymbals, the bass drum being used only for accents. Pianos and guitars no longer played steady time; instead they "comped"—played fragmented chord progressions in order to inspire the soloist. In general the beat became implied rather than felt. To play good bop a musician generally had to be more technically proficient than a swing-era musician. Unfortunately, perhaps, a be-bop listener had to be more aware of certain technical aspects of music than his swing-period counterpart. Bop marked the end of the road of jazz as a functional music.

28. Ulanov, pp. 246-249. To the boppers, Louis Armstrong, Fats Waller, etc., were clowns or entertainers, etc. Since the boppers were "artists" their work was to be accepted on their terms. Boppers turned their backs on audiences, refused to acknowledge applause and delighted in insulting eager but uninformed listeners.

    In the experience of this author, nothing stands out more than the occasion in 1953, when performing with a combo, I bowed to acknowledge applause and was roundly chewed out by the other musicians. "My man, that (i.e., bowing) was none too cool," said the combo leader.

29. Kenton never really defined "progressive jazz." One occasionally detected Afro-Cuban rhythms, splashes of Schoenberg, Stravinsky, Bartok, and other contemporary classical composers. Alas, when the soloists stepped into the spotlight, out came fair to middling imitations of Charlie Parker, Dizzy Gillespie, or J. J. Johnson (considered the father of contemporary jazz trombone style).

30. Among others, William Evans (saxophonist) became Yusef Lateef, Fritz Jones (pianist) became Ahmed Jamal. The conver-

sion to Mohammedanism was generally taken as an indication that the convert was showing his disillusionment with Western values. Just how orthodox these Negro Muslim converts became is a matter of dispute. In a radio broadcast on WBAA (West Lafayette, Indiana, February 14, 1966, "The Two Worlds of Jazz") Neshui Ertugen, director of jazz recordings for Atlantic Records, insisted that Mohammedanism among Negro jazz musicians was essentially racial in character, and thus not in keeping with Muslim theory. Mr. Ertugen is a Muslim.

31. Ulanov, p. 232, and Leonard Feather, *Encyclopedia of Jazz* (New York, 1955), p. 30. The recordings of the first "cool jazz" group (led by Miles Davis, arrangements and compositions primarily by Gerry Mulligan and Gil Evans) can be heard on Capital Records *LP*-F1974. Cool Jazz laid emphasis on group sound and orchestration as well as improvisation. As opposed to earlier styles, cool jazz was characterized by the relaxed approach of both soloist and arranger—theoretically the soloist always held something back.

"Cool" also referred to the tone qualities of the soloists. Each of the sole horns employed light, dry tones and practically eschewed vibrato entirely. The saxophonists in the group (Gerry Mulligan and Lee Konitz) obtained the origins for their saxophone sound and concept from a swing-era tenor saxophonist, Lester Young. Improvisers of the cool conception generally made a greater use of the lower and middle registers of their instruments and often "lagged," playing behind the beat.

32. For an example of how closely Rogers followed the style established by the Miles Davis group, hear Capital Records *LP* DC-294.

33. For Brubeck's photo and story, see *Time,* LXIV, 19 (October 8, 1954). One of Brubeck's earlier groups was also heavily influenced by the Davis group of 1949-1950. See Fantasy *LP*-3239.

34. *Metronome,* LXXVII, 9 (September, 1960), 12. One of the most popular West Coast groups, the Gerry Mulligan Quartet, usually added a chorus or two of collective improvisation (an old Dixieland practice) to the tunes it performed: Hence the origin of the term.

Originally, the expression was applied exclusively to the Mulligan group, but eventually it was applied to practically all the groups originating in the Los Angeles area. Use of the term was taken to imply that West Coast jazzmen were too cool, and disgustingly effeminate in their jazz (and sexual) outlooks.

35. Nat Hentoff, "Jazz and Jim Crow," p. 658, and *Time*, LXXX, 16, p. 62, both tend to agree that the success of the overwhelmingly white West Coast jazz movement, fired the surfacing of the "Crow-Jim"—Negroes discriminating against whites—attitude.

    My own experiences as an aspiring jazz musician bear out the above findings. With perhaps one exception, no young Negro saxophone player I knew wished to play a cool style horn, for this was identified with West Coast jazz and white saxophonists. Conversely, the vast majority of the white jazz aspirants I knew all played cool style horns and affected a lack of interest in other styles.

36. This term has been used in so many contexts that it has tended to lose its validity. Originally it meant that a jazzman played his instrument with feeling and energy or that the jazzman's concept was rooted in the blues and spiritual songs of the Negro past.

    In *Metronome*, LXXVIII, 10 (November, 1961), p. 14, three Negro musicians (Dexter Gordon, Benny Green, and Gene Ammons) were asked whether whites played with "soul" or whether Negroes possessed a monopoly on this capacity. Ammons, Gordon, and Green initially declined to answer. Finally Green spoke up: "Let's face it, jazz was created by the black man. He naturally knows how to play it best." This oblique way of answering the question mirrored the views of a large number of Negro jazzmen.

37. For an example of "Hard Bop," "Hard Funk," or "Soul Jazz," see "Horace Silver and the Jazz Messengers," *Blue Note*-BLP-1518. Hard bop combos often gave the tunes titles which made reference to Negro life in the South. One of the tunes from the above-mentioned LP ("The Preacher") proceeded to set a trend, the effects of which are still evidenced.

38. Stearns, p. 242, and Hentoff, "Jazz and Race," p. 658. In 1961, this writer suggested to Paul Winter, a white alto saxophonist, that he should pattern his solo style after Lennie Niehaus, an alto saxophonist then with the Stan Kenton orchestra. Winter voiced emphatic disagreement: "He [Niehaus] sounds too white."

    On another occasion, I teased several white musicians who were personal friends about their marriages to Negro females. There was some laughter and joking, but one answered quite seriously: "It's the best way to get some soul, man." A further query at a later date verified that the statement had been made in all sincerity.

39. A fair example of Negro dominance can be seen in the comparison of *Metronome* all-star jazz polls of 1949 and 1960. On the eleven basic instruments listed (alto, tenor, and baritone sax, trumpet, trombone, bass, drums, guitar, piano, vibraphone, and clarinet), white musicians won eight first places in 1949. The band voted the best of the year was Stan Kenton's; the combo voted most outstanding was that of Lennie Tristano (both white).

In the 1960 jazz poll of the magazine, on the same eleven instruments, nine of the first-place winners were Negro. The best big band was Duke Ellington's; the best small group was that of Miles Davis (both Negro). See *Metronome*, LXV, 2 (February, 1949), 10-13, and *Metronome*, LXXVIII, 2 (February, 1961), 12-14.

Among jazz critics, this ascendancy is even more pronounced. Of fifteen jazz instruments listed, Negroes were named the outstanding performers on all except clarinet—see *Downbeat*, XXXIII, 17 (August 28, 1966), 16-19.

40. For a frank discussion of Crow-Jim, in addition to the oft-cited *Time* article of October 19, 1962, see *Downbeat*, XXVX, 7 and 8 (March 15, 1962 and March 29, 1962).

41. "Free jazz" theoretically represents a step forward. Other than an arranged theme, chord changes, bar structure, the key signatures are dispensed with; any sound can become "valid," the will of the soloist being paramount. Drummers rarely keep a steady beat and meter is only suggested. The bassmen generally attempt to follow the soloist, or in some cases, spur him on.

For an example of free jazz at its best, see Ornette Coleman Trio, "At the Golden Circle—Stockholm," I, *Blue Note* BLP-4224.

42. Since 1961, LeRoi Jones and later Nat Hentoff have written consistently about certain disciples of the "new thing" (See Jones' column "Apple Cores" in *Downbeat* Magazine, Volume XXXIII and XXIV, and Hentoff, "The Jazz Revolution," *The Reporter*, XXXII, 10 (May 20, 1965), 42-45, and "New Jazz: Black, Angry and Hard to Understand," *New York Times Magazine* (December 25, 1966), pp. 10-11, 31-33. It is essentially a number of New York-based, all Negro jazzmen whose cause these critics seem most intent on furthering. These include Archie Schepp. Cecil Taylor, Sun-Ra and the Ayler Brothers, who have on several occasions manifested essentially leftist socio-political views and how these views are applied in their music. See *Downbeat*, XXXII, 26 (December 16, 1965), 11, 42; Paul D. Zimmerman

and Ruth Ross "The New Jazz," *Newsweek,* LXVIII, 24 (December 12, 1966), 101-108.

43. *Downbeat,* XXII, 26 (December 16, 1965), 42.

44. *Downbeat,* XXIII, 10 (May 17, 1966), p. 40.

45. The basis for this statement is personal experiences among "new thing" musicians in Chicago. The heroes of Shepp (DuBois, Malcolm X) are their heroes; their protest is more muted, but present. Many of the musicians are not particularly angry at anyone and simply hope to gain some kind of acceptance musically. The problem is that a small minority speaks out; the others who may have dissenting opinions keep quiet.

46. LeRoi Jones—see for example *Downbeat,* XXXIV, 2 (January 26, 1967), 11, and *Downbeat,* XXXIII, 17 (August 25, 1966), 13— frankly declares that the "new thing" is "black music"; an exclusively Negro art. The view of Archie Shepp—*Downbeat,* XXXIII, 10 (May 17, 1966), 40—appears to be that while he will hire a white musician they are limited in their potential as jazz performers by some combination of blood and environment.

Such jazz columnists as Martin Williams—see *Downbeat,* XXXIII, 13 (June 30, 1966), 21, and Leonard Feather, "Hierarchy of the Jazz Anarchy," *Esquire,* LXIV, 3 (September, 1965), 123, 188, 190, leave no doubt that they believe many of the left-wing avant-gardists are racists.

47. Hentoff, "The Jazz Revolution," p. 45.

48. *Ibid.*

49. See Jack Richardson, "Blues for Mr. Jones," *Esquire,* LXV, 6 (June, 1966), 108, and Jones' own work, *Home: Social Essays* (New York, 1966), ff.

50. *Downbeat,* XXXIII, 3 (February 10, 1966), 48.

51. In Chicago, avant-gardists have formed the Association for the Advancement of Creative Musicians (*AACM*). Similar attempts in New York in 1965 (New York Jazz Composers' Guild) failed miserably.

Electronic Music:
Past, Present, and Future

Walter Robert

"If music be the food of love, play on!" commands Shakespeare. To
which a humorist might add: "Play on what?" Music has been called
the *scientia bene modulandi;* it has been defined as an unconscious
exercise in mathematics by a mind not aware that it is dealing with
numbers; it has also been regarded as the art of expressing feelings
with sounds; it was felt to be the revelation of the invisible, infinite,
and inexpressible, the manifestation of the will, the creation of an
order in time by means of sound, and all sorts of other nice things;
it was the food not only of love, but at times of revolution and war.
With all that, it is not a disembodied spirit. Very material substances
are at its basis: skin, muscles, bones, brass, wood, reeds, sticks, felt,
the skin of flailed animals, horse-hair, steel, catgut, resin, ivory, and
probably a dozen other substances. I commune with an infernal
machine of wires, sticks, felts and ball bearings when I play the
piano; the queen of instruments that helps to uplift our spirits on
Sunday mornings has cables, blowers, and plastic buttons.

An assembly of huge amounts of these substances is made to give
off sounds by being blown into, hit upon, scraped, plucked, and
rubbed, under the leadership of a signal-officer: this is called a
symphony orchestra. The composition of this assembly has been
fairly constant for the last 150 years or so and any organization with
a life span that long begins to be regarded as a social institution de-
serving respect, or even veneration. But is it, therefore, "untouch-
able"? Much older institutions have felt the need for *"aggiorna-
mento."* Why not the symphony orchestra? And yet, any change in
the constitution of the orchestra has met with fanatic resistance and
derision. Trombones in a symphony? (Beethoven) Tubas in opera?

172

(Wagner) Windmachines in symphonic poems? (Strauss) A hammer in the concert hall? (Mahler) "Ridiculous! This is the end of music!"

It can be imagined what happened when the "Futurist," Filippo Marinetti the poet, and Luigi Russolo the composer, presented their new program in 1913 and, of all places, in Italy, the most tradition-bound country of Europe. Their "noisemakers"—(sirens, hissers, thunder-clappers, bombbursters, etc.)—were soon drowned out by the cannons of the First World War and what was valid of their aesthetic was further discredited by their alliance with Fascism.

Since about 1900, Edison's phonograph had caught on. It was conceived, of course, only as a sound reproducing device. Soon, however, composers began to fool around with the turntable, playing it backwards or changing its speed. By dubbing what they recorded they made sound-montages; youthful pranks, perhaps, but even men of stature like Ernst Toch and Paul Hindemith indulged in these experiments.

Then came the radio. Crystals captured the ether waves and translated them into audible sounds. But they also gave off ugly, piercing high sonorities. A Russian engineer, Leo Theremin, and a French musician, Maurice Martenon, invented gadgets to capture the radio "feed-back" and to make it musically usable. After years of residence in Paris, Theremin returned to his native Russia and was never heard of again. Martenon had success of a kind for some time, however.

But not until the advent of the tape recorders can one properly speak of electronic music. Only the magnetic band offered easy access to any and all sources of sound, indoors and outdoors; its reel can be controlled by a push button; its revolutions can be doubled, halved, and measured accurately; the ribbon can be spliced, cut, dubbed, and manipulated: the tape recorder was the *open sesame* to a New World of Sound.

At first, outdoor sounds were used predominantly. The French engineer Pierre Schaeffer based his experiments in tape-recording largely on locomotive noises, whistles, escaping vapor, and rushing water. The finished products, while not works of art, showed almost no trace of the origins of the sounds. Schaeffer manipulated the magnetic band so that the resulting pitches, durations, intensities, and timbres retained scarcely a sign of the concrete substances from which they had emanated. Nevertheless, the term *musique concrete* stuck.

How is the metamorphosis of sound achieved? Pitch is raised or lowered by speeding up or slowing down the reel. A multiplicity of recorders running at different speeds is used; the recorded pitches are dubbed together; their combination may be simultaneous or spaced in fugal fashion. The duration of each recorded sonority can be abbreviated or prolonged at will. It can be measured in inches or seconds by yardstick and stopwatch. The intensity (loudness) of each sound can be manipulated. Sharp attacks can be eliminated or shifted to the middle or end of the sonority; crescendos and descrescendos are in the technician's power, fading in and out can be controlled by a turn of a screw. Decibels can be multiplied or reduced at will. The timbre (tone color) of each sound or component can be altered by acoustical filtering. Sounds consist of fundamentals and overtones. Overtones, whole overtone regions, can be reinforced or suppressed. In this way cow bells can be turned into flutes and oboes into xylophones.

When all of these possibilities are combined, run forward and backward, superimposed upon each other, an infinite variety of mixtures and montages can be achieved. This potpourri of sounds can then be further enhanced by splitting the tape and running the bands "canonically"; reverberation and spatial effects can be added; the most usable sonorities can be catalogued and stored away as raw material, to be used and reused whenever and however needed. Indeterminate (white) noise can be added in any degree of intensity; it is the result of mixing all audible frequencies together, analogous to light where all waves of the spectrum are combined to give white.

To these processes must be added the latest advance in artificial sound production: the electronic synthesizer. It is capable of producing electronically the timbres of any and all instruments by duplication of their overtone spectrum, but it can also emit exotic sounds and sonorities never before perceived by man.

A truly immense new world has been opened up, something literally unheard of! At the same time, there was no reason to discard the traditional means of sound production; voice or voices, pure or subjected to manipulation, were combined with electronic sounds; works for solo instruments and tape recorder were written. Symphony orchestra and loudspeaker music were combined.

Did all this come about overnight? Was it a complete break with the past? Did technology destroy the foundations of music or can one argue that there is a line of development in music that made the new devices desirable, perhaps even necessary?

Western music was always based primarily on pitch relations and secondarily on rhythmic proportions. For many centuries, intensity (dynamics) and especially timbre (tone color) were almost negligible factors in the fabric of our music. Composers in the Middle Ages made no distinction between the human voice and instruments; they obviously were concerned primarily and perhaps exclusively with pitch. The dynamic scale and tempo are not indicated. It took generations of modern scholarship to re-establish the rhythmic patterns of old music with reasonable accuracy. Even if we reach back only as far as Bach we find works or parts of works notated without specific instructions "on what" they are to be performed. The prime example is the "Art of Fugue." Many works of Bach and his contemporaries can be performed equally well on any instrument within the required pitch range.

Even now it is the exception, not the rule, to find specific indications for registration (timbres) in organ compositions. Only a small part of this de-emphasis of timbre can be blamed on difficulties of notation. It was not until the advent of Impressionism that the pitch structure of music (organized into tonalities) began to crumble; now, for the first time color emerged as the primary concern of the composer. From there it was only a step to a musical pointillism which associated each single pitch inextricably with a distinct timbre. This was the step taken by Webern.

If contemporary composers of electronic music—perhaps temporarily—neglect structure and busy themselves almost exclusively with every new timbre and timbre combination, one may regret the losses, but one may have to admit that there is a line of development leading to the new emphasis.

There are contributing factors that need to be considered. The nineteenth century permitted the performer to deal rather freely with the vehicle he used for expressing himself, while the early twentieth century developed an aesthetic that elevated the text of the composition to the status of scripture. The performer is chastised if he does not remain the faithful steward and mediator. The aesthetics of Hindemith and Stravinsky give ample proof of hostility to the nineteenth-century style of performing.

At the same time, the demands and expectations of the composer rise to levels of difficulty and complexity that make faithful observance of the stringent and detailed indications in the score unattainable for fallible human beings, especially under the stress of public performance. Perhaps it was inevitable that the machine was asked to take over where the human nervous system and muscular response seemed to be insufficient.

We may regret the passing of the performing artist that is likely to occur if electronic music should be the only music of the future. The performer as we know him now will then join the ranks of the bard of old, the story teller of the Middle Ages, and the town crier of the early city. These all were "technologically displaced" when a broad public became literate. We may regret their extinction, but no amount of weeping will bring them back.

If electronic music is here to stay, whether it displaces traditional music or not, there are some gains to be noted. There is now an alliance between artist and scientist, two camps which have been eying each other with suspicion. Many composers are now taking a lively interest in acoustics; they learn to know the new tools technology has furnished them and make their decision to use or not to use them on artistic and rational grounds.

The cybernetics scholar has acquired a new respect for the creative artist; he marvels at the intuition of the musician who instinctively has hit upon solutions which higher mathematics is only just now gropingly able to encompass and to formulate. It may be that our age is on the threshold of a reappearance of the artist-scientist-inventor personality for which the Renaissance provided such glorious examples.

Another positive factor: the nineteenth-century composer felt isolated and withdrawn from society; the electronic media, however, are predicated on teamwork. Some centers, therefore, even publish "their" compositions as products of the organization. The composer may again be a *primus inter pares*, as he was in the cloistered singing schools in Christian Europe.

How will the public accept the new dispensation, if it accepts it at all? We go to opera and especially to symphony concerts almost as if we were heading for church. We dress festively; we are in our seats before the start of the ceremony; we refrain from conversation; we are disturbed by the rustling of our neighbors' programs. In short, we experience music in a somewhat reverential frame of mind. That this was not always so is well documented. Opera in the eighteenth century was a place to be seen, to converse, to flirt, to carry on illicit affairs, and only incidentally to listen to the music and to watch the stage. Rows of seats were not installed in concert halls until around 1800, and soloists complained as late as a hundred years ago about the loud talking that made their performances inaudible. The autobiography of Gottschalk, the first American-born pianist to become an international celebrity, is one of many such documents.

Let us also remind ourselves that concert music is a very recent historic phenomenon. Music for easing work ("Lift dat bale!"), music for the dance, music for ritual, for marching, for revolution, and many other purposes is older and has proved itself incredibly durable. It could be that the concert-hall type of performance, with its sociological basis and its aesthetic implications, will be relegated to a very minor role if electronics takes over. Undeniably a loss. But do we still have Courts of Love? Jousts? Horse Ballets? *Trionfi?*

Our public music making has even now taken on museum character. The safest method to keep the public away is to program contemporary music. The alienation that started in the nineteenth century has grown to frightening proportions.

What might happen if electronic music has the field more or less to itself? The performer will be largely displaced; the symphony orchestra will join the Zink, the Shawm, and the Crumhorn in the museum. "Live" performance will be a rare occurrence, aimed at an historical-minded intellectual elite. The Palio is still run in Siena and so might symphony festivals be staged as delightful anachronisms.

Loudspeaker music will perhaps be experienced much more casually but by many more people. It will be heard in connection with art exhibits, in functional buildings, as ballet and television accompaniment, together with color projections, and as incidental music for plays and films. These, it seems to me at least, are the most successful uses electronic music has served so far.

The much-discussed computer music is still too close to its infancy to permit evaluation. The complaints about machines displacing the human mind and gadgetry making imagination impossible may not be valid; a man still has to program the machine. The musical products of cybernetics so far have not been better than some of the worst avant-garde live music of our time and not much worse than our most inane popular tunes.

The use of the computer as a research tool in music is another matter entirely. Only the computer can cope with the vast possibilities of the intricacies of sound. The tools of the greatest acoustic scholar of the pre-electronic age, Helmholtz (1821-1894), were resonators that were of about the same sophistication for research in sound as Galileo's telescope had been for discovery in astronomy.

It is not only in the study of sound by the combination of computer programming with electric synthesizers that an enormous new field has opened up. With the aid of advanced mathematical concepts it seems that the total organization of musical works of art can be scrutinized in a completely new fashion. To give an example: Bach's "Musical Offering" is based on a sequence of eleven pitches (furnished by Frederick II of Prussia); the genius of Bach hit intuitively upon a number of valid musical structures based on these pitches. The computer can be "fed" a program to investigate how many more musically valid realizations might be possible, starting from Bach's individual solutions.

One of the criticisms levelled at "electronic" composers is that they are tape-and-scissors jugglers because they want to *"epater le bourgeois,"* or because they are not good enough to compose "normal" music, or because they are charlatans, or because of all three of these. Charges of this kind were levelled at anything new and disturbing in the Arts; Surrealism, Cubism, and abstract Expressionism suffered from association with a lunatic fringe, commercialism, and impotence. It is imperative, however, to cleanse one's mind of such prejudices; if composers like Varese, Krenek, Berio, Babbitt, Stockhausen, and others have adopted the electronic media for at least some of their work we must take these developments seriously.

Because of their vested interest in traditional music media it is difficult for most musicians to overcome an inner resistance to electronic music. The profession is threatened; they might become fossils, technologically displaced, unemployed, unless they are able and willing to be retrained. Not only is their livelihood involved, as are the investments of instrument makers and music publishers, but their total spiritual commitment to a musical ideal and their whole inherent way of feeling, experiencing, and expressing themselves are threatened with extinction.

It may be this bias which has prevented many from listening to electronic music with real enjoyment. Few of the sonorities emanating from a loudspeaker "send" people; few of the compositions have had effects other than to disturb, to annoy, and, for some, to nauseate. The impression often is of the experimental, the monotonous, the artless—potential raw material only. But, if distinguished people take electronic music seriously, it behooves other musicians at least to keep an open mind.

In 1786 *citoyennes* of Paris screeched with horror and delight when Galvani made frogs' legs twitch by electricity. Neither he nor they could foresee, however, that this same force of nature would some day spark our car and airplane motors. Even a great scientist like Maxwell did not foresee the miracle of messages reflected back from the moon by television cameras. Röntgen had no idea that rays similar to the x-rays he discovered would someday destroy cities but also heal bodies. My own parents were firmly convinced that electric light was harmful to the eyes. Gas light was much less glaring!

So, who can tell what the future of electronic music will be? In this future there are, perhaps, certain dangers, especially in America. The greatest dangers that I can see for the American scene in this as in many other fields of art are:

1. Gadgetry. The American is from adolescence on trained to use tools; he enjoys tinkering. Electronic music offers unlimited pos-

sibilities to indulge in this national pastime. Generally speaking, however, the amount of gadgetry employed stands in an inverse ratio to the artistic value of the end-product.

2. Related to this are the love of fun and the enjoyment of experimentation which I believe are characteristics of America. The young European musician is by his environment and by his schooling tradition-bound; more often than not he has to overcome by a hard inner struggle the fetters imposed upon him in his formative years. American art is more experimental, uninhibited, and daring. The electronic "hot plate" makes it easy to cook and serve musical pot-luck. The pot may turn out to contain not even stew, but hodge-podge, ragout, or slop.

Music is Order and we still have to wait for the composer who will be able to give shape and significance to the new sonorities so as to rival the musical architectures of the past. If this comes to pass, electronic music may bring a new message to our new society.

Folklore in Relation to American Studies

Richard M. Dorson

There is before me a new course proposal prepared for an American Studies program in a large Midwestern university. The syllabus recommends proven interdisciplinary authors: Boorstin, Hofstadter, Howard Mumford Jones, Matthiessen, Perry Miller, Nye, Persons, Henry Nash Smith. In this conspectus folklore plays little part. Again here is Robert Walker's survey *American Studies in the United States* (1958) analyzing ninety-one college and university programs in American Civilization. One examines curriculum after curriculum with extensive lists of fields or departments, but with no mention of folklore. One such list specifies "education, psychology, language, music, speech, art, zoology, geology, philosophy, sociology, economics, government, history, and English" (p. 61, University of New Hampshire). Or consider the contents of the *American Quarterly*. The articles and review essays cover a broad spectrum of the arts, literary and cultural history, regionalism, business history and technology, religion and philosophy, and seemingly every facet of American experience, but again folklore is rarely in evidence.

These examples raise the question whether the folklore approach may have any utility for even so eclectic a scholar as the American Studies savant. This question led me to ponder how in my own case an American Civilization program inveigled me ever deeper into folklore, and through folklore to see American culture from new angles. This program was initiated at Harvard University in 1938 under an interdepartmental committee chaired by Kenneth Murdock and it offered the first doctorate in American Studies in the United States. The new degree, titled "History of American Civilization," generated electricity among a memorable group of the faculty and some remarkable graduate students. The coming of Howard Mumford Jones to Harvard in 1937 coincided with the rise to fame on the existing faculty of Francis Otto Matthiessen and Perry Miller, and these American literature experts gave leadership to the loosely organized program. Bernard DeVoto had resigned from Harvard by 1938 but he had participated in the original deliberations and as a confirmed resident of Cambridge and close friend of the Americanists continued to make his presence felt. Ralph Barton Perry in philosophy and Benjamin Wright in government contributed actively to the committee. The American historians played a more passive role, having already discovered America, but the degree candidates had access to Arthur Schlesinger, Frederick Merk, Paul Buck, and Samuel Eliot Morison. First to attain the new degree was Henry Nash Smith, already an assistant professor, on leave from Southern Methodist University. The second was Daniel Aaron, the third Frederick B. Tolles, the fourth Edmund S. Morgan, and the fifth myself, an anomalous refugee from the tennis and squash courts. Like Morgan and Conrad Wright, I entered the doctoral program as a continuation of the Harvard College major in American history and literature.

The talk and the writing in those days was all of the American experience, now suddenly revealed as an independent, mature, intricate, and noble civilization. Notable books flowed from the inspired and inspiring faculty: Miller's *The New England Mind, the Seventeenth Century*, Matthiessen's *American Renaissance*, Jones's *Ideas in America*, Perry's *Puritanism and Democracy*, DeVoto's *The Year of Decision: 1846*. Henry Nash Smith wrote as his doctoral dissertation the work that would emerge as *Virgin Land*.

All this ferment and stimulation would seem to provide an excellent test ground for the interdisciplinary approach of American Studies. Yet it does not appear that the degree recipients abandoned the conventional disciplines. For the most part they entered history or English departments and functioned as intellectual or religious or colonial or literary historians. I remember Ralph Barton Perry saying that if the faculty on the committee had to take each other's exams they would all flunk.

The degree requirements at the time called for the mastery of six areas, five in American fields and one in a non-American field. For my outside area I chose folklore, being the first and the last candidate to do so. In the 1930's and 40's no courses in folklore were offered at Harvard, with one brief exception, a course called "Legend and Tradition with Especial Reference to Celtic Material" given by Kenneth H. Jackson, the Celticist on the faculty. One day I passed Henry Nash Smith in the catacombs of Widener Library and he stopped me to say he had recently met Jackson and learned of his interest in folklore. Smith knew that my own interest in the subject had arisen from an undergraduate paper on frontier humor that led to my publishing in 1939 a selection from the Crockett almanacs, *Davy Crockett, American Comic Legend*. The upshot was that I signed up with Professor Jackson for a special reading course in folklore and attended his lectures. Jackson had come from Cambridge University and would shortly return to the chair of Celtic Language and Literature at the University of Edinburgh. He introduced me to the mysteries of Stith Thompson's *Motif-Index* and the historic-geographic method of comparative folklore study. Since there was no category for folklore offerings in the Harvard curriculum, Jackson had to smuggle this course in as a Celtic-related subject.

The Crockett almanacs and the humorous literature of the old Southwest to which they belong offer a good case in point of the interrelation between American Studies and folklore. This forgotten subliterature that flourished in the three decades before the Civil War became visible once again through a sequence of notable scholarly anthologies and studies beginning in 1930 with Franklin J. Meine's *Tall Tales of the Southwest*. All the American literature members of the Committee on Higher Degrees in American Civilization relished and praised this newly resurrected body of writings which so happily supported their bright premises. Here indeed was a purely homegrown American prose, catching the idiom and accents of the backcountry and depicting a novel gallery of backwoods characters. Bernard DeVoto had demonstrated in *Mark Twain's America* (1932) how Clemens had learned his craft from this school of journalistic humor relying heavily on the techniques of oral yarnspinners. In place of, or at least alongside with, the tired beadroll of hallowed American authors in the genteel tradition emulating European models and mannerisms, Americanists could now speak of Augustus Baldwin Longstreet, William Tappan Thompson, Johnson Jones Hooper, and George Washington Harris, casual writers whose pieces appeared in newspapers and cheap paperbacks and hardbacks long out of print. Perry Miller lent me his own copy of Harris's *Sut Lovingood*, in the only known edition of 1867, during an undergraduate tutorial. I took it home with me to New York and promptly left it on the train. Panic-stricken I rushed to the Harvard Coop and ordered a new copy, not knowing what else to do. Astonishingly a copy did appear in response to this order, from the Fitzgerald Publishing Company, whose name was pasted in a label over that of the original publishers Dick and Fitzgerald. It seems that the successor company, who now specialized in drama scripts, had kept the original plates and run off a few copies every year in fresh bindings. Apparently Sut's yarns had retained a continuous if slender audience ever since their publication.

The humor of the Old Southwest was clearly an expression of the popular culture. It entered sportsmen's weeklies such as the now celebrated New York *Spirit of the Times,* the daily papers that in the thirties and forties served up a regular fare of entertaining stories, comic almanacs larded with woodcuts, knockabout one-act farces, lithographs and posters and drawings. Book publishers like Carey and Hart and their successors T. B. Peterson and Company, both of Philadelphia, developed a paperback series called the Library of Humorous American Works, whose individual volumes included a number of yarns and sketches first printed in the *Spirit* and other papers. The illustrations of Felix O. C. Darley superbly portrayed the scapegraces and slatterns of the stories and captured the lowbrow spirit of the series. One reason indeed that this humorous literature disappeared from sight when its vogue had passed was its lack of recognition or even awareness by highbrow literary critics. The Spirit's correspondents and the playwrights and actors of Yankee plays mingled freely with the character types they were depicting. The teller, the subject, and the writer might even merge into the same person, as in the case of Davy Crockett.

All critics have noted the dependence of frontier humor on oral storytelling, and this is the point at which the folklorist can render his service. Traditional folktales, reportorial sketches based on fact, and fictional narratives based in varying degrees on oral tradition lie side by side in the *Spirit.* Only a trained folklorist employing the system of type and motif-analysis can make these distinctions. In his generally excellent study of *William T. Porter and the "Spirit of the Times,"* Norris W. Yates does mistake a tale well-known in international tradition, "The Origin of the Twist in Pig's Tails," for a composed story. We should like to ascertain to what extent the Southern humorists drew upon floating anecdotes. Reading the new edition of *Sut Lovingood's Yarns* edited by M. Thomas Inge, which brings together some uncollected pieces, I came across this observation by Sut in an 1868 sketch titled "Sut Lovingood, a Chapter from His Autobiography." Sut is watching a glorious fight between his mom and old Mrs. Simmons. He says, "So I clomb a dogwood wif a chip in my mouth, an' sot astradil in the fork, to watch the fust fight I ever seed, whar I had no choise ove sides, so I meant to holler for bof ove 'em."

Now this seems a likely enough comment to come from "a nat'ral born durn'd fool." But one of Rowland Robinson's Vermont raconteurs, Uncle Lisha, tells of the farmer's wife who found her husband in the sheep-pen clasped by a great bear. "Go it, ol' man, go it, bear," she cheered, "it's the fust fight ever I see 'at I didn't keer which licked." The story is told as a Kentucky happening in an 1865 joke-book, as a Wisconsin incident in a 1944 folk booklet, and is credited to Lincoln.[1]

The folklorist can identify such small nuggets of tradition within larger compositions, and he can also locate narratives that are folk-tales in their entirety. Such narratives are strewn throughout the files of ante-bellum newspapers, with some papers of course being much richer than others in humor. Only one attempt has been made to ex-trapolate folktales from their journalistic beds, the article by Arthur K. Moore on "Specimens of the Folktales from Some Antebellum Newspapers of Louisiana" (*Louisiana Historical Quarterly*, XXXII, 1949, 723-758). Moore categorized the narratives according to their international types, as set forth in the Aarne-Thompson *Types of the Folktale*. Similarly the folklorist Ralph Steele Boggs identified the tale types placed by the North Carolina humorist Harden E. Taliaferro in the mouths of his raconteurs in *Fisher's River Scenes and Characters*.[2]

Literary historians recognize the presence of traditional anecdotes in the humor of the old Southwest, but they make much too exclusive a definition of this humor. In fact the folklorist is in a position to revise the whole picture. Tall-tale humor and ringtailed roarers are not confined to the old Southwest. In the same period one can un-cover other regional screamers, such as Zeb Short, the "Varmounter" who came out of the Green Mountains in a thunderstorm and slung a panther over the mountain by the tail when he was eight years old. A backwoodsman was not a shaving to Zeb, who once grappled a bear on the ground, pulled out its tongue by the roots, and pushed its head into the mud as if it were a child. According to the unknown storyteller, Zeb could tie a bear in a double bow knot around Davy Crockett and heave both where they would never see daylight again.[3] Or there is the "true Alleghanian boulder" who came clear from the forks of the Alleghany in York State alongside the Seneca nation, and who called himself the "raal prickly grit of America," although he turned out to be a Yankee trickster.[4] In newspapers and periodicals throughout New England, the Middle Atlantic, and the Midwest, as well as in the Southwest, there percolated a popular humor close to folk sources. Yet the conventional literary and cultural histories speak only of literary down-East humorists represented by Hali-burton's Sam Slick, Seba Smith's Jack Downing, Lowell's Hosea Big-low, and now the earliest of them all, Josh Strickland, the creation of

George W. Arnold and the discovery of Allen Walker Read.[5] Like the Southwestern humorists, these Yankee writers drew upon folk types and folk talk, although less obviously. In both regions, a large body of anonymous tales and anecdotes belonging properly to folk literature lies scattered through the organs of popular print. Feeling that the old Southwest had received undue emphasis, I turned to New England printed sources in my own doctoral dissertation to prove that the tall tale and comic anecdote did flourish down-East as well as on the frontier.

Individual studies already demonstrate that a flood of humorous folk narratives covered the nation in the ante-bellum years. The mood of the young republic—gregarious, mobile, sociable, buoyant —well suited the funmaking of tall yarn, capital joke, and sly sell. A folklorist can and should make visible this oral humor frozen in newsprint and analyze not simply the tall tale but also the trickster story, the local character anecdote, the jest, the numskull tale, and related forms of comic fiction. Now that Ernest W. Baughman's *Type and Motif-Index of the Folktales of England and North America* has finally been published after a long delay at the printer's, this task would be greatly facilitated. Such an anthology would show the vast store of traditional oral humor on which the literary humorists levied.

* * * * *

The folklorist belongs in the field as much as in the library, and the book that taught me most about American civilization was based on folk traditions collected in the field. Its title is *Bloodstoppers and Bearwalkers* and I wrote it. One day after years of reading works on American history and literature and society in the library and listening to lectures in the classroom, I found myself outside the university in the midst of real, living Americans brimful of Americana. The experience was heady and exhilarating and provided a totally new kind of education.

When I left Harvard in 1944 for a teaching post at Michigan State College, as it was then called, my initiation into the mysteries of folklore had aroused my desire to taste the field, and the Upper Peninsula of Michigan seemed made to order. Here a variety of ethnic and occupational groups co-existed under the same regional roof, and my purpose was to penetrate equally these separate traditions, rather than to identify with one alone, as collectors were wont to do. For five months I traveled around the friendly towns of the Peninsula, talking to lumberjacks, copper and iron miners, Great Lakes sailors, Finnish farmers, Cousin Jacks, French Canadians, and Ojibwa Indians. The Peninsula offered very much of an oral, even a garrulous culture; this was a free and open society, still close to its frontier spirit, devoid of bookstores but abounding in taverns. Now the great advantage of the folklore method for establishing personal relations became at once apparent, for with no previous contacts or acquaintances I was able to make conversation with hundreds of strangers and to enter quickly into their minds and memories.

What does the ivory-tower intellectual talk about when he finds himself face to face with the folk? Symbolism in Faulkner will not get very far, and the future of the Green Bay Packers will not last very long. But folklore topics bring the man in the street and the cloistered student of American civilization into an immediate community of interest. Before setting out on the field trip, the lore hunter should prepare himself by reading up on the available history and traditions of the region and blocking out a mental questionnaire that he can draw upon in his conversations. Once in the field he can speedily adjust, enlarge, and revise the set of leading questions.

The personal and emotional rewards of these five months in the field cannot readily be conveyed but some concrete findings may be noted. All the information procured bore out the initial assumption, that the Peninsula possessed a pluralistic culture, divisible into a number of coequal subcultures. Members of each ethnic and occupational group shared legends, sayings, anecdotes, beliefs, and customs, but the lore of one group never merged with that of another. The white man knew nothing of the Indian's private traditions, nor the lumberjack of the sailor's. One individual could participate in more than one lore, say if he were a Finnish lumberjack, but the traditions themselves remained separate. In addition to these group lores, the region itself had bred an all-enveloping lore that branded each Peninsularite, who could recite dialect jokes with expert mimicry and knew intimately the stereotypes of the uncanny Indian, the Indian-like Finn, the comical Cornishman and *Canadien,* and the whisky-drinking lumberjack. Yet the official culture of the Peninsula, such as it was, comprehended nothing of the fabulous folk wealth within its borders and boasted, through Chamber of Commerce releases designed to attract tourists, that the Peninsula had spawned America's two foremost legendary heroes, Paul Bunyan and Hiawatha. This substitution of fakelore for folklore by promoters is itself a typically American phenomenon.

By contrast, the writer who had faithfully and skillfully drawn upon the regional characters and folkways in short stories failed to attain recognition. John Voelker, prosecuting attorney for Marquette County, adroitly captured the Peninsula folk flavor in *Troubleshooter* and *Danny and the Boys,* books that won him little acclaim.

John, who wrote under the pen name Robert Traver, showed me a letter from a publisher suggesting he combine the short stories in *Danny and the Boys* into a novel with a connected plot, perhaps based on a treasure hunt. "But that's not the way I know these people," Voelker sighed. He took me to visit one of his favorite raconteurs, a Cousin Jack named Dave Spencer, who recited rhymes and sang a ballad of "Steve O'Donnell's Wake" that Voelker placed in his fiction and I in my folklore. Eventually Voelker capitulated and wrote for the New York publishers a courtroom novel, *Anatomy of a Murder,* that became the nation's number one best-seller for over a year. But it is far inferior to his short stories.

The history of *Bloodstoppers and Bearwalkers* was curious. Four trade publishers dallied with it for some time before deciding it was not another *Stars Fell on Alabama.* Their readers could not categorize the book. One said that as an American he could not consider the tales of immigrants part of American folklore. Finally I turned the manuscript over to our new university press at Michigan State, who took nine months to reject it, on the adverse report of a female dietitian, somehow on the Press committee, whose gorge rose in revulsion at the earthy contents. Harvard then took it in three months, sending me the report of their reader, who I believe was Howard Mumford Jones, saying it was the first manuscript he had ever read for the Harvard Press that he had to force himself to put down. So after six years the book found a home, but it never attracted much attention and, as I say, primarily served to educate me in the folklore approach to American Studies.

One obstacle that faces the American Studies folklorist in getting his message across is the professional resistance to local as opposed to national history. Fieldwork must take place in a necessarily limited area and the folklore collections that cover the whole nation or large regions inevitably must rely on second-hand printed sources. The bona fide field report, say Emelyn Gardner's *Folklore from the Schoharie Hills, New York,* will consequently be lumped by the academic scholar with antiquarian and genealogical studies on the local-history shelf. Theodore Blegen attempted to alter this emphasis with his persuasive plea for *Grass-Roots History,* but professional advancement will not be achieved through the Association for State and Local History. When I was presenting my case to the Mississippi Valley Historical Association, now the Organization of American Historians, one of the panelists, Merrill D. Peterson, author of *The Jefferson Image in the American Mind,* commented on my paper, "Who cares about a few obscure Indians?" Like myself, Peterson was a product of the Harvard American Civilization doctoral program,

and his identification of American civilization with the hallowed
figures of American history is certainly a majority opinion. One answer is "Jefferson. He cared and wrote about obscure Indians, as part
of his interest in the American scene."

In the Upper Peninsula, and on subsequent field trips, I encountered articulate Americans from the folk stratum whose life histories
deserved public recording. The American Studies folklorist is well
equipped to undertake the task of writing folk biographies. One example of such a document is John Lomax's narrative of Huddy
Ledbetter, better known as Leadbelly, the Louisiana Négro convict
who sang ballads and plucked a twelve-string guitar before concert
audiences after the Lomaxes discovered him. Similarly I have recorded the autobiography of James Douglas Suggs, the remarkable
Negro folk narrator I met in Calvin, Michigan. In *Lay My Burden
Down* Benjamin Botkin has assembled a number of poignant slave
memoirs and personal reminiscences. But by and large this kind of
folk source is not available for the student of American civilization.
In England, however, the publishing house of Routledge and Kegan
Paul, long sympathetic to folklore and folk-life books, has sought for
and printed several manuscripts of this sort. Routledge's editor,
Colin Franklin, has recently described this venture in an engrossing
article on "Publishing Folklore."[6] Franklin's most remarkable discovery to date is W. H. Barrett, now a bedridden invalid, who lived
most of his life in the Cambridgeshire Fen country. Routledge has
published in the last four years his *Tales from the Fens, More Tales
from the Fens,* and *A Fenman's Story,* all pungent chronicles of
Barrett's experiences and memories as a member of the powerless,
propertyless class in rural Britain fighting for breath with his wits
and nerve. His tales are not folktales but elaborate personal narratives, often punctuated with traditional motifs. This kind of oral
history lacks a convenient label but it exists and thrives in the folk
community, and I encountered such narrators in the Upper Peninsula. For want of a ready pigeonhole I grouped them in a final
chapter called "Sagamen." There Charlie Goodman recounts his
hunting and lovemaking exploits, Swan Olsen his heroic triumphs
over bullies and thieves, and John Hallen his psychic prophecies that
came true. A volume of these memoirs of uncommon common men
would inform us a good deal more about American life than another
tome on Jefferson.

A further difficulty the folklorist must overcome before he is fully
accepted in the American Studies brotherhood is how to translate collection into interpretation. The end product of fieldwork is usually a
gathering of tales or songs or superstitions, often regarded by readers

as entertainment. On my return from the Upper Peninsula I found myself in great demand as a speaker before all kinds of social and fraternal groups: Masons, Elks, Kiwanis, Zontas, P.T.A.'s, an endless wheel. They wished to hear my recitations of Upper Peninsula legends, and in these talks, and on a Sunday radio broadcast, I began metamorphosing into a performing storyteller. My own motive was to establish new contacts with potential informants, a hope that never properly materialized, while on their part the audiences expected amusement from hearing Michigan stories. They had of course no interest in my theories of folklore. My career as a performer ended when I related some unbowdlerized narratives to a P.T.A. convention. This popularizing aspect of folklore can and has injured serious folklore scholarship, and it is not easily avoided.

The fact remains that even the scrupulous, well annotated collection of field texts cannot greatly assist the American cultural historian. Texts recorded in the field today cannot be assigned to the nineteenth or eighteenth centuries, and texts divorced from the personalities of their carriers and from their social settings lose much of their historical meaning. A few praiseworthy exceptions to the conventional compilations of texts may be noted. Austin and Alta Fife debated whether to arrange their Mormon folk legends topically or chronologically and happily chose the latter option, making their *Saints of Sage and Saddle* a folk commentary on the main events in Mormon history from Joseph Smith's vision to the successful establishing of Deseret. Americo Paredes in *With His Pistol in his Hand* has used the ballad of the outlaw Gregorio Cortez to illumine the mutually hostile attitudes and folk stereotypes of Mexican and Texan along the southwest border. Vance Randolph in *Ozark Superstitions* has revealed hidden pockets of supernatural convictions in the minds of Ozark hillfolk. Yet one has to dig hard for these few instances of analytical and theoretical employment of American folk materials, and this is why folklore titles seldom appear in American Studies reading lists. Recently the ancient historian Frank Kramer in *Voices in the Valley* has attempted to utilize folklore in his interpretation of institutional myths and social symbols shaping the Midwest, but his concepts of myth and symbol are so vague and his insertion of folk tradition so artificial that the book serves as a warning against rather than a support for the folklore method. No one falls flatter on his face than an Americanist like Marshall Fishwick or Kenneth Lynn who tries to comment on folklore when he has no competence in the subject.

*   *   *   *   *

We have been considering contributions that folklore method can make to American Studies. Let us turn to the question where folk culture fits in relation to American popular culture. The usual view of this relationship communicated to me conceives of folk culture at the bottom of American civilization, with popular, mass, and elite cultures resting above on successive levels, as in the following representation.

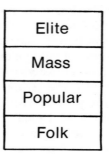

The organs of popular culture point toward the oral and grassroots culture, as in the ante-bellum newspaper. The organs of mass culture point toward centrally directed signals, as in the modern newspaper with its canned editorials and columnists and wire services. The elite or intellectual culture covers the small cerebral segment of the population at the opposite end of the pole from the folk. This is the picture Americanists seem to have in mind when they speak of folklore.

It is not an accurate picture. The folk culture does not relate more closely to the popular culture than to other spheres of American civilization. In Carl Bode's *The Anatomy of American Popular Culture, 1840-1861,* one will find only the scantiest indications of folk expression, in a passing reference to the folk art of carving and whittling. Yet this is a detailed examination of American taste and temperament in the mid-nineteenth century.

The relationships between folk, popular, mass, and elite cultures in the United States might better be presented this way:

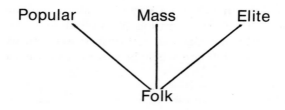

We may illustrate this model with the case of Davy Crockett. The legends of Crockett developed in the oral humor of the frontier and followed a universal heroic pattern common to folk epics. During Davy's lifetime and in the two decades following his death, the organs of the popular culture played with the oral yarns told by and about Crockett. In the daily press, in the comic almanacs, in the several versions of Paulding's farce about Crockett, *The Lion of the West,* in the graphic humor of woodcuts and cartoons, Davy blossomed as a popular and subliterary hero exhibiting chauvinistic and racist attitudes. The Crockett revival of the 1950's engineered by Walt Disney presented an all-American boy scout type as a mass-culture hero. In an elite view, Vernon Louis Parrington characterized Crockett in his *Main Currents in American Thought* as a frontier wastrel exploited by Whig politicians who constructed a romantic myth about the simple-minded rustic to advance their purposes. All four Crocketts interest the Americanist, but the oral, folk Crockett appears first historically.

Or we may take separate examples of relationships between the folk culture and the other cultures. At some points the intellectual culture does intersect with folklore. In the elite realm of religious thought and expression, one can point to Increase Mather's *An Essay for the Recording of Illustrious Providences* (1684) as a synthesis of theology and folklore. The president of Harvard, like other Puritan intellectuals of his time, believed in the providential interpretation of history, and accordingly he and his fellow ministers accumulated oral legends of poltergeists and spectral ships to compose the first book of American folklore. In *The Varieties of Religious Experience* (1902), William James brought together a number of vivid examples in religious history supporting his pragmatic proof of the existence of God. These mystical experiences, visions, and revelations dip into a common store of recurrent folk motifs and folk images.

A case of interaction between mass culture and folk culture is at once apparent in the urban folksong revival. Urban folksingers like Joan Baez have become national celebrities and the caricaturing of the left-wing beatnik songstress as Joanie Phoanie by cartoonist Al Capp developed into a national incident. The relationship between contemporary left-wing politics and the writing and singing of protest songs is being explored in an Indiana doctoral dissertation by a folklorist with training in American history.

A useful illustration of links between popular culture and folklore is provided in an article in the *Southern Folklore Quarterly* (December 1966) by Marcello Truzzi on "The American Circus as a Source of Folklore." Truzzi points out that circus acts have largely depended upon family tradition for their perpetuation, and he surveys the skills, techniques, personnel, superstitions, terms, legendary anecdotes, and tent-staking chanteys which form categories of circus lore. Circus folktales deal with tricks played by circus people on townsfolk, with origins of circus accessories like pink lemonade, with unusual capacities of circus animals, and with celebrated jugglers, clowns, and aerialists.

Such aspects of American culture permeated by folklore are the fertile research grounds for the American Studies folklorist.

The line of research pursued will necessarily depend on the special training of the inquirer, whether in literature, history, government, sociology, or art history. I remember Russel Nye once saying that when on occasion he teaches a history course he must shift gears from his usual critical analysis of a written work to a chronological consideration of events. The folklorist thinks in still a different groove, comparatively. Collecting in American folklore has been undertaken by scholars trained in medieval literature and modern languages or without formal graduate study. Among the new generation of students are some co-majors in folklore and American studies who will master comparative, historical, and critical thinking, and they may produce the sound, perceptive treatments of folklore in American literature or American history that are yet to be written.

NOTES

1. R. M. Dorson, *Jonathan Draws the Long Bow* (Cambridge, Mass., 1946), p. 227.

2. R. S. Boggs, "North Carolina Folktales Current in the 1820's, *Journal of American Folklore,* XLVII (1934), 269-88.

3. *Pearl and Literary Gazette,* III (December 21, 1833), 79, quoted in *Jonathan Draws the Long Bow,* 117.

4. New York *Spirit of the Times,* XV (July 19, 1845), 244, reprinted in R. M. Dorson, "Yorker Yarns of Yore," *New York Folklore Quarterly,* III (Spring, 1947), "A Mouthful of Pickled Dog," 12-17.

5. Allen Walker Read, "The World of Joe Strickland," *Journal of American Folklore,* LXXVI (1963), 277-308.

6. *Folklore,* LXXVII (1966), 184-204.

Even if, by all the Oxen in the World (a polemic)

William H. Gass

Consciousness comes too easily. We did not learn it like a language. It leaps to its work like a mirror. Yet consciousness can close and open like an eye; its depths are not illusory, and its reflection on itself is not mechanical. It's something-won, retrieved, conserved, as love is, and as love should be. It is with regard to consciousness, and the consciousness of consciousness, that I wish to examine popular culture in this country; and I shall simply suppose that cultural objects are created so we can become aware of them, and that those which are popular are so in a double sense: because they are widely approved and widely employed.

Imagine that a mirror, nothing falling into it, began reflecting itself: what a terrifying endlessness and mockery of light—merely to illuminate its own beams. You might think that an empty consciousness, like a vacuum, would immediately fill; that the nerves would pour in their messages like so many spouts from the roof of the skin, but sensing is not so simple as we sometimes suppose. Like falling, descent is easy only once we've jumped. Every consciousness has its rainless lands and polar wastes, its undiscovered and unventured countries. And there are simply boring stretches, like the Western Plains or the dry mouth's taste. Certainly consciousness is capable of subtle, wonderful, and terrifying transformations. After all, it is the dream we live in, and like the dream, can harbor anything. Although we are alert to changes in our physical and mental health, and have catalogued their causes and conditions, little has been done to describe adequately states of consciousness themselves or evaluate their qualities. Nonetheless, it is the whole of all we are at any time. At any time, if it is thrilling, we are thrilled; if it is filled with beauty, we are beautiful. It is our only evidence we live. Yet nothing seems more obvious to me than the fear, hatred, and contempt men have for it. They find it useful (an electric map of tracks and trains); otherwise it is embarrassing at best, or boring; at worst, it's threatening and horrible. Indeed, it's so much worse than simple black oblivion that only an obstinate, foolish will to live, the simple insistence of the veins which leaves have, cowslips, oxen, ants have just as well, can account for most men's going on, since such a will moves blindly, in roots beneath the ground, in bottleflies and fish, and our feelings are the price we pay for being brained instead of finned. Perception, Plato said, is a form of pain.

The working consciousness, for instance, is narrow, shuttered by utility, its transitions eased by habit past reflection like a thief. Impulses from without or from within must use some strength to reach us, we do not go out to them. Machines are made this way. Alert as lights and aimed like guns, they only see the circle of their barrels. How round the world is; how like a well arranged. This when desire is at an ebb and will is weak, we trail the entertainer like a child his mother, restless, bored, and whining: what can I do? What will amuse me? how shall I live? Then

> L'ennui, fruit de la morne incuriosité,
> Prend les proportions de l'immortalité.

The enjoyment of sensation as sensation, a fully free awareness, is very rare. We keep our noses down like dogs to sniff our signs. Experience must *mean*. The content of an aimless consciousness is weak and colorless; we may be filled up by ourselves instead . . . even flooded basements, some days, leak the other way . . . and then it's dread we feel, anxiety.

To tie experience to a task, to seek significance in everything, to take and never to receive, to keep, like the lighter boxer, moving, bob and weave, to fear the appearance of the self and every inwardness: these are such universal characteristics of the average consciousness that I think we can assume that popular culture functions fundamentally with regard to them.

But "before Plato told the great lie of ideals," Lawrence wrote, "men slimly went like fishes, and didn't care. . . . They knew it was no use knowing their own nothingness. . . ." Nothing keeps us back from nothingness but knowing; knowing, now, not necessarily in the sense of squeezing what we know into a set of symbols and understanding those; but knowing in the sense of seeing—seeing clearly, deeply, fully—of being completely aware, and consequently of being perfectly ourselves; for Lawrence lets his pagans speed to their mark as thoughtlessly as arrows. Must we be drunk or doped or mad, must we be dunced and numb to feed our animal halves? So it appears. The average man does not want to know how he looks when he eats; he defecates in darkness, reading the *Readers' Digest*; his love has an awkward automatic metal brevity, like something sprayed from a can, and any day his present sex may be replaced with plastic; his work is futile, his thought is shallow, his joys ephemeral, his howls helpless and agony incompetent; his hopes are purchased, his voice prerecorded, his play is mechanical, the roles typed, their lines trite, all strengths are sapped, exertion anyhow is useless, to vote or not is futile, futile . . . so in almost every way he is separated from the centers of all power and feeling; futilely he feeds, he voids, he screws, he smokes, he motorboats, he squats before the tube, he spends at least a week each year in touring and a month in memorizing lies— lies moral, religious, and political—, he beats the drum or shouts hurray on cue, he wears a neon nightie, swallows pills and chews his woman's nipples now because a book he's read has told him that he ought to; my god, he jigs, he swigs, he sings the very latest tra-la-las and sends his kids to scouts and all-white schools, he rounds his bottom to a pew, loves pulpitry, and contributes yearly to a cause; with splendid sexlessness he breeds—boards receive their nails with greater sensitivity—he kites the lies he's learned as high as heaven where they sing like frogs in trees, yet he sickens just the same, and without reason, for he's been to bridge and bingo, said his rahs as well as anyone, never borrowed on his insurance, kept his car clean, and put his three sons twice through Yale; but age, which is not real, hangs like a dirty suit inside his freshly pressed tuxedo; thus he fails, assumes another slumber, and dies like merchandise gone out of season.

Imagine for a moment what would happen if the television paled, the radio fell silent, the press did not release. Imagine all the clubs and courses closed, magazines unmailed, guitars unplugged, pools, rinks, gyms, courts, stadia shut up. Suppose that publishers were to issue no more dick, prick, and bobby books; movies were banned along with gambling, liquor, and narcotics; and men were suddenly and irrevocably alone with themselves . . . alone only with love to be made, thought, sense, and dreadful life. What would be the state of our nature, then, Mr. Hobbes?

It is the principal function of popular culture—though hardly its avowed purpose—to keep men from understanding what is happening to them, for social unrest would surely follow, and who knows what outbursts of revenge and rage. War, work, poverty, disease, religion: these, in the past, have kept men's minds full, small, and careful. Religion gave men hope who otherwise could have none. Even a mechanical rabbit can make the grayhounds run.

People who have seen the same game, heard the same comedians, danced to the same din, read the same detectives, can form a community of enthusiasts whose exchange of feelings not only produces the most important secondary effect of popular culture (the culture hero and his worship services), but also helps persuade people that their experiences were real, reinforces judgments of their values, and confirms their addiction. Popular culture occurs in public; it is as much an event as an experience; and it is reported on in the same spirit. There are therefore both participants and spectators, and in much of popular culture a steady drift toward voyeurism and passivity. As culture rises, it shatters; nothing remains in what were formerly the highest cultural realms but isolated works; isolated now by their character which repels all but the most devoted and cultivated love, and by the divisive nature of society which sets them apart in order to destroy them if possible. The objects of popular culture are competitive. They are expected to yield a return. Their effect must be swift and pronounced, therefore they are strident, ballyhooed, and baited with sex; they must be able to create or take part in a fad; and they must die without fuss and leave no corpse. In short, the products of popular culture, by and large, have no more esthetic quality than a brick in the street. Their authors are anonymous, and tend to dwell in groups or committees; they are greatly dependent upon performers and performance; any esthetic intention is entirely absent, and because it is desired to manipulate consciousness directly, achieve one's effect there, no mind is paid to the intrinsic nature of its objects; they lack finish, complexity, stasis, individuality, coherence, depth, and endurance. But they do possess splash.

It's in a way unfair to popular culture to compare it with the workmanships of artists since they do perform such different functions—nevertheless, this kind of comparison is not entirely unjust. Both shape a consciousness, but art enlarges consciousness like space in a cathedral, ribboned with light, and though a new work of art may consume our souls completely for a while, almost as a jingle might, if consumption were all that mattered, we are never, afterward, the same; we cannot unconsciously go on in the old way; there is, as in Rilke's poem, "Torso of an Archaic Apollo," no place that does not see us: we must change our life. Even Arnold Bennett noticed that we do not measure classics; they, rather, measure us. For most people it is precisely this that's painful; they do not wish to know their own nothingness—or their own potentialities either, and the pleasures of popular culture are like the pleasures of disease, work, poverty, and religion: they give us something to do, something to suffer, an excuse for failure, and a justification for everything.

If sixty percent of the people of a country are addicts of opium, then we are not rash in inferring there a general sickness of spirit; if alcoholism is epidemic, or suicide, or gambling, still another spiritual malaise can be confirmed; and if a great portion of any population is spending many hours every day driving all life from the mind, in worship of low cost divinities like the goddess of the golden udder, there's been another plague in spirit, and there are deaths to show for it, and endless deformities. Art does not, I hasten to say, have a hortatory influence; it's not a medicine, and it teaches nothing. It simply shows us what beauty, perfection, sensuality, and meaning are; and we feel as we should feel if we'd compared physiques with Hercules.

None of these complaints is new, and there would be little point in repeating them except that from time to time one senses an effort to Hitlerize the culture of the Folk; make it somehow spring from some deep well of human feeling, as if art were ever the triumph of sincerity over ineptitude, as if passion were a substitute for skill, as if, indeed, its gaucheries were not only charming, but *esthetically* so . . . this, in order to put out those high and isolated fires, those lonely works of genius which still manage, somehow, amazingly, now and then, to appear. There is no Folk, of course; there are no traditions; fine moral sentiments improve no lyrics, nor beautify their song; the occasional appearance of splendid exceptions does not soften, excuse, or justify anything; popular culture is the product of an industrial machine which makes baubles to amuse the savages while missionaries steal their souls and merchants steal their money.

How romantically he talks about it, you may say; what wretched little dramas he's made up—these wee morality plays from wild exaggerations. "High and isolated fires" indeed. Anything which surrounds us like the air we breathe, with which like wives and husbands we're easy and familiar, can't be so poisonous; we are alive, aren't we? Well, no, if you ask me, we aren't, or only partially. This muck cripples consciousness. Therefore no concessions should be made to it; and those who take their pleasure there should not be permitted to appear to lift those tastes to something higher with scholarly hypocrisy and philosophical pretense. The objects of popular culture are not art; their success or failure should not be judged as art's is; and the pleasures they provide, among goods, come last, even if, as Plato says, they are asserted to be first by all the oxen in the world.

List of Contributors

RAY B. BROWNE, author and editor of various works in American Studies and Literature, is professor of English, Bowling Green State University, Ohio.

RICHARD M. DORSON, one of the world's leading authorities in folklore, is Director of the Folklore Institute, Indiana University.

LESLIE A. FIEDLER, one of the most stimulating authors in American Studies, is professor of English, State University of New York, Buffalo.

E. McCLUNG FLEMING, Educational Director of the Henry Francis du Pont Winterthur Museum, Winterthur, Delaware, works widely in the iconography of the United States.

WILLIAM H. GASS, author of the successful *Omensetter's Luck,* is professor of philosophy, Purdue University.

C. HUGH HOLMAN, author and editor of many works in American literature, is professor of English, University of North Carolina.

The late FREDERICK J. HOFFMAN, prolific author of works in American literature, was professor of English, University of Wisconsin-Milwaukee.

VIRGIL L. LOKKE is associate professor of English and American Studies at Purdue.

WALTER ROBERT is professor of music at Indiana University.

LESLIE B. ROUT, Jr., an outstanding saxophonist, is on the history faculty at Michigan State University.

JAMES SANDOE, head of cataloguing at the University of Colorado Library, is ex-reviewer of detective fiction for the late New York *Herald Tribune.*

HERBERT M. SCHUELLER, Head of the English Department, Wayne State University, is Editor of *The Journal of Aesthetics and Art Appreciation.*

This book is set in Baskerville type face with chapter headings in Univers. It was printed by offset lithography on 70 lb. Clear Spring Offset stock by W. B. Burford Printing Company, Indianapolis, Indiana, and bound in Interlaken cloth by H & H Bookbinding Company, Inc., Indianapolis. Photographs and drawings are reproduced by permission of the various museums and societies mentioned in the captions. The jacket was designed by Dan Estes, designer with the Office of the University Editor, Purdue University, and printed by offset lithography by Owen Litho Service, Spencer, Indiana. Editorial and production work were supervised by Mrs. Eleanor Crandall, Assistant University Editor, Purdue.